BASILICATA

AUTHENTIC ITALY

BASILICATA

■■ AUTHENTIC ITALY

Karen Haid

Hiller Press, Las Vegas

Hiller Press
Las Vegas, Nevada

www.karenhaid.com

ISBN: 978-1-7348322-0-4
Library of Congress Control Number: 2020906522

Cover and Interior Design by David Provolo
Maps by Debbie Scott of Snappymap
Photos by the author

To me,

Lucania is genuine,

more so than anywhere else,

one of the most authentic places in the world.

Carlo Levi

CONTENTS

ITALY

*Adriatic
Sea*

★ Rome

PUGLIA

CAMPANIA *Eboli*

Potenza *Matera*

*Tyrrhenian
Sea*

Battipaglia

BASILICATA CALABRIA

*Reggio
Calabria*

*Ionian
Sea*

N

BASILICATA

N

10mi/16km

Melfi
Rapolla
Barile
Venosa
Mount Vulture
Rionero in Vulture
Ripacandida

PUGLIA

Bradano

Lagopesole
Acerenza
Irsina
Muro Lucano
Matera

Potenza
Tricarico
Grassano
Brindisi Montagna
Lucanian Dolomites
Miglionico
Brienza
Castelmezzano
Basento
Pietrapertosa
Ferrandina
Accettura
Bernalda
Lucanian Appennines
Pisticci
Metaponto
Craco
Aliano
Metapontino Plain
Agri
CAMPANIA
Tursi
Viggiano
Colobraro
Policoro
Grumentum
Moliterno
Senise
Valsinni
Lagonegro
San Costantino Albanese
Sinni
Maratea
San Severino
San Paolo Albanese
Viggianello
Gulf of Policastro
Rotonda
Gulf of Taranto
Pollino Mountains

Tyrrhenian Sea
CALABRIA

I.

WELCOME TO BASILICATA

Castelmezzano

1. ARRIVAL

I was on a train headed for Potenza. Coming from the south along Calabria's western shoreline, I passed through Basilicata's brief, yet strikingly dramatic coastline on the Tyrrhenian Sea. To reach my destination, I would continue on to Battipaglia in the region of Campania, where I would change trains and turn eastward towards Potenza. My train was *in ritardo*, late. Really? What train isn't, you might ask. Well, the one you need to catch when you're *in ritardo*.

I knew it would be close, and in my experience, the best thing to do in such cases is to find a train employee and ask him ever so kindly to call the next station and request that the connecting train be held for the two minutes in question. Conductors don't think to do this on their own unless their mother or girlfriend is on the train. And this isn't Switzerland. A minute or two in one direction or the other doesn't throw off a country of people for whom the phrase, *"Sto arrivando"* (I'm arriving), in a text message means your friend who is already ten minutes late has just thrown back his second *caffè* (espresso) of the day at his regular bar and is just about ready to start off for the appointment, whether it be a few minutes down the street or by way of a bus across town.

In this case, the problem was that I hadn't seen a conductor. Most public transportation relies on the honor system in Italy, so the apparent trustworthiness of my fellow passengers that day was working against me. As we got closer to Battipaglia, I actively sought one out, sticking my head out the window at the preceding stops, even stepping onto the platform for a look around — no conductor in sight. As the train pulled into the Battipaglia station, I was at the door poised to sprint, well, as best I could with my kaleidoscopic, medium-sized suitcase in tow. Without any indication on the platform as to when and where the trains would be leaving, I put the question to passersby as I quickly moved towards the stairs. "THE TRAIN TO POTENZA?" Shrugs. There was only one other in the station, so I hustled down a flight of steps and up the other, to discover it was the wrong one. The train for Potenza had pulled out, punctually.

Back down the stairs and up the other side to the station, sweaty and exhausted from the effort, I discovered the wait was just an hour. From the way the station emptied out, it would seem I was the only one who had missed the train to Potenza. Battipaglia was the final destination for those not continuing on to Salerno or Naples that day. To pass the time and more importantly find a bathroom, I walked across the street to a little bar with a *tavola calda* and *panini* sign over the entrance. The lunch hour had long since past and I was the sole wayward traveler looking over the array of hot items in stainless steel warming trays set up at the back of the storefront. A nice choice, but I opted for a sandwich with *pecorino* and *melanzane sott'olio*. The bread was fresh, the sheep's cheese full-bodied and the eggplant preserved in oil, delicate. What's more, the bathroom was clean and the server was so kind, I won't say that I skipped back across the street to the station, but I was certainly in better spirits than when I had left it shortly before.

I was ready to go up and down the stairs with my suitcase, but then I noticed a young man walking straight across the tracks at one end, right next to the sign *"Vietato attraversare i binari"* (crossing the tracks is prohibited). He wasn't even dragging luggage behind him. Emboldened, I looked both ways and as gracefully and nonchalantly as I could manage, I pulled my colorful suitcase up and down the small incline, seemingly put there for the purpose. The day was looking up. After a while, I boarded my train for Potenza, which seemed more like a commuter train compared with the regional train I had ridden earlier in the day. The trip was to be about an hour and a half.

I settle into my seat, the train pulls away and I gaze out the window, musing as to what I would find in Potenza, the capital of Basilicata. I happen to glance up at the computerized screen over the door that had a little map of the stops and then I saw it. The monitor flashed: *Prossima Stazione EBOLI* — Next Stop EBOLI!

I almost gasped. But *Cristo si è fermato a Eboli* — *Christ Stopped at Eboli*, I thought! Should I get off the train?

3

Seeing the station name, I realized that although I had read *Cristo si è fermato a Eboli*, I never knew where Eboli was. I assumed it was north of where the famous writer Carlo Levi had been confined in 1935-36. If I had to have hazarded a guess, I probably would have said somewhere in Campania, but I hadn't given it much thought. And there I was, approaching a town whose name had become iconic, the last bastion of the civilized world. Not even Christ himself would have ventured beyond this town into the dark recesses known as Basilicata.

The title of Levi's book was a condemnation in itself. He wrote about an abandoned people in a forgotten, arid land, in which the inhabitants themselves often said, "Christ stopped short of here, at Eboli." He told of his experience as an exile in the town of Aliano, a poor village built on rocky hills that seemed to be at the end of the earth. And in fact, that was the point; he was a prisoner, banished to live in a faraway place in Southern Italy. Train tracks stopped in Eboli.

Less than one hundred years later I was on the verge of entering this neglected region, on a nice train. I looked out at the people milling about on the station platform. All seemed normal, just one of many Italian train stations, seemingly unaware of the alleged hinterlands that lay beyond.

The train pulled out of the station. What did I expect as we left the municipality of Eboli behind us and progressed forward into the unknown? A barrenness, a nothingness. What did I see? A beautiful canyon. What? The train continued through this appealing countryside in southern Campania and entered Basilicata without my knowing it. The building of roads may have proposed a challenge, but I saw nothing unattractive with regard to the landscape unfolding before me. The ride flew by and before I knew it, the overhead monitor read *Prossima Stazione Potenza Centrale* — Next stop Potenza Central Station. I was to begin my exploration of Basilicata, a region rich in history, culture, folklore and art, nature, gastronomy and hospitality. My journey would be full of extraordinary beauty and delightful surprises, one I can now heartily recommend to others. So, at the risk of being accused of blasphemy, I would just like to say, "JESUS CHRIST, DON'T STOP AT EBOLI!"

2. BASILICATA OR LUCANIA

B ASILICATA IS MADE UP OF TWO PROVINCES, Potenza and Matera, with these two cities, roughly the same size, serving as the capitals of their prospective provinces. For most outsiders and tourists, Matera is the better known of the two. I had visited it years before I thought of embarking on an in-depth exploration of the entire region.

One day as I was enjoying breakfast in the lovely foyer of my hotel in Matera, the American couple with whom I was engaged in pleasant conversation took me by surprise when they casually referred to the region in which we found ourselves as Puglia. "Excuse me, but Matera's in Basilicata," I said. "No, we're on vacation in Puglia," they assured me. They had flown into the international airport in Bari, 68 kilometers (42 miles) northwest in neighboring Puglia, picked up their bicycles at baggage claim and rode to their first stop, which was, unbeknownst to them, in Basilicata. Admittedly, Italy has twenty regions and most visitors to Rome, for example, would be hard-pressed to come up with Lazio as the name of the region. Such geographical detail, particularly with respect to a lesser-known area, would be a lot to ask of the average tourist. However, the case of Basilicata's obscurity is not relegated to foreigners alone.

The opening words of Rocco Papaleo, protagonist and director of the popular Italian comic film *Baslicata Coast to Coast* (2010), puts it into perspective: "Okay, I admit it, I was born in Basilicata. Yes, Basilicata exists. It exists. It's a little bit like the concept of God — either you believe or you don't. I believe in Basilicata. I've seen it — it was during the night. Let's say, I sort of saw it. A great Basilicata…"

Papaleo's delivery is amusing, which the film's backer, the Basilicata region, hoped would sell, and it did. The film was a success, and many people for whom Basilicata had formerly been off the radar screen, became aware that Basilicata, in fact, did exist.

Before my first extended trip to Basilicata, a Calabrian friend, upon hearing of my destination, looked at me incredulously and said, "No one stops there. Basilicata is one of those places you pass through on your way to somewhere else." Harsh words from someone living in

Calabria, more often than not a region many travelers see as a pass-through from mainland Italy to the island of Sicily. The majority don't even go the handful of kilometers from Villa San Giovanni where the ferry leaves for Messina to visit the region's most important city and see the world-famous Riace Bronzes, a pair of exquisite 2,500-year-old lifelike statues in Reggio Calabria's archeological museum.

Basilicata, however, has an exception in Matera. In recent years, this city renowned for its atmospheric cave dwellings has gained in popularity to become a "must see" of Southern Italy, practically a Pompeii for international tourists in the know. I, too, had previously visited Matera on an in-and-out excursion from Calabria. The town has that unmistakable "wow" factor that enhances the prospectus of any organized tour. There's no denying that it's a special place, well worth its UNESCO World Heritage Site designation and the European Union's selection as the European Capital of Culture for 2019. But what about the rest of the region? Does Matera exist apart from Basilicata?

In the course of a brief TV interview during a stay in Potenza, I was asked to characterize Basilicata in a single word. My mind raced through a myriad of images. "The region is so diverse. To sum it up in one word would be very difficult." I spoke of the warmth of the people and finally came up with the word, *"meravigliosa"* (wonderful). Needless to say, the interviewer was satisfied.

A few weeks later, I happened to see a short promotional video for the region. Photographs of varying landscapes panned across the screen. As I was in the process of mentally placing each image, a text suggested the most probable country associated with the likeness.

An ancient temple: Greece? No, Basilicata.

A medieval castle perched on a hill with a lush green forest in the background: Scotland? No, Basilicata.

A cave with early Christian paintings: Turkey? No, Basilicata.

A sandy, coastal beach: Egypt? No, Basilicata.

A lone, windswept pine on the top of a snowy mountain: Japan? No, Basilicata.

And so forth... with each photo, a new wonder, another location in Basilicata: Metaponto, Brienza, Matera, the Ionian coast, the Pollino Mountains, etc.

Characterizing the essence of Basilicata is challenging, particularly in the 21st-century mode of summing up identity with a simple branding. The multifaceted region is sandwiched between Campania, Puglia and Calabria in the south of Italy. While Puglia is the heel, Calabria, the toe, Basilicata is the instep of the Italian boot. It's a high arched instep with mountains covering almost half the territory, and hills, most of the rest. Flat land accounts for less than a tenth of its area, which measures just over 10,000 square kilometers or almost 4,000 square miles. To give perspective as compared with the United States, the size is somewhere between that of the states of Connecticut and Delaware. Thus, Basilicata packs an impressive naturalistic diversity into its small dimensions.

Mountains reach up to 2,248 meters (7,375 feet), and as the name of the film *Basilicata Coast to Coast* would suggest, the region also has two coastlines: to the southwest, a very short, dramatic, rocky strip on the Tyrrhenian Sea, and to the southeast, a longer, sandy shoreline at sea level along the Ionian coast. The numerous mountainous areas and dissimilar landscapes have created natural separations within the region. In addition, there's the tendency to look towards the nearest neighbor with similar characteristics, which in Basilicata's case is often in one of the surrounding regions.

The population density is the second lowest in Italy, so spreading out a limited number of people over a vastly diverse territory doesn't lend itself to a strong unified identity. But as the actor says, "Basilicata exists," and it has existed for a very long time. The catch is that the region hasn't always gone by the same name. Even today, there are many people who grew up with Lucania as its official name. And to confuse the issue further, a citizen of the region is a *lucano* (masculine) or *lucana* (feminine). The Anglicized adjective or social identity would be Lucanian.

To give a little background on the history of the names, Lucania dates back to the 5th century BC and refers to an area that includes present-day Basilicata as well as bordering sections from the regions of Campania, Puglia and Calabria. The Lucanians were a strong people who migrated from central Italy, first occupying the coastal plains in Campania and then moving to the inland territories of Basilicata. By the 4th century BC, ancient sources described the land as the "great Lucania." Subsequent centuries saw the fall of these proud people followed by a series of dominations.

The name Basilicata came to the fore around the 11th century. The Normans are generally accredited with naming the region in honor of the majestic basilica in the town of Acerenza. However, the great Lucania never went away entirely and even today, the region is commonly referred to as Lucania. During the Fascist period, the classic name was revived to hearken back to times of former grandeur; thus, from 1932 to 1947 the region was officially known as Lucania. Although the name Basilicata was reinstated, the people are not called *basilicatesi* to reflect the designation, rather *lucani*. Furthermore, numerous towns include "Lucano" or "Lucania" in their names, Muro Lucano, Oliveto Lucano, Satriano di Lucania, to identify a few, but only one, Vaglio Basilicata, incorporates the current and also long-standing name of the region. Interestingly, Basilicata is the only region in Italy with this double nomenclature.

One could say that this small rocky region at the heart of Southern Italy has its heartstrings pulling in different directions, whether it be by a name, a particular landscape, an affinity towards an adjoining neighbor or by one of its own as an emigrant to a far-off land. I wondered how their geographical position, their long history and their present conditions would affect interactions with those passing through. As I traveled around Basilicata, with the exception of Matera, I felt as though I had the region to myself. Two, three or four nights in one location aroused curiosity. I must be there for work. No, I'm here to see what there is to see, to learn about the region, to get to know the Lucanian people.

"Ciao!" We had only just met. The first few times a local used the familiar with me, I was surprised. I wasn't used to this level of intimacy in other areas of Italy. Yes, amongst young people on the beach or in a family situation, jumping straight to or switching rather quickly after first meeting was normal, but Italians don't use "ciao" with strangers, contrary to what many English speakers may think. When you walk out of a store, *"Arrivederla"* or a bit less formal, *"Arrivederci"* are the appropriate salutations.

The familiar *"tu"* (you) is also not the accepted mode of address in a professional situation. However, in Basilicata the Lucanians switch quite easily to the *"tu"* form if they feel a compatibility. While I noted the practice, I never felt uncomfortable as I have in other areas when in a situation with a stranger who was trying to overstep accepted boundaries. After the first few times in Basilicata, I realized that the people just wanted to be friendly. It felt natural to them.

The Lucanians are a congenial people. They welcomed me in my exploration of their land, christened, *"il giardino segreto d'Italia"* (Italy's secret garden) by the region's tourist board. I visited Matera as well as the rest of the garden. When in the hinterlands, I was often asked if I was coming from or going to Matera. "Been there, done that, and I will return. However, on this trip I'm focusing on everything else. I want to get to know the entire region." And I can now confirm that Basilicata does, in fact, exist, even if it sometimes goes by the name Lucania.

II.
POTENZA

Teatro Stabile, Potenza

3. THE CAPITAL OF BASILICATA

I BEGIN MY EXPEDITION into the heart of Southern Italy at the center of what was once the "great Lucania," the area of Potenza. In Italian, the word *potenza* means power, vigor, authority, force, influence. The Romans gave the city its name Potentia, in Latin, for its physical characteristics. Located in a valley along the Basento River, Potenza sits on a perch, like a fortress, the highest regional capital in all of Italy with the old town reaching 819 meters (2,687 feet) above sea level.

On my first visit to Potenza, I arrived by train and was met at the station by my affable host of the bed and breakfast I had selected due to its proximity to the historic center and public transportation. The ride was short, but a steady climb — winding up to the right, then to the left and so on. I was staying near Piazza Vittorio Emanuele II and the old town was up the last hill. To reach it, I had two choices. I could go through the fancy, arched entranceway off the piazza and take the *Scala del Popolo* or the People's Staircase, which I'm sure was a godsend to those going to and fro back at its 1880s' inauguration. My other option would be more in line with my 21st-century sensibilities, that of the city's public elevators right next door — and they were free!

Potenza calls itself the *città verticale* or vertical city, which may seem odd, particularly in light of the fact that the tallest buildings hover between six to fourteen stories. However, in actuality, the *potentini* (people from Potenza) move vertically, or at the minimum on an inclination, all day long, going up and down staircases, escalators, elevators and streets in order to carry out their normal lives. They move up and down as much as side to side. And the fact that they've named the staircases, such as the "100 Steps" and the "Stairs of Thought," gives you the idea of their importance. In my humble opinion, it's a good thing for mechanization.

Now, alongside the many historic staircases the city fathers have installed a series of *scale mobili* or moving stairs. Alas, no rousing choruses of *"Funiculì, Funiculà"* in Potenza! Instead of funiculars, the *città verticale* boasts Europe's longest string of escalators to move people up and down the hills, 1.3 kilometers worth. The entire network, integrated with elevators and ramps, is made up of four lines that carry passengers from the periphery up to the center, from the banks of modern, high-rise apartment buildings, the industrial zone and the university to the old town with its shopping and entertainment. I found the *scale mobili* convenient and inexpensive, although I wouldn't recommend them for the disabled as I came across a number of yellow caution signs directing traffic to a few flights of the old-fashioned variety.

My focus in Potenza was the old town, which from my B&B was reached by way of the aforementioned elevators. And here I can attest to the fact that those accustomed to the unruly manner of *metropolitana* passengers in larger Italian cities will be quite impressed with the polite orderliness in which the *potentini* line up and wait their turns in front of the doors that open and close automatically.

The elevators lead to the "top of Potenza," as characterized by the locals. At one time, the old town was encircled by a medieval stone wall, an elongated oval shape corresponding to the form of the hill. Via Pretoria, another name hearkening back to the Romans, runs from one end to the other, from an eastern gate that no longer stands to the Guevara tower, the last vestige of a medieval castle, which I sadly spied through the webbed metal of a chain-link fence at the western end of the old town. However, despite the many disasters Potenza has had to endure throughout its history, most notably the devastating earthquakes of 1273, 1694, 1857 and 1980, the city still has a number of notable churches, patrician houses and simpler historic dwellings along its narrow lanes.

My visit started out a block up from the elevators in Piazza Mario Pagano at the center of both the old town and Via Pretoria. I hadn't ever heard of Pagano, but would learn that the "Plato of Naples," as he was nicknamed, was just one of many Lucanians who had made an influence outside the region. From Brienza in the Province of Potenza, he was a jurist and philosopher of the Enlightenment. Pagano lived his adult life in Naples and penned the constitution for the brief

Parthenopean Republic of 1799. This attempt at a republic in the territory of the Kingdom of Naples was a failure and Pagano became a martyr of the cause. However, Potenza's spirit of rebellion and alignment with the French during the tumultuous Napoleonic period led to the city's elevation to regional capital in 1806, a position held by the *potentini* since that time.

Piazza Pagano is a good size and functions as Potenza's outdoor living room, bustling with activity at all hours of the day. Friends, family and colleagues meet up and hang out in the square, as well as under the long portico of the large Fascist building that dominates its southern side. Opposite, the *Palazzo del Governo* or government building serves as the backdrop for many cultural events, festivals and concerts held in the piazza. Performances of a much more intimate nature are given in the adjacent *Teatro Stabile*. A 19th-century jewel, the small theater features classic red velvet seats and gilded cherubs in the elegant, three-tiered playhouse.

A young woman working in the small tourism office on the theater's ground floor graciously showed me around the building. She seemed pleased to have someone come into the office that morning and was very happy to tell me about the city. Perhaps I asked a lot of questions, but we must have chatted for close to an hour, and by the time I was ready to leave, I had such a load of tourist materials about Potenza and the region that we decided I'd take just what I needed to visit the old town and pick up the rest at the end of the day.

I came across even fewer visitors in Potenza than I would have imagined. The locals moved about the old town, in and out of shops, bars and businesses, without the clutter of tourists, and I couldn't help but notice how willing the *potentini* were to respond to questions and assist in any way they could, showing genuine surprise in meeting an American without a family connection to Potenza who took an interest in their city. Small exchanges of information had a way of developing into full-fledged conversations, which ended with big smiles and hearty handshakes.

Via Pretoria is the main street, the place where the *potentini* go to shop in well-appointed stores, but more importantly to *fare una passeggiata*, to take a pleasant walk and see friends, at any time of day, but particularly in the evening. I had to laugh on my second visit to Potenza when on Via Pretoria I heard my name called out. In an Italian city of about 67,000 inhabitants, could there be another Karen on that street at that very moment? Well, as it turned out I had met the woman a few days earlier in another town in the province. It's a small world and a rather narrow main street, making it easy to spot friends.

The city's architecture is mixed, with attractive, light-colored, rectangular stonework characteristic of much of the antique construction. The handful of remaining medieval gates and watchtowers have been incorporated into later structures that have grown up to replace those fallen by earthquake, fire and war. Numerous churches can be visited, such as *Chiesa di San Francesco* situated in an angle of Piazza Pagano. Built over a much earlier chapel, this tall, slender, starkly simple, single nave Church of St. Francis was founded in 1274 together with a convent that no longer exists. The *Chiesa di San Michele Arcangelo* on a side street to the east of Piazza Pagano is a beautiful 12th-century Romanesque church with a harmonious stone façade and a matching four-story bell tower. The stonework continues on the interior arches that divide the largely unadorned three-nave church dedicated to Saint Michael the Archangel.

The *Cattedrale di San Gerardo* on the west side of the old town was built in the 12th century over the remains of an Early Christian Church and renovated in the 18th-century to the neoclassical style seen today. The church is dedicated to San Gerardo La Porta or St. Gerard of Potenza, who served the community as bishop from 1111 to 1119 and became patron saint of Potenza. His miracle of note is changing water into wine for a procession of thirsty priests accompanying him on his return to Potenza. Of course, by today's thinking, nothing quenches a thirst like a nice glass of water; however, perhaps a people who actually climbed stairs and scaled hillsides needed the added calories in the wine. St. Gerard's remains reside in a chapel on the right side of the cathedral along with his statue that is carried through the streets during Potenza's annual festival in their patron saint's honor.

Right around the corner from the cathedral is a museum not to be missed. Most people pass through Potenza with a brief stroll in the old town, a quick pop into a church or bar and go on their way, which is unfortunate, but the upside for my visit was that I had the place to myself. The *Museo archeologico nazionale della Basilicata "Dinu Adamesteanu"* is housed in the early 16th-century Palazzo Loffredo, one of the few patrician houses that have survived the area's many earthquakes. Interestingly, the museum is named after a Romanian who is considered to be the father of archeology in Basilicata. Through aerial photography he was able to map out the various urban areas of the early peoples in the region, and the museum gives an excellent overview of its archeology, starting from the indigenous populations of the 9th to 8th-centuries BC before colonization through to the settlement by the Lucanians, Greeks and Romans. This museum is one of eight in the network of archeological institutions and parks throughout the region, which also include those in Grumentum, Melfi, Venosa and Muro Lucano in the Province of Potenza and Matera, Metaponto and Policoro in the Province of Matera.

My first surprise upon entering the museum was that the *biglietto intero* or full-priced ticket was only 2.50 Euros. However, I wasn't surprised when the woman behind the counter didn't have change for my 5-Euro note. The lack of petty cash is endemic in Italian businesses, and as a matter of course, employees look into their own wallets and those of their colleagues for change, even at state-run institutions. It would seem that waiting on the interminable bank lines isn't in anyone's job description. Once the 2.50 change was located, I headed over to the first exhibit room and began to read the introductory information panels when another employee approached me and deferentially pressed a brochure about the museum written in English into my hand. I thanked her and said I was okay with the Italian as we turned into the room and I saw what appeared to be a large wooden door with attractive bronze decorative features lying in a case. Extraordinary, I exclaimed. The woman's face immediately lit up and she launched animatedly into an explanation of this relatively recent find. The pair of

6th-century BC doors came from the entrance to a ceremonial hall in ancient Torre di Satriano, which is in the countryside near Potenza in today's Tito. To think that such fine specimens are still out there for the picking and that the silver fir trees were chopped down so many centuries ago to construct these elaborate doors. The ancestors of Basilicata would have pushed them open at a time when the population was in a period of flux, with influences coming from all directions. Groups of indigenous peoples — the Enotrians and the Peuketiantes — inhabited the interior; the Greeks were settling the coasts; and the Lucanians were moving into Basilicata's inland territories.

The museum was full of highlights, and I was particularly drawn to the contents of several female tombs. For example, an early 8th-century bronze crown with trains of circular button-like ornaments was amongst the grave goods of an Enotrian woman in the southern part of the region in today's Tursi, where the Iron Age people were found buried in the fetal position. From an inland hilly zone of Northern Basilicata near Potenza, the late 6th-century tomb of a young princess made the biggest impression. Children's deaths are sad in any epoch, and this six- or seven-year-old was buried in a crouched position with all of her would-be wedding jewels, from a gold diadem most likely made by the area's Greek settlers to the large amber necklaces, whose stones would have come from the Baltic. The little princess was of the Peuketiantes people, similar to the Puglians.

I spent quite a number of hours in the museum, surely more than most, but it was fascinating, particularly in light of all the ancestry research of late. The staff member who told me about the ancient wooden door came back after a bit with several books and brochures about the museum and the area. It would seem that when you show an interest, the *potentini* pull out all the stops. She said she was still looking for a few more things, so I asked her if she could hold them at the front door. When I was ready to leave, the expanded pile was ready for me in a very large document envelope. I signed the guest book, the very first of the day in the late afternoon, although I had seen two or three other guests during the course of my visit. I headed back to the theater to collect the other books waiting for me there. So much for traveling light, I thought, as I went down the elevator back to my comfy B&B.

4. FIRST TASTES

S IGHTSEEING MAKES ME HUNGRY. Well, lots of things make me hungry, and the late night Italian dinner hour can be a challenge. Sure, a big meal for lunch might hold me through to the evening, but two big meals a day? Not to mention the risk of an afternoon lethargy. A snack? "Don't ruin your appetite," says the little voice in my head, as I ogle the slippery-slope delicacies lining the cases of bars and pastry shops.

I wasn't even tempted as I had enjoyed such delicious pastries at my B&B on that first morning in Potenza. No soft, oddly moist, dented croissant in plastic wrap or dry, Zwieback-style crackers masqueraded as a continental breakfast that day. My host was the daughter of *pasticceri* (pastry chefs) and prepared a beautiful array of baked goods for her guests, from a plum *crostata* (a lattice topped pie) to a ricotta and chocolate cake, an apple pastry akin to a Viennese strudel, a pile of light, crispy, flaky sticks filled with various jams, an assortment of cookies and even traditional sugar donuts. And to my delight, a few persimmons, my favorite fruit, topped the buffet's fruit bowl — just one, a meal in itself. How could that group of four Austrians actually ask for sliced meat? I thought, seize the day, start off with an organic yoghurt! So when I returned in the early evening after a long, rewarding day of sightseeing, I wasn't about to offend my host and eagerly accepted her kind offer of a nice cup of tea and a few pastries to ward off those nasty hunger pangs until dinner. She had desserts in all sizes just for such an occasion.

My lunch had been healthy and quite filling, a large bowl of *cicoria e fagioli*, chicory and beans, at a *tavola calda* around the corner from the archeological museum. The pleasantly bitter greens and cannellini beans were prepared simply and served with their own boiled liquid and a good-sized hunk of bread. The range of choices and down-home offerings usually found at the cafeteria-style "hot table," as these establishments are called, suit many a palate and mood. A couple of local businessmen with whom I shared a small table dined on the traditional *primo* and *secondo*, first and second courses, but the earthy beans were more than enough to energize my afternoon at the museum and not spoil my evening meal.

For my first dinner in Potenza I headed back up the elevator to a restaurant in the historic center. Its antique interior walls and arches of variously sized stone and irregular bricks were complemented by warm lighting and a contemporary décor. As I looked over the menu, the friendly waitress pointed out the card sitting on the table promoting their tasting menu. The 16-Euro price that included the *coperta* (ubiquitous cover charge in Italy) seemed tough to beat even though the focus of the offering was a steak, which I'm not in the habit of ordering. Somehow, the waitress convinced me of its specialness although the price made me doubly dubious.

The antipasto of *tipicità lucane* or Lucanian traditional products arrived on a wide platter, the contents of which would have been enough to sate my appetite even without the steak. The little cup of soup with various grains and beans, the portions of greens and grilled vegetables, slices of *pecorino* (sheep's cheese) and *caciocavallo* (a semi-hard cheese in the shape of a little sack on a string) were all tasty, but for me the pièce de résistance was the ricotta. Sitting unassumingly at the edge of the plate in the telltale miniature plastic basket in which this cheese-like product is sold all over the country, the ricotta was not like any I had ever sampled. The consistency was much, much thicker, almost approaching in both taste and texture a buttery whipped cream, which would seem incredible for a milk-based product made from just the whey. But who could think of the whys and wherefores in the face of such a delicacy? It was simply to be enjoyed.

The final appetizer arrived on its own plate and provided a taste sensation about as far from the ricotta as I could have imagined. Two deep red, shriveled, oblong peppers glistened on the dish. These were Basilicata's famous *peperoni cruschi. Peperoni* doesn't have anything to do with the salami that tops pizzas all over America but is the Italian word for pepper. *Cruschi* is the adjective that describes this sundried sweet Italian pepper with great onomatopoeic effect as the letter "c" is pronounced as a "k" in both syllables. The *peperoni cruschi* is like the potato chip of Basilicata — delightfully crunchy!

The type of pepper used has a thin, glossy skin that is characterized for its low water content and is red when mature. In the countryside and in smaller towns, these red peppers can be seen hanging out to dry, intertwined in long strings and suspended from balconies or any available hook. The town of Senise, located in the northern part of the Pollino Mountains in the south of the region, is the hometown of this pepper, called the *Peperone di Senise*. Preparation of *peperoni cruschi* is quick, fried in extra virgin olive oil for a few seconds and then removed to cool down, crisp up and given a sprinkling of salt. Frying up a few eggs in the same oil is also traditional at home. In restaurants they are served as appetizers as well as an ingredient in first and second courses.

To taste, they're sweet, very mild peppers and of course, crispy, making them fun to eat by themselves, and when incorporated into other dishes, they add an interesting textural component in addition to the flavor. A classic example of a first course would be *strascinati con peperoni cruschi e mollica di pane*, a delicious dish from the annals of the Lucanian *cucina povera*, or cuisine of the poor, in other words, good, simple food prepared with economical ingredients. In this case, a wide, flat pasta made by a dragging movement of the hand (*strascinare*, to drag) is dressed with broken pieces of *peperoni cruschi*, oil and bread crumbs. A popular second course is *baccalà con peperoni cruschi* or salted codfish that is boiled, drained and served with the crunchy peppers and their cooking oil.

I would eat many a *peperone crusco* in Basilicata, offered enthusiastically by restaurateurs, and I must admit that when artistically balanced, *peperoni cruschi* do make an impressive presentation. To wash down this culinary mainstay and pretty much everything else eaten in the region, the drink of choice is the excellent Aglianico wine. Well known outside the region, this full-bodied red wine is grown in the volcanic soil of the spent volcano, the Vulture. The house Aglianico accompanied me throughout my evening of first tastes in Potenza.

The main course was a *tagliata podolica*, a steak of the robust Pod-olica cattle breed found in Southern Italy. This hearty race is adaptable, able to survive in difficult natural environments, thus suited to Basili-cata's mountainous terrain and vegetation. I must say that I was very pleased with the succulent, intense flavor of this free-range animal that clearly benefitted from its varied, wholesome food sources, and I found myself uncharacteristically searching it out on future menus.

The meal concluded more than satisfactorily with a glass of the re-gion's classic bitter, the *Amaro Lucano*. Served in its signature glass, the sweetish bitter was formulated by a pastry chef in the town of Pisticci, Province of Matera, in 1894. Before ever tasting it, I was well aware of the *Amaro Lucano* due to a series of national commercials in which elegant in-dividuals who seemingly have everything they could ever want are asked, *"Cosa vuoi di più della vita?"* (What more do you want from life?) And they respond, *"Un lucano."* (An *Amaro Lucano*.) My evening was complete.

5. PARADE OF THE TURKS

YOU HAVE TO COME BACK for our *Sfilata dei Turchi!* The *potentini* are enthusiastic about their festival. It's a big deal — several days of celebrations, a parade with almost 1,500 characters dressed in period costumes, an incredibly long pole made of cane to be set on fire in the piazza, not to mention the procession of the city's patron saint. I made plans to return.

The Parade of the Turks is held on May 29th, an excellent time of year to be in Potenza. The locals say that the festival coincides with a change of season. "It's always beautiful for the parade" — warm, sunny days that cool down at night due to the elevation. The sun certainly shone on my visit, and the old town's streets and squares were buzz-ing on the evening before the parade. Vendors peddled candies, nuts and toys from long booths set up along city lanes. Various stands sold food in the piazzas, and child, amateur and professional performers provided entertainment in stage areas.

La Cantina del Portatore (The Wine Bar of the Saint's Bearers) had a large stall offering food and, yes, wine in Piazza Pagano. Industrial-sized metal trays were filled with a first course of pasta and a second of *baccalà* in a tomato and olive sauce. I chose the pasta, tasty and a bit unusual. Presented on a sturdy, plastic plate, the homemade, medium-length *cavatelli* pasta was flavored with sautéed bread crumbs, raisins and a sprinkling of *parmigiano* cheese — a traditional dish for the festival, according to the server. To wash it down, I went over to the booth's wine area, where a smiling young man in a *Portatori del Santo* (saint's bearers) T-shirt and synthetic gloves was eagerly pouring red wine out of a large pitcher into small plastic cups in exchange for a donation to their association.

Where are you from? No! *Un'americana?!* He wanted to tell me all about his festival, which included teaching me a few local words with the proper inflection. *"Effess.....!"* (An exclamation articulated with the utmost of enthusiasm and the raising of an outstretched hand.) I would learn over the next couple of days that this was an important acquisition for my *bagaglio culturale* (cultural knowledge) of Potenza, particularly when drinking was involved. The *potentini* sum up a wonder, amazement or approval with a drawn out *effess...!* We worked on my pronunciation, back and forth, until I found myself in the center of a bemused cluster, each contributing his own two cents. *Uagliò* (*ragazzo* — guy), the young man called out to a friend to help fill up the cups. *Gn vdemm* (*ci vediamo fra poco* — we'll see each other soon)!

I had to work on that last phrase quite a while before it met with my teacher's gleeful approval. And needless to say, this particular carrier of the saint also had a string of more colorful phrases up his T-shirt's sleeve.

Down the street, another group was starting a new tradition. The association *La Nave del Santo* (the Saint's Ship) was selling sandwiches, prepared with the winning recipes in the festival's first contest, *La Potenza di un Panino*, in which gourmet panini were meant to characterize the city and the events of the celebration. I was unfortunately too full to partake in the sandwich eating, as mouthwatering as they appeared. I had to pace myself.

Many different organizations participated in the *Sfilata dei Turchi*, each with its own area of expertise. *La Nave del Santo*, for example, took care of St. Gerard's ship, which carried the holy man as a young boy. But in addition to the parade activities themselves, groups also sponsored other cultural events. For instance, earlier in the day *La Nave del Santo* held a conference entitled, "Symbolism of the ship in the period of emigration," which made me think. We often focus on the immigrant experience, but what is the perspective of those left behind? Even during their yearly festival, the *potentini* reflected on the period in which great numbers of their countrymen left Basilicata. They were not forgotten, nor were the feelings surrounding their departure.

But what links St. Gerard, the Turks and a ship? Although commonly referred to as the *Storica Parata dei Turchi*, the parade isn't a specific historical reenactment, but an amalgamation of various events from different time periods that have been fused with popular tradition and religion. St. Gerard, the city's patron saint, is the central figure. In the parade, the saint is represented as a child, sailing through the crowd on a ship, which begs the question, what does the ship have to do with Potenza?

The popular story recounts that St. Gerard, with the help of warrior angels, stopped the Turks from invading the city on the Basento River. The catch is that the waterway isn't navigable today, nor was it a thousand years ago. Additionally, there wasn't a Turkish invasion in St. Gerard's time. Despite these overwhelming discrepancies, the legend remains, and the saint's boat is pulled through the parade route by costumed Turkish prisoners.

Numerous experts have put forth multiple explanations as to how, why and when the story came to be. One such version accounts for the legend by citing the defeat of Catharism as the victory attributed to St. Gerard. The Cathars were viewed as heretics by the Catholic Church because they believed in dual gods, representing good and evil. This medieval Christian sect blossomed in parts of northern Italy and when they descended into the area of Potenza, St. Gerard managed to neutralize their effect on the Catholic citizenry. Interestingly, scholars of

Potenza's dialect identify northern Gallo-Italic influences, which date from this period of late medieval immigration. With regard to the parade, the *potentini* merged the memory of their saint as religious savior together with the enemy of future generations, thus creating the imaginative Turkish defeat attributed to St. Gerard.

Another version finds its source in a simulation of the 1571 Battle of Lepanto, a naval conflict in which the European Christians defeated the Ottoman Empire. In 1578, the *potentini* presented a reenactment of the battle as a welcoming gesture to Don Alfonso de Guevara, who would be the sixth count of the city. This pageant was then repeated and combined with Potenza's patron saint. Other ideas as to the origins of the parade have been proposed over the years without a consensus. However, regardless of the historical circumstances on which the parade has drawn, the association of St. Gerard and the Turks is firmly rooted in the culture and is there to stay.

On the day of the festival, the city bustles in preparation. The aforementioned *Portatori del Santo* put on an al fresco lunch in an old town square, but I stumbled into a different meal in Piazza San Michele alongside the lovely Romanesque church of the same name. The "Team Over 40," a group usually focused on soccer, organized a charity lunch that requested a mere 10-Euro donation. The piazza was already almost full when I arrived — rows and rows of long wooden tables and benches lined with paper and plastic place settings. I spied what seemed to be an open spot at a table that looked as though it would be in the shade throughout the afternoon. I don't think anyone would have chosen those particular three young men as my table mates, and I may have surprised them myself when I asked if the seat was taken, but we got along swimmingly. And yes, "Over 40" also served wine that flowed freely.

The menu was taped down to the table as the wind gusted now and then, swirling around empty cups and plates: *Antipasto di prodotti tipici lucani* (antipasto of typical Lucanian products), *cavatelli e fagioli* (pasta and beans), *salsiccia con uova* (sausage with eggs, after which was written the aside, "greatly appreciated by Londoners"), *salsiccia con i broccoli* (sausage with broccoli), *soffritto* (simmered innards), *fave fresche con formaggio stagionato* (fresh fava beans with aged cheese), *dolci* (sweets, accompanied by the words of wisdom, "Don't throw it away, save it for later"), *vino* (wine, with the tongue-in-cheek comment, "We hope there's enough"), *acqua alla fontana* (water from the fountain).

Members of the "Over 40" group not only organized the event but also served the food to the very large crowd, so the plates came out slowly with lots of time in-between to talk, drink, sing, sway and dance on top of the benches, and in a few cases, the table, as the afternoon wore on. The group was quite mixed from parents with young children to older folks. Everyone was excited about the festival. My table mates had worked the nightshift the previous evening to have a couple of days off so they could attend and then recuperate from the celebrations. They were friends and coworkers at the Fiat plant in Melfi about 60 kilometers (36 miles) north, but commuted from the capital.

The lunch started at 1:00 pm and dessert wasn't served until well after 6:00, to give a sense of the time frame. Every once in a while, someone at my table would catch one of the waiters running past and say, "We have *un'americana*, here," especially when they wanted the wine containers refilled. And I must say that they snapped to attention, returning quickly with the requested item. Personally, I had enough to eat just with the antipasto that was presented on a large plastic serving platter. I thought it was for the table, but then platters were placed in front of everyone, which left very little room for wine cups and elbows. Each large plate contained about 20 slices of salami, a couple slices each of *capocollo* (a cold cut made from neck meat of the pig) and prosciutto, a good portion of ricotta, about 10 pieces of pecorino (sheep cheese), 2 small, fresh mozzarella balls and a tasting of eggplant preserved in oil. If my value at the table hadn't been thoroughly appreciated with regard to the service received, it certainly gained ground as I shared a large portion of what was on my plate. Apparently, it takes a lot of energy to build the Fiat 500x.

I could have walked away then and there, having consumed more than my money's worth. The courses to follow were equally generous, and the band, composed of a concertina player and singer, a drummer and a couple of synthesizers, played on as the *potentini* passionately joined them in song. A small wooden wine cask made the rounds and elicited lots of cheering. Held in the air just high enough so that the spigot didn't touch the mouth (Italians are quite meticulous about such things), the little barrel emptied its contents all over the face and clothes of those perhaps a bit too well-oiled to finesse the keg. In the spirit of the event, I gave it a whirl, but after a hasty drizzle, flipped my wrists back so as not to soil my shirt. To be sure, quantity not cleanliness would have lent a greater esprit de corps. *"Effess.....!"*

At a certain point, I felt a vibration in my pocket and I realized I had ten phone messages from my host at the B&B. Leaving the piazza so I could hear the call, I would discover that my car was about to be towed from what the city information had stated to be a parking spot not affected by the parade route. She had tried to move it but didn't know how to drive an automatic. What an irony, I thought, as I got my hand stamped and hurried down the street and the city elevator. And then, it dawned on me. I can't drive — I've been drinking! She assured me I looked fine and I didn't have any wine stains running down the front of my shirt, so I cautiously got behind the wheel and followed her to a secure parking lot. She then returned me to the elevator and back up to the old town as I was told that I couldn't miss the *soffritto*.

The innards were roughly chopped, bathed in wine and sautéed in a large terracotta container with onions and herbs, then cooked slowly in tomato sauce. Going from table to table with the enormous ceramic vessel, the servers ladled out abundant helpings of the chunked internal organs. As this type of dish is somewhat of an acquired taste, I ate a respectable portion and justifiably pleaded satiation.

I didn't last until the very end of the meal, which probably coincided with the passing parade a few hours later, but said goodbye to my gracious table mates and hurried off down the hill on the long escalators that conveniently led to the city stadium, the staging area for the procession.

Costumed participants and decorated animals were waiting their turn for the start of the parade, which was 4 kilometers (2½ miles) up

a long hill to the cathedral in the old town. After soaking up the atmosphere behind the scenes and watching it get underway, I went back up
the escalator and enjoyed the happenings from the window of my B&B.

The parade represents three historical periods, each with its own cast
of characters, including *contadini* (peasant farmers) and *nobili* (nobles),
beautiful horses and oxen. The procession kicks off with joyful *contadini*
of the 1800s, playing concertinas and dancing the tarantella. The *iaccara* follows shortly thereafter. This long pole made up of cane and wood
is an important element of the parade. The tightly wrapped bundle of
reeds is 12 meters (almost 40 feet) long and weighs about a ton. The
iaccara is carried on the shoulders of the *Portatori della Iaccara*, fifty
young men plus assistants dressed in old-fashioned rustic garb accented
with red neckerchiefs and cummerbunds. Construction of the *iaccara*
begins the preceding January with the gathering of the cane and continues throughout May with the assembly of the slim tower. At the end of
the parade, the *iaccara* is raised in a piazza and one of the young men
climbs up to light the brush attached to the top. The tower takes hours
to burn down in a roped off area with firemen standing at the ready. In
olden days, torches for lighting were fashioned in a similar manner.

As the parade proceeds, various groups of participants pause, do a
flag-throwing routine, a belly-dancing spectacle or a folkloristic perfor-
mance of some kind. As the *iacarra* came up the street past my B&B,
the *Portatori della Iaccara* stopped, put down the long pole and started
singing a song about St. Gerard, directed right up at Mariangela and
me, leaning out the window. What else could I do as they finished up
but yell out, *"Viva San Gerardo!"*

The next historical period to pass was the 1500s with elegantly costumed ladies, lords, knights and cavaliers on horseback. The corpulent
Grand Turk *"Cippollino,"* so named for the classic headdress that resembles an onion, sailed past, sucking on a large hookah pipe as he sat
contentedly surrounded by his warriors and harem. He had chillingly
mastered his role as I found myself almost afraid of snapping his picture
for the scowl shot out in my direction. Templar-clad Christians and
loose-pantalooned Turks clashed swords in his wake.

Representing the 1100s, the earliest period, were the saint's boat and his warrior angels. Four groups of flag throwers accompanied by drums and herald trumpets symbolized the four historic gates to the city. And last but not least, the caped *Portatori del Santo* carried the little temple of St. Gerard on their shoulders through the applauding crowd. A contemporary band brought up the rear with a distinctly American sounding march.

Up to the old town they all went, to the cathedral. May 30th, the following evening, would be the stricter religious festival in which St. Gerard was once again processed through the lanes of the historic center and into the *Cattedrale di San Gerardo* to culminate in the saint's solemn mass. But as for the *Sfilata dei Turchi*, its torch burned into the night, finally extinguishing itself as the new day began.

III.
THE SACRED AND THE PROFANE

Il Maggio Festival, Accettura

6. CASTELMEZZANO AND PIETRAPERTOSA

I F A PICTURE IS WORTH a thousand words, a glimpse of Castelmezzano is worth a thousand pictures. I had seen photos. The town clutched onto the edge of a cliff at the base of gargantuan, spikey rocks that looked more like a giants' playground than a village for mere mortals. But there was no substitute for the impact of its in-person, three-dimensionality, which I would discover on a daytrip from Potenza.

Castelmezzano and neighboring Pietrapertosa, a gem of similar proportions, are two of Basilicata's six communities amongst *I Borghi più belli d'Italia*, the Most Beautiful Villages in Italy. To become a member of this exclusive club and have bragging rights as one of Italy's *più belli*, the *borgo* must be under 2,000 people, have a rich and harmonious architecture within a naturalistic setting and also advocate policies and initiatives to maintain and enhance the community's environment, as well as to develop and promote the village for tourism.

Castelmezzano and Pietrapertosa fit the bill. No doubt amongst Italy's *più belli*, the two villages are wedged amidst the pinnacles of the Lucanian Dolomites, so named for their visual similarity to the better-known Alpine Dolomites, although they are geologically different. *I Borghi più belli d'Italia* characterizes Castelmezzano as *"l'anfiteatro delle Dolomiti lucane"* or the amphitheater of the Lucanian Dolomites and Pietrapertosa as being *"tra le rocce e il cielo,"* between rocks and sky. To stimulate tourism, these enterprising villages, both fused to craggy outcroppings and surrounded by forest, have hitched their wagons together, literally. At a distance of about 16 kilometers (10 miles) or a half hour drive by road, Castelmezzano and Pietrapertosa have cleverly reduced the distance and created reasons beyond beauty to visit these hill towns.

Why don't you do *Il Percorso delle Sette Pietre*, the Path of the Seven Stones that goes between Castelmezzano and Pietrapertosa? The husband of my B&B host was full of ideas. I was looking for a daytrip from Potenza and I didn't have a car, so my hosts set about sifting through online schedules of various local bus companies and making telephone calls to ascertain the particulars. There wasn't a bus that went directly between the two villages, and each was served by a different company. The plan was to start out in one town and walk to the other along an old trail that had been revitalized to immerse visitors from near and far in the beauty of the natural setting, and incidentally, cut the distance between the villages to around 2 kilometers or a little over a mile. It sounded like a good idea. The limited bus schedule determined that I would start out in Castelmezzano and return from Pietrapertosa.

Early the next morning, my host dropped me off at the bus stop, which was quite a ways from the old town and although there was undoubtedly a connection, figuring it out would have entailed more time than taking me there. The bus pulled up about a half hour late, I entered and asked to buy a ticket, and the driver informed me that there was an extra charge if purchased on the bus. He pointed to a store a short distance away and said I could buy the ticket there. "But I want to take *this* bus." "We'll wait," he responded calmly. I looked at the three passengers sitting in the full-sized vehicle and they appeared equally unperturbed. So rather than offend him by not taking advantage of the Euro savings, I hustled down the street and into the store, which I might have done previously, but for the fact that it wasn't right behind the stop and I didn't want to take a chance of missing the bus. So as politely as possible, stating my necessity for quick service, I interrupted a pair of locals making their daily lottery picks, and they, too, seemed unruffled.

All eyes were on me as I stepped back onto the bus. What was this foreigner going to do in Castelmezzano outside the tourist season and where was her car? I thanked them all for waiting and took the initiative to satisfy their collective curiosity. *"Americana?"* Which village were my ancestors from? I thought they might be disappointed when I said I didn't have roots in Basilicata, but it was just the opposite. Not that they wouldn't have been pleased to have met a Lucanian from America, but without any blood relation, their curiosity doubled. Here was someone interested in them, their land, their story, no familial strings attached. Pride swelled.

One of the older women got out at her stop just before we pulled out onto the highway. The other offered us individually wrapped hard candies and talked with the young woman about her mother. The bus driver joined into the conversation. They all knew each other. Usually, they knew everyone who got on and off the bus to Castelmezzano, which was about 35 km (22 m) from Potenza. They told me proudly about their *Volo dell'Angelo*, a zip line that whizzed people through the air from Castelmezzano to Pietrapertosa and back. Would I take the "Angel's flight"? Probably not, I told them. Neither would the older woman nor the driver. The young woman had done it numerous times, but she worked for the concession during their summer season.

I was more concerned with the Path of the Seven Stones and in which town they recommended I eat lunch. I needed to plan my day. How long does the walk take? The young woman was the only one who had done it. "It depends," she said. "A half hour to a couple of hours." And this is when it first dawned on me that it might not be a carefree walk in the park.

After pulling off the highway, we dedicated a good amount of time to mountain switchbacks and then, without warning, Castelmezzano appeared, a fantastical landscape of gray, sawtoothed, sandstone boulders with a cluster of houses protectively huddled in their crook. With each hairpin curve, the vision came nearer until the bus stopped at the start of the main street. I waved goodbye to my traveling companions as the bus driver pointed out one of the restaurants where I could lunch.

Today, just under 1,000 people live in this fairytale village that preserves its medieval layout of terraced houses sheltered in the rocky hollow. The center road is steep and the side lanes and stairs that branch off of it are even steeper. No one living in this town need pay for a gym membership, I thought, as I passed the nicely preserved old stone homes lining the inclined lanes. A few grander doorways marked entrances to the occasional noble palazzo. In the center of the village sat the stately, squared-off mother church whose doors opened out onto the principal piazza and a stunning view of houses clustered in multi-levels against the dramatic backdrop of the irregular Lucanian Dolomites. The church was built in the 13th century next to an elm tree *(olmo)*, representing the tree of life, and was thus dedicated to Santa Maria dell'Olmo. Historic devotion to the saint is shown in the locally sculpted, rather sophisticated folk art statue of St. Mary of the Elm, which was carved early in the life of the church and hangs on the wall above the altar. The church was enlarged in the 19th-century and has a façade of local stone with an interesting frieze of flowers, lions, two-headed eagles and bull heads.

The most intriguing feature of the church, however, is on a lateral, outside wall and is a sign that the Knights of the Templar visited the town. The knights passed through Basilicata and the evidence, literally carved in stone, indicates that Castelmezzano, today a remote hamlet, was on the map in the days of yore, as a point of repose and prayer for those headed to do battle in the Holy Land. A secret, east-facing door was revealed in a church restoration. Crowning its ancient stone framework is a pediment on which the characteristic cross of the Templars has been carved. This well-known Maltese cross of equal-length arms that broaden slightly from the center with indented, V-shaped ends, is in plain view just off the main street. Further up the road, the town hall displays Castelmezzano's coat of arms that highlights this historic period with an image of two knights dressed for battle and sitting upon a single horse.

The main street narrows as it continues to climb in the direction of the towering boulders. Small shops and houses line the stone road and as it nears the great rocks, the buildings are either crammed into or emerge out of the natural slabs. Up and up past the last dwellings at the base of the mammoth stones lie the remains of a castle, just a small piece of a wall built by the Normans during their time of dominance beginning in the 11th century.

The adjacent *Gradinata Normanna* or Norman Staircase is a longer lasting reminder of these northern people who conquered much of Western Europe and the Mediterranean so many years ago. The steps carved into the rock almost look like the work of modern rock climbers, but they were actually sculpted into the stone to aid the military garrison in reaching the highest point in order to keep watch over the

Basento River Valley. I couldn't see myself walking up the arched rock face, so the metal fencing and locked gate were a bit of overkill in my particular case. However, Castelmezzano attracts adventurous types, and in the summer season offers a *Via Ferrata*, which translates as Iron Way, and is an international term for a technique of scaling rocks with iron aids and cables fixed into the face. The Lucanian Dolomites have two such trails, one up to Castelmezzano and the other to Pietrapertosa, which are connected by a Nepalese-style bridge.

For me, just walking around the old town to this incredible viewpoint at the base of the *Gradinata Normanna* was exciting enough on that morning in mid-October. Although very few tourists were in Castelmezzano that day, I met a pair of friendly Germans who were staying in the old town and who also planned on doing the *Percorso delle Sette Pietre*, but lunch came first. They had sandwiches and perhaps already knew that despite the recommendations of my fellow bus companions, the three restaurants in town were all shut up tight. Ascertaining this at ten to one without anything to eat, I felt a bit panicky. I hustled back up the street to the little grocery store, only to discover they were out of bread. Its deli man recommended I go down to the bakery for a roll and return with it to be filled. Back down and around the corner to the indicated shop and then up again to the grocer's, I had my sandwich complete just before they locked up for the afternoon. Not quite like sitting down to a plate of pasta, but I couldn't have had a better view as I enjoyed that deli sandwich sitting on a bench in the piazza gazing out onto the picture-postcard, life-sized nativity scene that is Castelmezzano. Maybe, just this once, I lucked out on the apparently unusual, universal restaurant closures.

Finished eating, I head in what I thought was the direction of the *Percorso delle Sette Pietre*. The distance to the start of the *percorso* seemed as long as the prescribed walk itself. Finally, after long stretches and hairpins, alone on the hot pavement as everyone else was at home enjoying the midday meal, I arrived at the town cemetery. Its caretaker looked at me a bit quizzically but confirmed the path was just ahead. Sure enough, as I descended into the forest, the official sign welcomed me to the precipitous jumble of pebbles and stones of a downhill trek that I would have forgone if not for the long road back up to Castelmezzano. As I slowly and carefully chose where to place my feet on the slippery stones, picturing myself going down in a tumble in an area with less than sketchy cellphone reception, I heard voices and music coming out of the surrounding wood. A lively camp group, I thought, as I concentrated on staying upright. The forest fell quiet for a while, and suddenly, there it was again, strangely similar to the previous outburst. Arriving at a large, primitive sculpture, I heard the entire segment once more. I wasn't delirious; it was the art, entitled *Delirio* (Delirium).

I didn't come across any campers that day, just one Northern Italian woman, dressed in Italy's version of L.L.Bean with regulation walking poles, a bit winded but striding confidently up the precipitous slope I was so cautiously going down. I would discover that the *percorso* was not just a physically challenging walk, but was conceived as a literary and artistic itinerary, based on a book by Castelmezzano's own Mimmo Sammartino. Each stage along the path features a stone sculpture and a recorded excerpt, transmitted from speakers under the rocks. The seven scenes are: fates, spell, witchcraft, witches, flight, dance and delirium. I was taking the trail in reverse order, so my fates were yet to come.

Engaging, at times a little spooky and with a good dose of quirky, the *percorso* wasn't a random literary selection, and the *streghe* (witches) weren't haphazardly chosen as its centerpiece. Sammartino's book *Vito ballava con le streghe* (Vito Danced with the Witches) is based on local stories passed down orally over generations, from a grandmother's lips to her grandson's computer. The witches were said to anoint themselves with enchanted oil collected from the cavities of olive trees and safeguarded in terracotta pots. Their monotonous, delirious voices echoed throughout the woods as they flew into the night on the backs of white dogs. In Sammartino's story, Vito, the *contadino* (peasant farmer), caught up by a love spell, dances with the witches.

Sorcery? Witchcraft? Such images were vivid in the *contadino*'s world, not so very far in the distant past. Castelmezzano was, in fact, known for its witches, and an interpretive sign in the middle of the village boasts of its *Mago della Lucania* or Wizard of Lucania. Giuseppe Calvello, known as Ferramosca referring to his small stature or more familiarly, Zio Giuseppe (Uncle Joe), was one of the most famous sorcerers in all of Basilicata. Although usually the domain of women, Zio Giuseppe dominated the magical and supernatural life of Castelmezzano and the surrounding villages. He was born in 1867 and lived in an isolated cottage in the shadow of the rocky pinnacles, where he practiced as an occultist and miracle worker, dissolving and conjuring spells, telling the future, curing all sorts of illnesses with herbs, stones and secret magic formulas, and calling forth and driving away evil spirits. Zio Giuseppe was a godsend to many Lucanians, Puglians and Calabrians, and was even studied by the Italian anthropologist Ernesto de Martino. He died in 1963.

The *percorso* plunges the visitor into this world of the *masciari* (the local word for *streghe* or witches) and their magic formulas in accordance with ancient rites. I felt the eeriness, and then, as I approached the waypoint of the *streghe*, a black cat ran across the path right in front of me. No way could I turn around and not pass the spot. I had seen Italians make U-turns in such a situation, but I had come too far. I had to forge ahead.

Did I put stock in such notions? At what point are these ancient superstitions and beliefs abandoned? I would venture to say that it is based on the community's collective thought. If most people believe in the *malocchio* or evil eye, it exists. The receiver of ill will is perceived as cursed until an experienced practitioner brings drops of oil into play, together with a mysterious chant and physical gesture. At that moment in time, however, my fear wasn't a curse, but physical exhaustion. I needed a modern conveyance to airlift me out of the forest. I would have settled for the back of a white dog or even a witch's broom. I was beginning to think the *Volo dell'Angelo* zip-line flight would have been the more conservative choice, although the ride was closed for the season. I would later find out that the elevation change along the path itself was 110 meters down (361 ft) and 260 meters (853 ft) up, almost doubling those numbers to reach the tops of the villages.

Despite my discomfort, I enjoyed the nature and walking across the valley floor. An interpretive sign near an old stone structure reminded me of the *briganti* (brigands) and the many hiding places afforded by the mountains of Basilicata. As it happens, Castelmezzano's patron saint dates back to the 19th century and the consequences of concealing brigands. A Napoleonic general was sent to destroy the area for their collaboration. As the fire was about to be lit, the officer's gaze turned to a fresco of St. Rocco of Montpellier on the wall in the mother church. Recognizing the face of a countryman from his hometown in France, the general immediately gave the order to suspend the sentence and Castelmezzano was spared.

Eventually, the *percorso* began to wind up a seemingly never-ending hill. I passed donkeys and sheep, who paid me no mind, and I found myself appreciating the difficult lives of the people in such mountain villages. This trail served the poor inhabitants and their animals for epochs, and it was no doubt a walk in the park compared to the distances they traversed afoot or the suffering many of them endured throughout their daily lives. Of course, it's all a matter of perspective. I would later find out that my B&B host's husband, who recommended the *percorso*, was a marathon runner. Finally arriving in the center of Pietrapertosa, I ran into the German couple I had met that morning. We looked around the village together before they needed to return to Castelmezzano to be out of the woods before dark. They had hiked the Himalayas.

Pietrapertosa has the distinction of being Basilicata's highest town, at 1,088 meters (3,570 feet) above sea level. With this bird's eye panorama over the Basento Valley, the Romans had already established a fortification at the spot where future generations would build the castle that is just ruins today. The village's architecture of note include the mother church, a convent devoted to St. Francis and a chapel dedicated to St. Catald, a 7th-century Irish monk who was credited with bringing Christianity back to many areas of the south after the Saracen domination. And to that point, the *Arabata* section of town is Pietrapertosa's oldest. Its small stone houses hug the dolomites, packed together on the steepest, narrowest, most austere streets of the village.

As with Castelmezzano, the jagged peaks loom over the dwellings. Making the final ascent to the bus stop at the upper part of the town, the homes and I were dwarfed by a pointy stone behemoth. The bar was setting up for happy hour and I got a cold drink, but the *tabaccaio* (tobacco shop) that sold bus tickets wouldn't open until after the scheduled departure. I don't think the driver was kidding when he said he couldn't sell me a ticket, but I entered the van, a more appropriate size for the slender roads and curves, and said I was going to Potenza with or without a ticket. I was relieved to be seated amongst the handful of passengers, regulars judging by the conversation. I felt as though I had traveled back in time and couldn't wait to return to a comfy, 21st-century bed.

Later that evening, mulling over my adventure and the trail of the *contadino* with its challenges and superstitions, I decided I would someday return to experience the latest, state-of-the-art mode of traveling between the two villages in the form of the *Volo dell'Angelo*. I didn't really think it through all that carefully. I was told a 92-year-old archbishop had done it. So, on a busy weekend the following spring I found myself pulling up to Castelmezzano, not seated in a bus, but at the wheel of a rental car. I parked on the outskirts, picked up my reserved ticket and waited for the shuttle that transported the "angels" to the start of the flight. We wound up and up the usual curvy road and then the driver stopped and indicated where we should start walking. What? How far? About 20 minutes. Flashback to the *Percorso delle Sette Pietre*, but this time just uphill, trekking along the mountain slopes to reach the start of the flight. Maybe the archbishop brought his own angel wings, but more than likely, he was whisked up in a small off-road vehicle.

The hike was as beautiful as it was arduous. I didn't see anyone who approached the archbishop's age group that day, but I didn't see anyone in my age group, either. The impact of what I was about to do didn't hit me as I waited in line or put on the harness and helmet, but when one of the technicians instructed me to lean forward as I was being strapped in. I looked down at the webbing that was between me and the valley floor below — 1,119 meters or 3,671 feet, to be exact. *Mamma mia!*

The netting, although just around the starting platform, had a purpose. The helmet?

"*Uomo, 84.*" That was how the guy in front of me would be remembered. The last words, spoken into a walkie-talkie to the technician at the other end. Man, 84 kilos. He would fly through the air, face down, a distance of almost 1½ kilometers or slightly less than a mile reaching 120 km or 75 miles per hour. So what does the person-who-just-relied-on-that 92-year-old-archbishop think in that brief minute hurtling through the air over that sheer drop? Just a few more seconds left. You're still alive.

Wings, from what I understand, are what physically characterize the classic angel. The only instruction I received was to keep my arms pinned back, gripping something at my side. On the one hand, I was whizzing forward, but I also had a strong sensation of the wind, playing with me and erratically pushing me from side to side. Maybe the technician hadn't gotten my correct weight, as he hadn't ever heard of pounds. I found myself thinking of a bird and how their tiny weight would react to this wind, but more specifically of their eyes, those strange, beady orbs. I was wearing my sunglasses, as recommended, but they weren't enough. Birds had all sorts of specialized eyelids for such situations.

The zigzags of the road are far, far below. All of a sudden, I see an obstacle ahead of me. I can't possibly fit through that! A few seconds later, I recognize the other platform and the space becomes just wide enough as I whiz through and, YANK! An unpleasant jerk with a metallic noise of the pulleys hitting the end of the line and me, ricocheting back. I made it. I felt completely disoriented as I was helped out of the harness and I staggered back toward the shed to hand in the helmet. My sunglasses were wet with tears. Why didn't they supply goggles? "They disappeared early on," I was told, which proves that those who came before me weren't angels at all.

I watched others flying in as I waited for the shuttle to Pietrapertosa, where there were several eateries with their shingles out. I needed to sit down and bolster my strength, but I couldn't overdo for the return flight. I had a delicious plate of homemade pasta with local mushrooms and then continued my walk along the main street and up to the flight station, thankfully just at the other edge of town. The zip line back was different and included on the round-trip ticket. I don't recall the start. I suppose I was already an old hat on the second go-round. Relax! Enjoy the view! Castelmezzano was in my sights. YANK, and I had arrived, once again.

The *percorso* and the *volo*, the walk and the flight, two completely different experiences, neither without effort. The first made me think of the place, the culture, the inhabitants, and the longevity of a people and their traditions. How would I have fit in? Am I superstitious? Will I twist an ankle? For the second, I focused on the technical. Where do I keep my telephone and wallet? How *ever* do I get into this harness? Am I going to die? Nature and witches versus steel cables and wind velocity. But in the end, both experiences got me there, to see two of the most enchanting *borghi più belli d'Italia*.

7. ACCETTURA: ANCIENT MARRIAGE OF THE TREES

M ANY MONTHS BEFORE Accettura's renowned *Il Maggio* festival, the town's two small hotels were long booked. Nearby localities still had some availability, but I didn't want to drive back and forth on the tortuous mountain roads, particularly by myself at night. Racking my brains for any connection I might have had with someone in the community, I got in touch with an Italian journalist friend who had attended and written about the event several years earlier. Bingo! Within a couple of hours, I had an option on a small, unused house in the old town.

Like all good Italians, Enzo recommended I ask something off the price, but the woman's voice on the other end of the line hardened as I discreetly skirted around the subject. She said there were three rooms that could sleep several people. How could I push for a discount off the 50 Euros per night she was asking for her spacious, well-equipped lodging?

Although the entire festival takes place over an almost two-month period, I was interested in attending the central days of the event, the marriage of the trees. I would be in the company of the *accetturesi* (people from Accettura), of whom fewer than 2,000 reside in the town with many more returning from all over the world. *Il Maggio* is also popular with tourists, particularly Italians within a few hours drive. The gathering offers a peek into an ancient agrarian ritual, the reawakening of spring, an homage to Mother Earth. Similar festivals take place in a number of communities in the mountains of Basilicata and adjoining Calabria. In Basilicata's regional park, *Parco Gallipoli Cognato Piccole Dolomiti Lucane*, tree rituals are practiced in Accettura, Oliveto Lucano, Pietrapertosa and Castelmezzano, and the municipalities in its Pollino Mountains include Rotonda, Viggianello, Terranova di Pollino and Castelsaraceno.

The isolated locations of these mountain villages, far away from the powerbrokers who prohibited such pagan activity, enabled the ritual to survive alongside Christianity. From its roots in agrarian mysticism, *il Maggio* gradually developed into a collective identity for the people in these communities as well as for their descendants scattered throughout the globe. Today, the festival in Accettura is completely integrated with the devotion to their patron saint San Giuliano (St. Julian of Sora), including religious services, processions and the saint's omnipresent image.

The event spans from the first Sunday after Easter, which is also celebrated as the Day of Ascension in Italy, to the Feast of Corpus Christi, and begins with the selection of the trees. On the Sunday after Easter, a group of volunteers goes to the nearby Montepiano Woods to choose a large oak tree, specifically the *Quercus cerris* or turkey oak, of all names, although the tree is native to southeastern Europe and Asia Minor. The following Sunday, a holly is selected in the Gallipoli Cognato Forest. A Mass is held in the Montepiano Woods on the official Thursday of Ascension. Then, on Pentecost Sunday the trees are transported from their respective forest locations and united in the center of Accettura. The next day features processions of the saints and the day after, the putting together, raising and scaling of the trees in the square along with another religious procession. Various entertainments and fireworks cap off the important evenings and the tree is taken down on Corpus Christi.

On the afternoon before the main festivities were to commence, I was at a festival in Tricarico. Already leaving later than I would have liked, I called the homeowner to advise her of my departure time. "No problem. Call again when you pull into town." Not only wasn't there any traffic, but for most of the 42-kilometer (26-mile) route, I hardly saw a vehicle. The views were lovely. I even had enough light to stop and take a few pictures of the irregular, patchwork landscapes of beige and brownish fields, rocky hills and green clumps of brush and trees before entering the Gallipoli Cognato Forest, where darkness fell in a picturesque canyon. Along the drive, I wound up to and through the village of Garaguso. As I slowly zigzagged back down the hill on its other side, a small water balloon splatted down on my windshield. I was undoubtedly an easy mark, as I cautiously negotiated the curves. Perhaps the youth of Garaguso looked forward to the influx of vehicles, but I was thankful I had a place in Accettura, so as not be subject to juvenile exuberance on the twists and turns back and forth to the festival.

I did not expect such numerous decorative street lights, large carnival rides and the noise level I encountered as I pulled into town. A band was testing out the sound system. Yes, we can hear you, but I couldn't hear to make a telephone call. The village appeared larger than I had thought. I got out to ask the *vigile* (traffic warden) where the homeowner's pizza place was. Just up the street—no problem for a car. I turn up the indicated road and stop almost immediately thereafter. I remembered the guy at the rental car company smiling and explaining all the dents on the car, "The Germans visit our villages and think they can get through any tight space." I was happy that the vehicle was already scraped and dinged to the max, but not about to push my luck as an *ape*, one of those little three-wheeled trucks, pulled ahead with little room to spare. So I just stopped in the piazza in front of the fully booked Hotel San Giuliano where I was finally able to get a call through. "My mother will meet you there in about a half hour." Huh?

I couldn't go forward and I couldn't back up. People milling about sort of looked at me. I moved a few inches here and there when someone needed to get by, but I had no idea how I would turn around between the cafe tables, restaurant-sized grill, flowerpots and cars in the small piazza. A large American-sized car pulled up and filled what was left of the space. A paunchy couple, bickering as only a married pair can do, unloaded a suitcase the size of an armoire. No wonder there wasn't any room at the inn. Someone came out from reception to help them back the car out, but no one asked me to move. I must have had my reasons for being there.

45 minutes later, her parents arrived and assisted my maneuvering out of the piazza. I was to follow them. Round and round, up and up. Accettura wasn't a village. The town traces its origin back to the time of Greater Greece, and in the hundred years prior to 1960, its population fluctuated between four and six thousand, after which the numbers dropped drastically. We were climbing to the top of one side, to another piazza completely full of cars. Everyone was in town for the festival, but I managed to squeeze into a spot that was good enough for overnight.

I had a small rolling bag and a large backpack. Oddly, the proprietress' father didn't make the least motion to help me bump over the cobblestones or down the uneven stone steps to the house—very strange for a man in the south of Italy. It was the same as they showed me the house. The light in the bathroom didn't work and he suggested that I climb up on a rickety chair to change the bulb, which was taken from another fixture that remained without. I was a bit shell-shocked from the past hour of inhospitableness, so gave it my best, as did his wife before he finished the job.

The lodging wasn't quite what I had anticipated, but it gave me a good idea of the dimensions of a typical dwelling. The kitchen had its own separate entrance a couple steps down the street, but I wouldn't have a need for the drab, un-stocked room during my brief four nights there. Back on the street, the door to the living quarters was up a couple of steps and then a handful more once inside. A small living area with a narrow old fireplace accommodated a little table and a couple of twin-bed mattresses piled on top of each other along the other side. The bedroom had a large, comfortable bed with thankfully clean sheets and a small desk. Although it didn't look as though anyone had lived there for a while, the wardrobe was full of old clothes and linen. Used odds and ends, including a disposable razor and a couple of toothbrushes, littered the soiled sink area in the bathroom, grimy but well-equipped with two small hand towels. The next morning I would discover that the heavy rolling shutters were rusted permanently in their three-quarters down position.

I was beginning to feel less and less grateful for the apartment in town, when I stepped outside my door and Teresa's head popped out of her entranceway across the narrow staircase-street that separated the houses. "Would you like a coffee?" In great contrast to the proprietors, she was warm and helpful. The evening before, the same energetic little lady appeared through her plastic, anti-fly, string curtain with a big smile at the first thump of my suitcase. She was my welcome party, this tiny woman full of goodwill. Had I eaten? "Have some *zeppole*," as she handed me a paper plate piled with large fried dough rings. "And put this plastic bag over it so they keep better." She spoke more or less in dialect, but we didn't have any problem communicating. "Tomorrow I'll show you the easy way to walk down to the square."

Easy? She meant the most direct route through the maze of stairs and streets between the houses, a course I would never remember in either direction. I just knew that I had to keep going down or up and I'd eventually get there. Teresa scampered down the large, uneven steps like it was nothing, and later bounded back up. She had clearly run up and down those stairs—too many to count—her whole life. When I made the reservation, it hadn't occurred to me that the distance from the top to the bottom of the town could be further than side to side.

By the time I arrived in the main piazza, a little before 9 o'clock, the *accetturesi* who dedicate themselves to the trees were already up in their respective forests. The *Cima*, or treetop, is only cut after dawn that morning, so the leaves will remain fresh for the festival. This holly tree, at a height of approximately 10 meters (33 feet), has a long journey from Gallipoli Park into town, taking about 12 hours to traverse the 15 kilometers on the shoulders of the young *accetturesi*. There are frequent stops to rest, eat and drink, not necessarily in that order.

The *Maggio* with a length of roughly 30 meters (98 feet) had been chopped down ten days before, and the branches cut off to facilitate its dragging from the Montepiano Woods. I took a shuttle bus to join the *Maggio* cortege already in progress and waited along the road with the ever-increasing crowd. And then I heard the fife and drums leading the procession. Over the next few days, I would see and hear those five music makers, who had more stamina than any I've seen, playing hour upon hour without break. The fife player led four percussionists, two on snares and one each on a small bass drum and triangle. They were *Il Maggio*'s strolling musical accompaniment, this blue-vested, red-capped "*Associazione culturale U Sciarabal*" or Cultural Association named after a public transport for the poor in the form of a one-axle horse cart. They hailed from Carbonara, a quarter in the city of Bari in neighboring Puglia.

I'm not sure if the beat of the drums or the embellishments emanating from the fife roused the oxen to step lively in their task, but the ensemble appeared well-versed in the event's procedures. The oxen, on the other hand, looked to be following instructions as best such animals not accustomed to working for their keep, are able. However, when these magnificent beasts enter the scene, they become the scene—60 glorious pairs, 120 massive oxen of the *podolica* breed. Their enormous bulk is blanketed by their mostly whitish pelts tinged with gray, just a handful of darker versions among them. Their large horns curve gracefully skyward. Numerous of the mammoth heads are crowned with colorful flowers and San Giuliano prayer cards. Tinkling cowbells blend with the drums, the shouts of the handlers and the excited buzz of the crowd. The procession is quite long as in addition to *il Maggio*, there are also six other trees that will be used to hoist the larger oak into place.

The trees are dragged along between the pairs of oxen. Handlers walking alongside and balancing on the trees themselves prod the animals forward. Historically, this breed was reared for work purposes, but with mechanization, they are now bred for meat and milk, so the oxen that participate in *il Maggio* are raised exclusively for this occasion. Not used to working, there's a bit of practice involved in the days leading up to the actual event. Once the colossal creatures get going, the pace is rather quick; however, the onlooker need not worry about the procession passing by too quickly, as they move short distances at a time. Frequent shorter stops and quite an extended longer one for a Mass and picnic lunch in the woods allow for plenty of time to immerse in the festival. Sausage, salami, cheese and cooked dishes are served from the back of conveyances that range from a makeshift horse-pulled cart to vans outfitted with casks and kegs to cars with trunks full of local specialties prepared by the townspeople, such as my neighbor Teresa, who was chopping up liver to add to her casserole earlier that morning.

Spontaneous musical entertainment also breaks out during the rest stops. A few of the old-timers gather around a *zampogna* player, who hugs the bagpipe's large goatskin bag and leans into his accompaniment. Various singers with whittled canes and walking sticks cup hands to their ears and with heads cocked intone songs that hearken back centuries. An older gentleman neatly dressed in a button-down shirt, closes his eyes and sways side to side, perhaps remembering his father and grandfather, as he delivers the high-pitched chant with an earnest supplication. The sharp tone cuts. Several animal handlers join in the emotive display, one gesturing to emphasize the lyrics, which remain a mystery for all those capturing this folkloristic image on their smart phones. The oxen stand aside, chewing nonchalantly.

Wanting to catch some of the *Cima*'s itinerary as well, I caught a ride back to town, where I reposed in an air-conditioned restaurant and hooked up with a lively group of Puglians dining at the next table. They had driven over for the day to see what the *Maggio* was all about and were tickled to have happened upon a local author and historian in the piazza. The writer invited them back to his house, which made quite an impression. They couldn't believe that a learned man who had taught history at a university in Bari lived in such small, simple quarters. From what they described, his home had dimensions similar to Teresa's, basically, a kitchen and a bedroom. They had purchased several copies of the author's books—local history and poems in the Accettura dialect—for a total of 20 Euros, a bargain that almost seemed to top having met and conversed with the man himself. So at that point, I told them that I had written a book about Calabria. Two authors in one day! And an enthusiastic round of photos followed.

After lunch we piled into Ciccio's jeep and headed out to meet the *Cima*. The procession followed a main road, so there was great discussion as to where to park in order to view the cortege without getting stuck behind it for hours. Of course, in the end a traffic jam is inevitable, but the Puglians acquitted themselves nicely.

In general, younger people carry and follow the *Cima*. When not at rest, the freshly cut holly tree moves along at a good clip on the shoulders of its youthful volunteers—a sight worth seeing, although the drunken behavior of many in its wake tends toward the unseemly. The onlooker needs to have his wits about him, lest he find himself doused in a shower of red wine. With the *Maggio*, the tendency is to forget the unpredictable nature of the oxen. The space can be quite narrow when passing through the woods. It only takes one slip of a hoof on the uneven rocky surface for one of the oversized beasts to lumber in your direction. And on one occasion I found myself scrambling up an embankment as fast as I've ever moved, thankfully into the helpful embrace of fellow spectators.

The day's climax comes with the greatly anticipated meeting of the two trees in the piazza. As the *Cima* was running late, the *Maggio* with its entire retinue of oxen, participants and observers had to wait for what seemed an eternity for its final entrance from the edge of town. To pass the time, we took pictures posing on the *Maggio*, and then, one of the Puglians got carried away, asking a handler if the American could sit up on an ox. They thought it was a good idea even though no one else was doing it. They egged me on—I'd be the only one in America with a photo of myself riding an ox at the festival in Accettura! I actually got to the point of putting my foot in the handler's cupped hands, but it was too much to swing my leg over, because I was afraid of grabbing hold of the animal's fur, not to mention the sheer size of the creature. Admittedly, it would have been a good photo next to the one of me flying like an angel at the *Volo dell'Angelo* in the Lucanian Dolomites.

At last, the tired oxen descend the final slope and haul the *Maggio* the remaining distance as briskly as their handlers are able to convince them. The *Cima* rushes into the piazza with a popular song, and the trees meet to the roar of the crowd. Butcher shops and food trucks grill up sausage and meat, women go through the crowd with baskets of *zeppole* on their heads, folk and pop musicians entertain as the grand event is celebrated into the night with a fireworks display.

The following day is another busy one for the men, who debark and smooth out the *Maggio* as well as the other oaks destined to assist in the lifting of the grafted trees. For me, it was a day to relax and visit with Teresa. She explained that the town was getting ready for the wedding of the trees, and even though in everything I had read, the festival was referred to as a matrimonial ritual, no one put it as simply as she did. "There's *lo sposo* (the groom) and *la sposa* (the bride)." She didn't use *Maggio* and *Cima*. Her reference was more direct and I realized that she viewed the event not as a representation of marriage but as a real matrimonial union. The trees embodied their respective masculine and feminine spirits. Fortune, health, wealth and fertility were manifested in plant life, always in a state of regeneration. Just as in the most traditional of marriages, the bride and groom were accompanied by their families from their place of origin to the point of union. Their fates would then be grafted together.

Teresa spoke very matter-of-factly as we sat together in the front room of her house. The door to the outside opened directly onto her eat-in kitchen with a small hearth and all the modern conveniences. To the right of the entrance sleek fixtures and a new washing machine gleamed in her spotless bathroom. She showed me the bedroom in back of the kitchen. Her father had slept in the larger bed to the left until his death the year before. To the right there was a single bed. All neat and tidy, Teresa was obviously a conscientious homemaker.

She also crocheted beautifully. Sitting in a petite wooden chair so her feet could comfortably touch the ground, she occasionally peered through her reading glasses at her deft movements and back over them to continue the conversation. She showed me a delicately executed fabric she had made with the image of San Giuliano and insisted on giving me a lovely crocheted table decoration as a souvenir.

Teresa worked for the *forestale* (forestry service) and was happy to have a couple of days off. *"Zappo."* (I hoe.) She was talking about a simple farm implement, not a motorized weed whacker of any kind. Teresa was a manual laborer who cleared brush, along the roadside or wherever needed. In fact, her two hoes were soaking in a bright blue bucket of water, the long wooden handles leaning against the tiles around her fireplace. With use, the blades became loose, so she soaked them for the wood to swell back up and tighten to the sturdy blade. Not only were this little lady's legs in tremendous shape, she must have had arms to match the heavy steel blades. And these were quality tools, made years ago, most likely passed down in her family.

Later as I was leaving, she pressed a small sausage and salami, both in shrink wrap, into my hand. I couldn't refuse her homemade delicacies and they were delicious. She was a busy bee with a garden in the countryside and a workroom somewhere else in town. Perhaps fresh produce accounted for the rather large refrigerator for an Italian home. I happened to notice there were a couple of refrigerator magnets stuck to it, so the next day I brought over one from Las Vegas I had in my bag. She thanked me and said she would put it with the others from Taranto, which is a few hours away in neighboring Puglia. Her sister, who lives in Taranto, had given her the magnets. One had a red double-decker bus with "London" written on it, and the other featured an Alpine house with "Camigliatello," a tourist village in Calabria's Sila Mountains. I started to say that her sister must have visited England as the magnet was so traditional and it even said London right on it. And in the way she looked at me, I realized in that moment, she didn't know how to read. I was surprised as she was my age or perhaps younger. She was able to do all kinds of things, but reading wasn't amongst them. Perhaps her father hadn't known how to read, either, or her brother, who came over for lunch. Although I had heard so much about the lack of opportunities in the south, I had assumed that children more or less attended primary school from the 1960s onwards. Teresa clearly wasn't afraid of work, hard work. And granted, she may have had a specific issue, but my gut feeling was that I was looking at a statistic, a consequence of the country's disregard for or inability to assist a family in need. Teresa, on the other hand, turned out to be a kind, generous person, well-integrated into her society, and I for one, was very happy to see her smiling face each time it popped through the plastic string curtain that covered her door.

That evening after Mass was the procession of *il piccolo*. Teresa's use of "the little one" in reference to the statue was not disparaging in any way. She just told it like it was. The town's San Giulianicchio statue, as it is called, is indeed a small San Giuliano. According to popular belief, he represents the saint's grandson, teetering back and forth atop the pedestal that raises him high up in the air. Bright red banners with images of San Giuliano hang from the balconies and greet the procession as it winds through the narrow streets. Bringing up the rear is a painting of St. John and St. Paul that arrived in a morning procession starting out on nearby Mount Valdienne. These saints have an important connection with the pagan element of the festival as their holy attributes include rain. Without their presence at the spring celebration, the town could risk a drought.

The climax of both the religious and pagan festivities occurs on the following day, a Tuesday. The trees are put together and the larger San Giuliano statue, *il grande*, is carried through the streets on the shoulders of the *accetturesi*. The procession is led off by many candles, historically attached to maidens' hats. Today, the candles are lined in tiers that resemble a square, multi-layered wedding cake, and are carried on the heads of whoever wants to participate. Children as young as eight or nine years old are topped with miniature versions and even men carry them. Quite a balancing act, particularly when a group of them breaks out in a conservative tarantella. My neighbor Teresa stood almost twice as tall with the candles crowning her head, and I'm sure her neck is as strong as the rest of her.

The local marching band, an ensemble that ranged from middle-schoolers to adults and were unified by peach-colored ties, played dirges for the martyr saint as well as more upbeat tunes. On a completely different note, ancient strains of the *zampogna* and the *ciaramella*, a double-reed instrument with the nasal tone of an ancient oboe, lent an earthy historicism to the event.

Meanwhile, the stage was being set for the raising of the tree, literally. Every year, the floor of the small amphitheater in the piazza is dismantled and a section hollowed out in the center to bury the base of the tree. Piles of stones lay to the side as the workmen secured the trunk in a manner that has been passed down over generations. The *Maggio* and *Cima*, *lo sposo* and *la sposa* have been married with large wooden pegs. An enormous pulley together with a coordinated human force to balance the 40-meter (130-foot) *Maggio* gradually raises the unified tree in increments, a tiny bit higher at a time. The aforementioned fife and drums accompany the hoisting of the tree as they did for the dragging of the *Maggio* from the forest. What endurance these Southern Italians have!

The final distance to the complete vertical is only completed when San Giuliano reaches the piazza. The crowd cheers and all of the bands burst into song for the majestic *Maggio*, smooth and straight with its leafy *Cima* that towers over Accettura. The supportive beams and ropes are removed by courageous climbers. The sun begins to go down, the colorful lights of the festival turn on and the *scalata* (scaling) commences. No special clothing, shoes or gear, no safety net, just a piece of a rope that reaches around the tree.

One climber used the cord methodically, placing his foot in makeshift knots as he went up the tree; others scooted up quickly by the strength of their legs. Only three made it to the top, performing acrobatic maneuvers on the way—swinging legs and doing scissor movements as they hugged the *Maggio* high above the ground. The first to enter the *Cima* climbed without fear through the upper branches, retrieved and threw down the bouquets of flowers that had been attached before its raising. The climbs were expert and exciting, made all that much more atmospheric in the twilight. I noticed that one of the climbers was older than the others, perhaps close to fifty, and commented admiringly as such to the woman watching the spectacle next to me. She was from Accettura. "They're *contadini*," she replied, as if that type of athletic prowess was expected of people who work the land. Well, it seemed out of the ordinary to me. I had seen him earlier managing a pair of oxen with a cart. "The world needs more people like him," I said.

Accettura is noted for this festival, and ironically, the first person to photograph the *Maggio* and bring the event to a larger audience was a political prisoner. In 1930, Lojze Spacal, an artist from northern Italy suspected of antifascist activities was sentenced to confinement in what seemed like the end of the earth for the country's powers that be. So, like Carlo Levi who was banished to nearby Aliano and subsequently wrote about it for what eventually ended up an international audience, Spacal documented the *accetturesi* and their festival. Today, it isn't easy to get a photo at the event without capturing the image of multiple photographers who seem to think that everyone showed up to watch them snapping closeups. I think they even confused the oxen.

In the end, the *Maggio* belongs to the people, its true beauty rooted in the salt of the earth. From its ancient pagan origins, the festival has endured through the dedication of the *accetturesi* who embraced Christianity, merged the liturgical observance of San Giuliano with the marriage of the trees and have carried forth the tradition through today. Two rounds of fireworks topped off the evening. A few weeks later, the *Maggio* would be dismantled. The wedding was over and it was time to get back to normal life. When I left the apartment the next morning, Teresa's head didn't pop out of her doorway. She was already out wielding her hoe.

IV.
THE VULTURE

Cathedral of Acerenza

8. MOUNT VULTURE

When I was a young boy, upon leaving my nurse Pullia's house,
I fell asleep on Mount Vulture, tired from playing and overcome
*   with drowsiness,*
and the fabled doves covered me with tender fronds.
Marvelous for the people of Acerenza, perched on high like a nest,
for Banzi surrounded by woods, and the fertile Forenza down
*   in the valley,*
That I slept safely from poisonous bites of vipers and bears,
blanketed under a pile of sacred laurel and myrtle leaves,
I, intrepid child, not without protection of the gods.

Horace, *Odes*, Book III, iv

IN BASILICATA, the name Orazio is thrown about with a certain frequency and in a manner that says, anyone who is anybody has heard of him. So to avoid any possible embarrassment, I looked him up. Quintus Horatius Flaccus (65 BC – 8 BC), commonly known as Orazio in Italy, is none other than Horace to the English-speaking world. The Roman lyric poet was born in Venusia, today Venosa, a town in Basilicata's Vulture area. Although Horace moved away for education and career, he remained attached to his homeland, which he referenced in his poems.

In the above excerpt Horace fondly recalls exhausting himself with amusements on Mount Vulture and reflects on the locations and sensations of his childhood while heralding his poetic destiny. The carefree poet-child amidst the wilds of the Vulture manages to avoid danger through the sacred laurel of Apollo, the god of poetry, and the sacred myrtle of Venus, goddess of love, the source of poetry.

Mount Vulture is a prominent feature of northeastern Basilicata's landscape in the Province of Potenza. This extinct volcano, which made an impact on the young Horace, has given the area a rich naturalistic identity. Interestingly, the Vulture is the only major Italian volcano east of the Apennine chain. The former crater has formed two lakes, called the *Laghi di Monticchio*, which are surrounded by a lush forest of beech, pine, fir and chestnut trees. The woods boast an extraordinary biodiversity, a prime example of which is the rare European Bramea. Discovered in 1963, this night moth that has been flapping its wings from as far back as the Miocene period, makes its exclusive home in the Vulture.

Jumping millions of years forward to the time of Frederick II, King of Sicily from 1198 and Holy Roman Emperor from 1220 until his death in 1250, the Vulture is said to have inspired the sovereign ruler's falconry treatise *De arte venandi cum avibus*. In fact, Frederick chose his castles of Melfi, at the base of Mount Vulture, and nearby Lagopesole as his summer residences. *The Art of Falconry* details the birds' capture, training and hunting, information that is still valid today. Melfi even has a group of falconers that have taken the name of Frederick's book for their organization and for the park in the Maddalena neighborhood where the regal birds are kept and shown. Almost a thousand years after Frederick's scientific study, the organization trains birds of prey on the very land where the emperor refined the practice to an art form.

The woods of the Vulture have also attracted the religious minded. Early Christians sought refuge in caves carved out of the volcanic rock. The picturesque St. Michael Abbey eventually developed from such simple places of worship. Overlooking the smaller of the two lakes, the abbey is a welcome sight after winding around the base of the mount. With a car, the drive is easy, but I imagine back on September 28th, 1847 when artist and writer Edward Lear stepped out of the woods, the panorama must have been that much more noteworthy. He chronicled the moment in his *Journals of a Landscape Painter in the Kingdom of Naples*:

> Through the branches of the tall trees we saw the sparkling Lake of Monticchio, and the Monastery of San Michele reflected in its waters. A more exquisite specimen of monastic solitude cannot be imagined. Built against great masses of rock which project over and seem to threaten the edifice; the convent (itself a picture) stands

immediately above a steep slope of turf, which, descending to the lake, is adorned by groups of immense walnut-trees. High over the rocks above the convent the highest peak of Monte Voltore [sic] rises into air, clad entirely with thick wood: dense wood also clothes the slopes of the hill, which spread as it were into wings on each side of the lakes.

The reflection of the solo edifice in the circular pond, so white and pure, completely surrounded by the luxuriant wood rising steeply on all sides, transmits both a sense of intimacy and grandeur, a communing with nature, and perhaps even a higher power.

The abbey was constructed around a large grotto carved out of tuff and used as a place of worship by Basilian monks, who sought out nature's spirituality nestled in the side of the crater. Over the following millennium, the church passed to the Benedictines, Capuchins and the Order of St. George. Pilgrims flocked to the area, which brought about several expansions to arrive at the large multistoried convent and 18th-century church seen today. The abbey's beauty as seen from across the lake is matched by the sanctuary's interior, and somewhat surprisingly as the entrance on the side of the building opens up onto a nondescript hallway that leads to a long staircase. At the top is a large three-nave church with unadorned white walls, functional floor tiles and solid wooden pews. The focus, however, is at the two ends of the sanctuary, the primitive apse carved out of the native rock with 11th-century frescos that serves as a dramatic backdrop for the altar and the spectacular view of both lakes out of the back windows. This religious edifice truly embodies the meaning of the word "sanctuary" in its many significances: a place of refuge or safety, a nature reserve, a holy site, church or temple. The sanctuary embraces them all.

Presently, nature lovers and day trippers seem to enjoy the church as much as those for prayer. A natural history museum of the Vulture fills in the space left behind by empty abbey cells; however, as with all small operations with limited personnel, phoning ahead is a good idea, particularly if one has a strong interest in such unique exhibits as those dedicated to the area's exceptional moth.

The Vulture is also rich in water with natural effervescence, which is bottled to much acclaim. However, the area's quintessential beverage of international renown is the Aglianico del Vulture, Basilicata's only DOCG wine (signifying both controlled and guarantied designation of origin). The fragrant, robust red wine comes from the Aglianico grape that was imported by the Greeks in the 7th-century BC. As the legend goes, Hannibal used this wine as a medicine to put on the wounds of his soldiers. The Aglianico is also remembered as the favorite wine of Pope Paul III, reformer of the Council of Trent; and Francis II is said to have attempted to drown his sorrows by guzzling twelve bottles at his last meal as ruler of the Kingdom of the Two Sicilies in 1861. I imagine countless bottles have since been consumed by Southern Italians disappointed in the outcome of unification.

9. MELFI

Melfi noble city of Apulia, surrounded by stone walls, famous for its healthy air, for the affluence of its people, for the fertility of its fields, has a castle built on a very steep cliff, an admirable work of the Normans.

Frederick II, Holy Roman Emperor

SO MANY CASTLES, so little time. Basilicata's topography seems to be made for constructing fortifications on the tops of hills. I was on a bus heading north from Potenza in the direction of Melfi and Venosa, and the image out of the left window flashed me back to earlier times. No doubt there would have been more trees in the surrounding countryside in days of yore, but the panoramic vision of the massive stronghold at the center of the broad landscape seemed to linger in a timeframe more in keeping with the pace of an historic diligence than a bus rolling along at a modern clip. I sometimes wonder how humble folk, not used to cities full of monumental buildings, must have perceived such an imposing structure. Even today, this dramatic Castle of

Lagopesole, about halfway between Potenza and Melfi, leaves an indelible impression. Rulers ought to have felt quite comfortable behind the thick walls of the rectangular fortress, from where they were able to survey great distances in all directions, including an excellent view of Mount Vulture. Together with the castles of Melfi and Palazzo San Gervasio, Lagopesole was a favorite summer lodging of Frederick II, who relished hunting in the environs.

The legacy of this Hohenstaufen Emperor is vaunted throughout Basilicata, particularly in the Vulture area. Of his twenty-nine fortifications and residences around the region, many in ruins or only a memory, Melfi is one of the best known, and the town holds a grand *Corteo Storico Federiciano* or historic parade dedicated to the former emperor on the last weekend of October, with falconry events, a medieval tournament, and tastings of local chestnuts, Aglianico del Vulture wine and other typical products. Melfi's castle is prodigious and as with that of Lagopesole, dominates the crown of a hill and the town at its feet. Its historic center is completely encircled by a turreted wall over four kilometers long. Despite the many modifications through the years, the castle and its bulwark reflect the medieval origins of the eleventh-century Norman construction. This stronghold was where the Normans started out on their conquest of Southern Italy. Melfi was the first capital of the Duchy of Puglia and Calabria, as well as the host of five *Concili di Melfi* between 1059 and 1137, each organized by a different pope. Notably, at the Third Council of Melfi in 1089, Pope Urban II proclaimed the First Crusade.

The Hohenstaufens succeeded the Normans, and when Frederick II came to power, he selected Melfi as an administrative capital, central gold treasury, prison, archive and superior court. He even established an early zoological garden with animals that accompanied him as he moved between various towns and castles. Amongst the creatures was Europe's first giraffe, a present from Sultan Al-Kamil at the conclusion of the Sixth Crusade. Noblemen and vassals arrived at court to render homage to or receive privileges from Frederick. Throngs of the faithful, crusaders, pilgrims and all types of miracle workers came to Melfi, as well.

In addition to his treatise on falconry, Frederick also set his mind to the law, and together with great jurists of the day composed the Constitutions of Melfi, a legal code for the Kingdom of Sicily that he put into effect from the castle in 1231. The constitutions' three books address public law, judicial procedure and feudal, private and penal law. One highlight is the equality of citizens before the law with the abolishment of trial by ordeal, where guilt or innocence was decided by surviving an experience, which was painful at best, painfully mortal at the worst. Sicilian law would be based on the Constitutions for 600 years.

The Castle of Melfi was at its height of splendor during Frederick's reign, after which it passed to the Angevins and the Spanish. A bleak event, perhaps Melfi's most tragic, occurred in 1528 when a French army sacked and burned the city during the Siege of Melfi or more commonly Bloody Easter. The bulk of the population was slaughtered, estimated at three to over four thousand people. Melfi was repopulated by residents from nearby communities as well as a colony of Albanians. A couple of years later, in 1531, Charles V gave Andrea Doria, admiral and statesman from Genoa, the title Prince of Melfi together with the city and its lands, and the family was in possession of the castle up until the 1950s. Edward Lear stayed at the castle in the 19th century and declared Melfi to be, "a delightful place of sojourn…. What a home one might make of the Castle of Melfi, with its city below and its territory around—the beau ideal of old feudal possession and magnificence." Shortly thereafter, Melfi was shaken by one of many devastating earthquakes throughout its history. Today, the castle is home to the National Archeological Museum of the Vulture-Melfese, which is the area in the very north of Basilicata and includes twenty communities around the spent volcano at the border of Campania and Puglia.

The museum was at the top of my list of things to see in Melfi. The public bus dropped me off at the train station on the outskirts and I had a little bit of a walk as Melfi is a good-sized town with about 18,000 inhabitants. Just before entering the walled center, I walked through a pleasant park that sat across from the last remaining historic gateway. A statue of Francesco Saverio Nitti (1868-1953), economist, politician, writer and antifascist, stands at the center of the garden, a tribute to Melfi's native son, who was at the forefront of *Meridionalismo* or the study of the problems of Southern Italy after unification. In the old town, a medieval maze of lanes lined with modest homes branched off of a handful of straighter arteries with several stately buildings dating back to the 16th century. All had weathered natural and other disasters, and been subject to much renovation and rebuilding. Along the very eastern side of the town was a more modern neighborhood of small, single-story houses arranged in perpendicular blocks that were constructed after the big Earthquake of Irpinia and the Vulture in 1930.

Of the cathedral, originally built by the Normans, only the Romanesque bell tower still stands, a square campanile with fantastical animals depicted high up on its face. A quick climb to the top rewards with a nice view over the tiled roofs to the castle and out to the surrounding fields. The cathedral itself, subject to countless ruinous events, has been restructured many times. Inside, a lovely Byzantine painting of the Madonna hints at the area's long ecclesiastical history, which is also evidenced in several *chiese rupestri* or cave churches that were carved out of volcanic tuff in the local countryside. The Santa Margherita *chiesa rupestre* even has a fresco called "The Contrast of the Living and the Dead" that is thought to portray Frederick II together with his wife and son dressed in falconer's clothing facing off three skeletons.

The bishop's residence next to the cathedral was initially erected by the Normans, but the present palatial quarters are of an 18th-century Baroque structure and house Melfi's diocesan museum. I particularly enjoyed the frescoed rooms and the bishops' hats designed into the tiled floors on the *piano nobile* (noble floor).

On my way to the castle at the northwestern edge of the old town, I passed streets with names like *Vico Albanese* (Albanian Road) and *Vico Pellegrino* (Pilgrim Lane). The wider *Via Normanni* (Normans Street) led to the fortification. Laundry waved on balconies and on makeshift lines strung along walls at the ground floor of the two-story buildings. I was taking a picture of rows of beautiful red peppers hanging on a balcony under a protective covering with a white T-shirt swinging out in front when I spied an old woman following my movements from the building next door. She was the type of old-fashioned, matronly woman who would never dream of donning a pair of slacks. I smiled and waved. She greeted me warmly and asked where I was from. She must have seen lots of people walking up *Via Normanni* to the castle in her years. *"Sei una straniera?"* (Are you a foreigner?) A couple of sentences later came, *"Sei da sola?"* (Are you by yourself?) Undoubtedly, she could whip up a batch of homemade pasta or bottle a year's supply of tomato sauce in her sleep, but she couldn't fathom visiting an unfamiliar town in a foreign country without a man at her side. *"Ti trovo io un bel compagno italiano, signora."* (*I'll* find you a nice Italian companion, ma'am.) Southern Italy is full of would-be matchmakers.

So I approached the castle with a smile on my face. The final block of dwellings was particularly unpretentious, seemingly all the more scaled down in relation to the fortress on higher ground. The drawbridge had been replaced with a permanent stone structure that invited me across and through the open archway to the castle's interior and erstwhile haven of emperors and popes. What was formerly impenetrable as an irregularly shaped polygonal fortification with ten towers, is today a museum of archeological antiquities. The exhibits range from artifacts of prehistoric indigenous peoples through the Roman period. Old stone walls give some sense of the location as does a section that has been renovated in Baroque style with a couple of paintings on hunting themes. But alas, Frederick's spirit must be conjured from the very walls themselves. Or short of that, the castle of nearby Lagopesole has a multimedia production with special effects projected on the walls that evoke the lives of former inhabitants, for those who go in for such dramatic presentation.

Melfi's archeological museum is excellent. The adjoining town of Lavello (ancient Forentum) is especially featured with a wealth of grave goods from the Daunian people (7th-3rd centuries BC) who were centered in northern Puglia, as well as objects from the period of Greater Greece (4th-3rd centuries BC). Daunian ceramics with geometric patterns, archaic bronze armor and a young noblewoman's otherworldly trousseau with elaborate gold jewelry are highlights. Ancient Rome is also represented, most notably with a grand, marble sarcophagus from the 2nd-century AD that attests to the importance of the area at the time. The tomb was discovered on the Appian Way near neighboring Rapolla.

Finally, of immense historical interest is an *askos* from the 3rd-century BC that shows the process of the zone's romanization. This ancient Greek vase found in Forentum may look a bit primitive at first glance; however, the transitioning between the Daunian, Greek and Roman cultures can be seen within the one object, in which elements relative to dress and customs, myths and musical instruments from the three societies are depicted in a decorative funeral scene. The vase is an excellent example of how civilizations and their traditions have been overlapping for thousands of years.

With these thoughts and images in my head, I descended back through the old town, past the modern district to the train station. Construction played havoc with the official bus stop, so I made sure to clarify the exact location of pickup with the station's barista. A Puglian who had long lived and worked up north was already waiting. He didn't look too happy and then explained that he had to get off the train and take a bus to complete the last stretch of his journey to Puglia because of work on the line. I was headed to Venosa for a couple of days, and when the appointed time neared and then passed, I waved down every bus that came by and asked where it was going no matter what was clearly stated on the front. The schedule was rather sporadic so I didn't want to get stuck. I even went over to the other side of the street to make sure. The transplanted Puglian waited patiently, to his detriment, as he would find out too late that his driver didn't pull up at the official alternate stop. I left him cursing the buses, the trains, the powers that be, Italy. My bus was empty, just the driver and me. We had a nice ride through the Vulture, passing Rapolla with its rows of wine caves built into the hills. This was the community where the large Roman sarcophagus was found. I would return, but Venosa beckoned.

10. VENOSA

Carpe diem . . .

Horace, *Odes*, Book I, xi

I DOUBT HORACE had the killing of one's wife and lover in mind when he penned the now famous phrase. However, that's just what Carlo Gesualdo, Prince of Venosa, did when he caught the couple *in flagrante delicto*. The particularly gruesome execution became the talk of the town in late 16th-century Naples, and even when Gesualdo da Venosa is discussed today, the question lingers as to whether it is wholly due to the man's talent as a composer or that the macabre details of his personal life have boosted interest in his musical compositions. That the bizarre attracts attention is certain; however, as an artist, Gesualdo's gifts are undeniable.

Horace put Venosa on the literary map, and Gesualdo (1566-1613) has caused many a serious music lover to reach for an Italian atlas to pinpoint the late-Renaissance composer's birthplace. To say that he was innovative is banal; his compositions in context of the period's prevailing musical harmony are nothing short of extraordinary. Surely, his great wealth gave him the leeway to explore, not to be bound by convention or a patron who demanded a run-of-the-mill style. And perhaps the pain of his own life pushed him to the edge of dissonance and to a chromaticism that wouldn't be approached again for well over 200 years. His madrigals and secular vocal music must have been startling to the ears of his contemporaries. Today, program notes fascinate audiences as much as the music.

Gesualdo was born in Venosa although he spent much of his life in other homes, such as in Naples, where he committed the double murder, and in the town of Gesualdo, not too far over the border in Campania. Shortly before his birth, the family was granted the title Princes of Venosa together with the accompanying feudal lands and castle, which was built in 1470. (An earlier castle in Venosa had been turned into a convent.) Carlo and his son Emanuele transformed the imposing for-

tress with its four cylindrical towers and wide, dry moat into an aristocratic residence. They added the loggia that faces the inner courtyard
and substituted the drawbridge with a permanent stone structure decorated with two lion heads dug up from the town's Roman ruins.

During the time the Gesualdo family were feudal lords of the man-
or, Venosa attracted artists and intellectuals, and was an important cultural center. Today, the castle hosts an archeological museum in underground stone chambers. I would have preferred a late-renaissance
drawing room on the upper floors, but perhaps that will come. Gesualdo may be a bit obscure for the average visitor, but he certainly spices
up local history. I even ate in a restaurant named after his butchered,
two-timing wife. The risotto made with the local Aglianico del Vulture
red wine was delicious, but the slightly reddish color that, shall we say,
bled a bit onto the pecorino gave me pause.

The castle museum divides its focus between a prehistoric site about
nine kilometers (6 miles) from the town center and Venosa's Roman period. The Stone Age archeological park called Notarchirico dates back
600,000 years and can be visited with a reservation. Numerous animal
remains, Paleolithic tools and the femur of a woman who lived 300,000
years ago were discovered there.

Jumping forward to antiquity, the area of Venosa was inhabited by
the Samnites, an ancient Italic people, from the 6th century BC. Rome
drove them out in 291 BC and moved in 20,000 Romans to establish
their first colony in Lucania, which they named Venusia in honor of
Venus, the goddess of love. The construction of the Appian Way, which
passed right through the center of Venusia on its route from Rome to
Brindisi, brought prosperity and development. Venusia would become
a Municipium, giving its inhabitants citizenship and the right to vote.

A highlight of the museum is the collection of inscriptions that
show the various phases of inhabitation. The memorial stones written
in the Oscan language of the Samnites, the funerary etchings in Hebrew, Jewish images and early Christian artifacts are particularly interesting. Exiting the castle and going back over the bridge to the piazza
from where the main street through the historic center began, I was

struck by both the flatness and the orderliness of the town. Edward Lear had a similar impression many years ago and remarked that it was "a most picturesque place ... on the brink of a wide and deep ravine, its cathedral and castle overlooking the whole area of habitations. Extremely clean streets, paved from side to side with broad flags of stone, like those in Naples; numerous bits of columns or capitals, mediaeval stone lions, and the machicolated and turreted towers of the old castle, gave great hopes of great employ for the pencil."

I wouldn't be drawing Venosa as he did, but I enjoyed the features of the old structures and the town's tranquility. And walking on the smooth, wide paving stones down the main street, I came across several ceramic shops, each with an artisan concentratedly hand-painting detailed images on a variety of clay pieces. From fulfilling commissioned orders to objects for the tourist trade to fine decorative arts, the execution was excellent. I would discover that Venosa has historically been known for its ceramics and that evidence of production goes back to antiquity.

In the first shop I entered, the range of articles spanned from cute refrigerator magnets to large plates and vases of a serious nature. The famous Lucanian brigand Carmine Crocco looked benevolently out at me from a framed ceramic portrait, Horace's laurel-wreathed profile graced a souvenir plate and I recognized an homage to Lear in a Venosa landscape on a large platter. A young woman in a white smock was working on a house sign in the characteristic position of the fine paintbrush in the right hand with the left gently supporting the wrist. She looked up from her project and greeted me with a warm smile. The shaping, firing and other production aspects were done in a larger location on the outskirts of town, but as for the painting of just about everything on display in the center shop, she was a one-woman band. But of all the lovely pieces including reproductions of ancient Greek vases, the image that popped out at me and obviously spoke to her as she repeated it in various forms was the *gufo* or owl. I remembered the charming simplicity of the wide-eyed owls on the red and black ceramic cups of ancient Greece in Melfi's archeological museum. I had even snapped a photo. Her contemporary interpretations found the whimsical in this popular symbol of wisdom and created an historical bond through the reworking of the traditional image.

Further down the street, a retired art teacher was busy painting a large lamp. Her body was very still as she balanced the brush delicately between her fingers. A beautiful set of personalized dinner plates sat on a worktable next to a pile of translucent paper with hand-drawn designs. What patience and dedication—meeting these women, watching them work and examining the ceramics, I was struck by the spirit and artistry that went into the creation of each piece and the genuine value in such one-of-a-kind objects.

Venusia would have had numerous kilns to keep up with the needs of the local population, much greater than today's approximately 12,000 people. And as the modern town didn't grow up directly on top of the ancient Roman one, the remains of this once-thriving culture can be visited in the good-sized archeological park just a few minutes walk along the main street outside the center. The ruins feature an elliptical amphitheater that would have held 10,000 spectators in its heyday, Roman baths, a Domus and other houses lining the old Roman roads. Habitation of the site continued into the medieval period.

Of all there is to see in Venosa, however, Lucanians usually zero in on one thing: *"Hai visto l'Incompiuta?"* Have you seen the incomplete? Huh? I suppose there is a grand fascination in the monumental project left undone, so great a venture that one-thousand years later, the unfinished complex is still called the *Incompiuta*. In Venosa's case, the project was the enlargement of a medieval church. If the plan had been to build a destination, whether it be for flocks of pilgrims or tourists, the Benedictines succeeded in their task. The official name of the *Incompiuta* is the *Abbazia della Santissima Trinità* or the Abbey of the Holy Trinity. Italians have been waxing poetic over the complex for a long time and designated it a National Monument in 1897 together with the cathedral in nearby Acerenza. Basilicata's third national landmark is Matera's cathedral, added to the list in 1940.

Over a thousand years before the *Incompiuta* was conceived, a pagan temple dedicated to Hymen, the Greek god of weddings, was situated on the site. In the 5th-6th century, Early Christians constructed a church over the ancient house of worship and left behind sections of mosaic flooring with symbols of fish. Other remnants underfoot include mosaics from an upper-class Roman home of the Imperial Era, and part of a patterned, multicolored medieval floor in small brick-tiles. These elements coexist within the large Romanesque church, of an uncertain date but built prior to the arrival of the Normans and successively modified.

The cathedral's entrance is rather modest. To its right, an attached building that originally served as guest lodgings houses a handful of miscellaneous architectural sculptures. The foyer features an attractive 13th-century marble entranceway and what is known as the Friendship Column, a well-worn Roman pillar that gets its name from the tradition of going around it in tandem with hands held, hugging the stone, to augur eternal friendship. Young brides squeeze in the narrow space between the column and the wall to herald fertility.

The sanctuary would become the final resting place of several high-placed Normans of the Hauteville family, most notably William Iron Arm and Robert Guiscard. With the abbey's increasing importance, a larger, monumental complex was conceived, and work began in the 11th century. When the Benedictines lost favor with the pope, the project was passed to the Knights of Malta, and the enterprise eventually fizzled out to leave the *Incompiuta*.

Aerial photos give a good idea of the incorporation of the old church into the new plan in the shape of a long Latin cross. The entrance is through the archeological park, past the ruins of one millennium to those of another and through a stone portal over which the Agnus Dei, a lamb with a cross, the symbol of the Knights of Malta has been carved. Only the outer walls and numerous pillars were erected, with much of the building material coming from the surrounding ruins of ancient Rome. Mellifluous chiming of the large, three-eyed bell-gable, a 16th-century addition, welcomed me into the atmospheric inner sanctum. I waited until the tour group finished their rounds and were led out, perhaps down the main street to Horace's house and then on to the castle. A few moments in silence between the walls and columns, I felt the *Incompiuta* was the way it was meant to be, big plans, borrowed building blocks with the occasional symbol from another era, all stacked haphazardly in medieval order under the open sky.

Churches, castles, Roman ruins and perhaps a line or two of Latin are what one might expect on a visit to an Italian town, maybe even the distant hooves of a crusader or the dissonant strains of a Renaissance madrigal. Venosa surprises with Jewish catacombs. A Hebrew community already existed in Venusia by the 1st century BC, and its population grew with the destruction of Jerusalem in 70 AD and the diaspora of the following century.

I had the good fortune of stumbling on a private tour of the catacombs with the proprietor of my bed and breakfast. I had selected the accommodation primarily for its location, but the choice turned out to be much more than having a door key to one of the lovely, 16th-century buildings in the historic center. My hosts were armed with that essential information needed to plan smooth days, not to mention rides to the bus stop and even as far as Potenza when our schedules coincided. The word helpful doesn't begin to describe their generous spirit and the warmth imparted, and as an added bonus, a remarkably informative tour of the catacombs.

I had been to catacombs in Rome and had always associated them with early Christians, who excavated large underground burial areas that reinforced the sense of community. Venosa also has a Christian complex of tombs next to the Jewish one, which experts take as a sign that the two religions tranquilly resided side by side. There was no ghetto in Venusia. As in Rome, the catacombs of ancient Venusia were excavated out of tuff rock beyond the city boundaries, and today they lie just two kilometers from the historic center continuing northeast along the road that passes the archeological park. These catacombs are easily accessible, just a walkup to a doorway built into the side of a hill, due to the shifting earth that brought the underground passageways to light in the mid-19th century after having been long forgotten.

590 entombments have been identified in Venosa's Jewish cata-

combs. From the inscriptions on the walls, the tombs can be dated between the 4th and 6th centuries AD. However, in an open-air cemetery between the Roman amphitheater and the *Incompiuta*, Hebrew epitaphs have been found on gravestones through the 9th century. Inside the catacombs, oblong recesses line the walls, corridors and arms of the subterranean passageways. Although the physical beings are long since gone, catacombs give off that sense of mystery and the unknown. Are the spirits still lingering? Do the souls of the people who walked the earth in ancient times and who filled the niches for centuries lurk somewhere within the cramped spaces or the porous volcanic stone, itself?

The wood-paneled walkway and recessed lighting contrast the ancient chisel-markings that cover the walls. Inscriptions are etched on the burial chambers in Greek, Latin and Hebrew, with Latin predominating over the Greek in later years. Many epitaphs are in two languages, and both seven- and nine-branch menorahs are painted on the walls in red. The pièce de résistance, however, can only be seen in photographs as the arm where it is located has collapsed. The fresco in vivid gold and red is in one of the larger, arched tombs and depicts a menorah, Etrog (citron), shofar (ram-horn trumpet), amphora of oil and lulav (palm branch). These symbolic objects are as relevant for Judaism today as they were in the period of the catacombs, but not in Venosa, as the Spanish expelled the Jewish community from Southern Italy in the 16th century. Sadly, they would have to *carpe* their *diem* elsewhere.

Horace is famous the world over for this Latin quotation, often translated as "seize the day." His poetry, which is principally collected in *Satires*, *Epodes*, *Odes* and *Epistles*, is known for its stylistic elegance and uncommon irony. Venosa honors the poet with a full-length statue in the old town's center square, Piazza Orazio (remember, Horace in Italian). And there is even a *Casa di Orazio* or Horace's house, despite the fact that no one really believes he lived in the ancient structure. However, the building just off the main street does date from the Roman period, so he could have lived in it if the old stone walls hadn't been proven to be part of a bath complex.

Walking through the heart of the historic center, I couldn't help but notice another of Horace's phrases written on, of all things, a country-and-western bar, complete with images of cowboys, their boots and a wagon wheel: *Nunc est bibendum* — Now you must drink. Not bad advice, particularly at midday. I was reminded of Lear's culinary experience in Venosa: "The cuisine is of a much more recherché kind than is usually met with in the provinces, and we are particularly directed to taste this dish of *seppia* or cuttlefish, or to do justice to those mushrooms. The wines, moreover, are super excellent, and the little black olives the best possible; and all things are well served and in good taste."

I had worked up an appetite for lunch that day and found a nice, centrally located restaurant in which to dine. I was seated at *"tavolo 1"* or table #1, according to the marking on top of the small glass jar filled with a couple of dried, bulbous peperoncini at my place. A pile of Lucanian *peperoni cruschi* spilled over a platter on the restaurant's serving table, together with a dish of fresh peperoncini and a jar with peperoncini in olive oil. Later, I popped my head into the kitchen, where bunches of these important ingredients hung from a hook in the center of the room. I wouldn't be surprised if Basilicata's scout motto was, "Be prepared with *peperoni cruschi*."

What would Horace have said about the bright-red, shriveled peppers? He certainly enjoyed eating, but peppers arrived in Europe much too late for him. By his own account, he was a man of simple pleasures, and in his first book of *Satires* professed contentment with his unpretentious lifestyle and mentioned a comfort food that is still typical of the region: "I return home to my bowl of leeks, chickpeas and *lagane* (short, flat fresh pasta)." On that day, I opted for a characteristic *orecchiette con ragù di salsiccia* (ear-shaped pasta with a sausage and tomato sauce) and ordered the house wine, which I thought to be rather good, a local Aglianico del Vulture.

An Italian couple at the next table happened to be ordering as I was in the midst of devouring my pasta and I couldn't help but overhearing the discussion with regard to their wine choice. The waiter volunteered the merits of the house wine and the woman asked numerous, very specific questions. The ordering process can sometimes be quite lengthy in Italy. She seemed satisfied with the responses, tasted and ordered it, and from what I gathered was pleased with what, in my humble opinion, lined up with Edward Lear's.

After finishing my sizable portion of pasta, I proceeded with a grilled, sliced beef that was served with a generous pile of rucola and long pecorino shavings on top. It was the type of presentation that makes red meat seem like the healthy choice. At the end of this abundant second course, I was too full to even listen to what tasty desserts might have been available that afternoon; however, I never feel amiss with a good digestif after a large meal. The waiter recommended the house-made grappa, which wouldn't normally be my first choice, but he exuded such enthusiasm for the fragrant brandy. Wow, was that grappa ever smooth! And such a delicate flavor. My exclamation, something to the effect of *"una grappa per le donne"* or a lady's grappa got the attention of the couple at the next table, who wanted to try it. We then began to talk and as it turned out, the woman's family was in the wine business from nearby Barile. Her companion was a down-to-earth intellectual who spoke passionately about the historical *transumanza* or migratory herding of sheep and cows along the ancient paths that corresponded with the Appian Way and other such routes of the Romans.

Often in life, a pleasant half hour of conversation with strangers ends then and there with that momentary good feeling, but perhaps because it was Venosa, we seized the day and exchanged information for the next time I passed through. As Horace said in the ode with a phrase that would become more recognizable than his own name:

In the moment of our talking, envious time has ebb'd away.
Seize the present; trust tomorrow e'en as little as you may.

11. RAPOLLA: VISIT TO AN ITALIAN SPA

THE YOUNG MAN at the front desk advised me to get a number early the next day in order to avoid waiting all morning to see the doctor. I tried to convince him to just give me a number that evening, but he said he couldn't do that. So I rolled out of bed earlier than I would have liked, only to discover that I probably could have nabbed a number on my own the night before. I just had to take a ticket from the little gadget like the ones in old-fashioned American bakeries. Eight or nine people were already seated in the waiting room. You can't beat the Italian elderly. Being the first at the doctor's office to take a number is a way of life.

The doctor hadn't arrived yet. I was at the *Terme di Rapolla*. Usually translated as spa, *terme* are hot springs or thermal baths. The word refers to the facility that makes use of the therapeutic properties of the thermal spring water. While beauty services are often offered as well, the main business of a *terme* is medically related and treatments are largely covered with a prescription from one's primary-care physician within the Italian health network. Patients then have to see the spa's doctor to confirm the validity of the prescriptions (in other words, to weed out fraud). As a client not affiliated with Italy's national health care system, I have also visited a couple of *terme* in Calabria, so I was familiar with the services. They're quite reasonable when compared with an American spa experience. The complete lack of pampering may account for the difference. The indulgent spa also exists in Italy, but not on the government's dime.

Basilicata has two *terme*, in the towns of Latronico in the Pollino National Park and Rapolla in the Vulture. They're seasonal and generally operate between May and October. Looking for a spa late in the season, I was pleased to find the *Terme di Rapolla* still open and offering an excellent *pacchetto* or package of treatments in combination with their hotel. Of course, the specific thermal ministrations were contingent upon an official medical visit. According to the brochures at the front desk, the spa's salty-sulfate-bicarbonate-alkaline waters were especially

71

indicated for curing rheumatic pain, the gout, sciatica, arthritis, arthrosis, the after-effects of fractures, rhinitis, sinusitis, pharyngitis, laryngitis and bronchitis. My goals were a bit more modest: to breathe a bit easier and to rest my tired muscles and joints under a heap of hot mud.

The waiting room was fairly full by the time the doctor arrived. Most of the people lived within an hour's driving distance. A woman sat down next to me, smiled, and after a couple of pleasantries said, *"Voi non siete da qui."* (You're not from around here.) No, I'm American. *"Un'americana… vi conosco! Voi siete una scrittrice."* (An American… I know you! You're a writer.) I don't know if the woman was clairvoyant or just had an excellent memory, but she said she had seen me on TV in the interview I had done for a local channel about the Parade of the Turks in Potenza. The station apparently had the tendency to run programs over and over. And then I thought back and I realized that I happened to be wearing the same bright-blue shirt. Maybe she really did recognize me. She definitely seemed pleased. And then my number came up.

The medical visit was similar to other Italian spas. I basically told the doctor which treatments I was interested in and why I needed them. He took my blood pressure, deemed me fit to withstand hot mud and sulfurous inhalations, and checked off the boxes. Six days of therapeutic mud, curative baths, aerosol, inhalation, nebulization and massages, plus one aesthetic treatment of my choice for good measure. It was a full package. I took the *prescrizione medica* or medical prescription to the front desk and they set to work on arranging my appointment schedule while I had a quick breakfast at the bar, over which hung a poster of a *cornetto* with a cup of tea and the words, *"Il benessere a colazione"* or Wellness at Breakfast. At least I was getting a good, Italian-style start to my day.

My wellness plan looked more intense than a college student's class schedule as the treatments were only ministered in the morning during the shoulder season. Perhaps because I was a foreigner, one of the administrators extended the courtesy of taking me around to the various rooms, introducing me to the staff and explaining the drill. Donned in the spa's large, white terry-cloth robe, I was ready to begin my course of treatments.

I had my work cut out for me, starting my mornings with a battery of inhalations. I was advised that I could beat the rush if I got there before 7:30, which wasn't difficult as my hotel room was up one flight of stairs, and judging by the lengthy rolling I heard from daybreak, I was above the mud area. Those heavy buckets traversed a very long corridor.

The aerosol and inhalation were done in a room lined up with rows of partitioned sinks. The setup is what I would imagine to have encountered back in 1930s America when the likes of FDR were taking the cure. Not that the equipment was necessarily old, but it seemed to be saying, "If it works, why change the design?" One day I was placed in front of a newer row, a variation of the old style except for the abandonment of the ceramic sink for an all-in-one plastic design, a computerized on-off switch, and aqua-colored accents. The tube that conveyed the therapeutic stream to my nasal passages was exactly the same.

The attendant handed out paper bibs to catch the vapor and its runoff from the patient's face and little plastic appendages that fit in the nostrils to personalize the end of the water tube. Some patients got a circular attachment that covered the nose and mouth. I assumed this was as per the doctor's directive, based on the only word written in the annotation column of my prescription: *forcella* or forked, which I deduced was the divided nostril accessory I received. Thus, the aerosol treatment consisted of inhaling small particles of thermal water for the benefit of my respiratory system. Next came the open-mouth inhalation of the spa's curative waters in the form of a mist. The vapor billowed out of a larger tube, and with eyes closed and mouth agape, I breathed in the hot steam. I could feel my sinuses beginning to drain, although I could in no way compete with select elderly gentlemen whose mucous, from the sound of it, could have filled a claw-footed bathtub.

The final respiratory therapy, the *nebulizzazione* could be done at my leisure as the cure was imparted by way of a nebulizer or a device that produces a fine spray from a liquid. Fewer people were signed up for that as it was an additional charge under the Italian health care system, according to a lovely woman I met amidst the medicinal haze. A large misting machine filled the modest space with the sort of grayish fog that shrouds coastal towns in horror movies. About twelve stackable plastic garden chairs were lined up along the wall, although you could sort of kick one before you saw it. The room didn't really lend itself to chitchat as you couldn't get a good look at who you were talking to. I did notice the glow of cell phone screens, though. I don't remember how our conversation began but we got onto the topic of traveling in Basilicata. She wanted to recommend places to explore, all of which I had already visited, to her surprise and delight. Nothing endears you more to Lucanians than taking an interest in their region.

My *fango e bagno terapeutico* or therapeutic mud and bath treatment took place in one of a row of rooms set up for the purpose. I was prepared for the type of odiferous experience usually associated with the presence of sulfur, but surprisingly, the smooth, shiny brown mud didn't stink! Sitting up on the covered table, I watched the no-nonsense woman dressed in scrubs unceremoniously lob large hand-scoops of mud behind me. She then instructed me to lie back on the warm, squishy substance while she slung more mud on my shoulders, elbows, hips, knees and feet. It felt so good. My wrists and hands were waiting for their turn when she began to wrap me up in a cocoon. *"Ma le mani?"* (But my hands?) They weren't X'd off on the diagram, she said. Maybe there was a reason. She didn't want to hurt me. I tried to assure her that it was just an oversight and it wouldn't be a problem. No, I would have to get it in writing from the doctor. *Mammamia*, I thought. I tried to push it out of my mind as I relaxed into the warm, weighty mud. This was truly the feeling of *benessere*, wellness. No matter how long I lie in hot mud, it is never enough.

Reality returns with the woman dressed in scrubs. She draws the bathwater and helps me extract myself from the gooey matter. I was to leave as much as possible in the gauze and plastic, then try to make it the two steps across to the tub without slipping and giving myself a real reason to return to the spa. The residual mud dissolved into the warm thermal water, and my skin soaked it all up until the timer buzzed. As per my instructions I pulled the plug, rinsed off with the same thermal water using the handheld sprayer and went to a room across the hall where I lay down and was covered with a hot blanket. A little time to repose.

I returned to the doctor early the next morning. No line on a Tuesday and he scribbled his okay for my wrists and hands. I would come to find out that many people had prescriptions for just one shoulder or one knee. I had wondered how the older people I saw shuffling up and down the hallways could have managed not falling on their faces as they tried to maneuver in and out of the tub with the slippery mud all over their bodies, not to mention their hands and feet.

After the mud, I had no time to dally as I had my half hour massage appointment and the physical therapists had full schedules, as well. I would repeat the routine for five more days. One morning I even managed to fit in a facial as my optional beauty treatment. And the thing about the *terme* is that you work up an appetite because you're really working on your "cure." My package included *pensione completa* or full board, where the word "full" could refer to all three meals or to your feeling after eating them. Every day, there was a little form to be filled out for lunch and dinner, three choices for the first course and two for the second.

The food was good homestyle cooking, and as I staggered away from the table after the first lunch, I remembered the doctor saying that you had to pace yourself as the portions were *abbondante*. Even the wine was served in copious quantities. Rapolla is a community noted for its wine production, and the spa's house red was excellent; however, there I am at my table-for-one and the waiter brings me a liter pitcher, full above the line! So I asked him if any women really drank a liter of red wine at lunch, and he didn't hesitate, *"Alcuni, sì."* Some, yes. He never placed less than a good half liter on the table and I never came close to finishing it, but I was still in need of a nap afterwards.

First courses ranged from a lighter *risotto con zucchine e vongole* (rice with zucchini and clams) or *vellutata di verdura* (a velvety puree of vegetables) to a heavier, heaping portion of *orecchiette in cartoccio* (ear-shaped pasta en papillote) that could easily have served two. I recall the traditional aroma of sausage, tomato sauce and cheese that gently rose with the steam emanating from the mound of orecchiette as I opened the packet. I had trouble pushing it away before reaching the bottom.

A little while later my beef stew with mushrooms and potatoes was served. That weighty experience convinced me to check off the *orata in crosta di zucchine* (zucchini encrusted sea bream) the next day and the *baccalà in umido* (codfish stew) the day after. Yes, I wanted the *salsiccia ai ferri* (grilled sausage), but I was there for my health, after all.

In an attempt to work off a few calories I walked up to the historic center on free afternoons. Rapolla has quite a history. Even Hannibal encamped in a section of town now known as *Querce d'Annibale* or Hannibal's Oaks from where he engaged in skirmishes with the Roman Consul Marcus Claudius Marcellus in 209 BC. Marcellus died the following year in neighboring Venosa, where he is said to be buried on the Appian Way. Other testaments to the community's ancient history include the remains of a Roman villa and the aforementioned magnificent sarcophagus of a consul's daughter that is on display in the archeological museum of Melfi.

My wanderings in Rapolla (population around 4,400) took me up the very steep, narrow lanes of the old town that has been battered by earthquakes over its long history. The 13th-century cathedral at the top of the hill is particularly attractive as the evening light bounces off its facade. Perhaps the most interesting view is looking across to the opposite hills that are lined with wine caves dug out of the tuff rock in every crest. Wine is important in this neck of the woods.

On one of my evenings I was invited to the home of an affable couple I had met in Maratea the week before. When they asked me what angle of Basilicata I would be exploring next and I said Rapolla, they laughed incredulously. They lived in Rapolla! Originally from the Naples area, they treated me to a homemade feast of a Neapolitan classic, the *pizza fritta*. Being in their kitchen was like an invitation to a private cooking show and they made enough of those little fried pizzas to feed a whole studio audience. But I was a guest, so there was also a whole *arista di maiale al latte* or pork loin roast cooked in milk and fried potatoes. Delicious food, great conversation, an overwhelming hospitality.

The next day at lunch (those meals just kept coming), in addition to the usual fruit for dessert (and in no way does the word "usual" diminish that tasty, nutritious tradition) the waiter placed a slice of chocolate crostata in front of me. I had been missed at dinner the previous evening and he had saved me a piece. The waiter was a man of few words, but significant gestures.

On my final day I didn't know if I would be able to finish my entire routine before check-out, but I was reassured I could take my time. So I stayed a few extra minutes in the nebulization room and had a good chat with my massage therapist. And staring at the floor through the donut hole, I discovered another coincidence. Remember the couple with the winery that I met at a restaurant in Venosa? My therapist was also the masseur of the vintner's mother. It's a small world and even smaller in Basilicata.

As I'm paying my bill, literally, as this was still an old-fashioned place where they didn't take an imprint of my credit card at check-in and I paid the entire sum at the end of the stay, and saying my goodbyes to the staff, I heard, "Kar-ren, Kar-ren!" It turned out to be the nice woman I had talked with in the nebulization room. I would never have recognized her out of the mist, but I was the foreigner so it was a little easier for her. She introduced me to her friend and we talked about more places I could visit. My rest was over. I was going to have a light lunch…maybe tomorrow.

12. AGLIANICO DEL VULTURE

No verses written by water-drinkers can please or be long-lived…. the sweet muses have usually smelt of wine in the morning.

Horace, *Epistles*, Book I, xix

I HAD SEEN THE ROWS of doorways built into hillsides of several communities in the Vulture. Now I was parked in a turnout on a narrow street across from a succession of them in the town of Barile. These doorways were entrées into an ancient wine tradition, and I would soon get a gander at what was within. Even before I was aware of the official designation of the *Parco urbano delle cantine* or Urban Park of Wine Caves in Barile, Rapolla, Roccanova, Pietragalla, Sant'Angelo Le Fratte and Tolve, I instinctively felt there was something important going on behind those closed doors. Each portal exuded a personality, even those that appeared abandoned or suffered from neglect. The doors had been carefully painted at one time or another. Locks of various shapes and sizes secured the contents. Each entryway had a street number. Some were flush to the hillside and others had what looked to be a little antechamber built out from the earth. To me, the urban wine park held a certain fascination.

After all, the evocative grottos carved out of the volcanic stone have been prime locations for wine conservation for thousands of years. The prestigious Aglianico grape has found a happy home in the hilly, volcanic soil of the Vulture and a fitting maturation within the area's tuff caves. Tradition goes back to the Greeks and the importation of the vine that the Romans would call *ellenico* in reference to the Hellenic civilization, according to a probable theory as to the derivation of its name. The Aglianico grape yields an intensely ruby-colored, harmonic, full-bodied red wine with a rich tannin structure that becomes silky with age.

A chance meeting in a Venosa restaurant over a year earlier introduced me to a family with a Barile vineyard that had been passed down over generations. Then betrothed and since married, the couple responded enthusiastically to my e-mail and we were to meet at their *cantina*, which I quickly located amidst a row of caves along the hillside leading into town. A pair of industrial-sized double doors in brown-painted metal were fitted into the stone facade. This grotto was the hub of a thriving family business, one that had historically focused on growing high quality Aglianico fruit for others. Of course, the Mastrodomenico family had always made wine for personal consumption, but it wasn't until the 21st century that they decided to take the leap and create their own label. From the initial 1,000 bottles that quickly sold out in the first year, the winery today produces 30,000. Amazingly, almost the entire production is carried out in the rather modest *can-*

tina, just one of many along the row of nondescript doorways built into the hillside.

The cave was maximized to its fullest with gleaming, state-of-the-art stainless-steel containers filling the space up to the domed ceiling. Banks of French oak casks lined a side wall. Emanuela excitedly told me all about the production as we sampled the must from the recent harvest. The not-yet-wine was a gorgeous pinky-red color and its taste boded well for the vintage. We sat down at a small table with folding chairs and she popped open a bottle that we enjoyed together amidst animated conversation. The family was entwined with the land and its people. Their work was a labor of love in a process that wasn't only biological, but each and every step from the growing to the maturation to the bottling was traceable by way of a matrix barcode on the bottle.

We drove out to the fields in a very Italian manner, assuredly but a bit wild on the up-and-down winding roads. The vineyard's leaves were turning a rich red and contrasted elegantly with the deep, velvety blue of the grapes that were still to be harvested in a section in which the fruit was destined for a meditative dessert wine. Hmm, the Appian Way would have passed nearby... A wind farm was visible off in the distance, but as it was approaching dusk, it was best not to stray too far from the car. The wild boars could be dangerous.

Later on, as we took our leave, Emanuela pressed a local stone into my hand. I should take a piece of the Lucanian terroir back to America with me. That terroir was certainly more than a rock formed from the Vulture's ash. She was giving me a memory of the land, its people and traditions. I would visit other wineries of the area. Each had its distinct style and its own microclimate within that of the Vulture. One winery had excavated an enormous cave out in the countryside. As the oversized door slid aside, I expected 007 to come racing out of the underground bunker. The setup looked too modern for Batman.

Another winery that made an impression on me was in the heart of nearby Rionero del Vulture. When I pulled up to the Cantine del Notaio, I thought that there was perhaps a mishap with my navigation system. How would I be able to visit the wine cellars in the middle of town? Answer: Grottos under the street level that had been dug out as far back as 1600. The cellars used by Franciscan monks still provide the perfect balance of temperature, humidity and ventilation for the maturation of wine. Descending into the grottos, I found the humidity oddly refreshing. The engaging owner led the tour with passion, and as with Emanuela, I became caught-up with his enthusiasm for the family enterprise, the wine and its terroir.

Such encounters could really get a girl drinking. I made a note to return to the area during one of the community festivals in which the *cantine* doors would be thrown open, and local products and tastings could be had: cured meats, cheeses, honey, chestnuts in the fall, and of course the "Prince" of the Vulture, the Aglianico.

13. ACERENZA, RIPACANDIDA AND LAGOPESOLE: FAVORITE CHURCHES

GUIDEBOOKS, especially those in Italian, tend to wax poetic about churches, and they count an extraordinary number of *gioielli* amongst the religious art within. While these jewels don't always appear to be of top priority with regard to conservation, their numbers are sufficiently significant to overwhelm the casual church visitor as he peruses an informational pamphlet distributed by the local tourist board. The region of Basilicata is no stranger to beautiful churches, many *gioielli* in themselves. Traveling throughout the Vulture, I was struck by three that oozed history and transported me back to another time even without cracking open a guidebook.

The cathedral of Acerenza had been recommended by several Lucanians interested in the next stop on my itinerary. I was assured that the monumental church was *vale la pena* (worth the effort), which was a good thing as my route to the town turned out to be much longer than it needed to be. I had missed my exit, thus considerably extending my journey, driving up and down hillsides, past fields, forests and wind turbines. Finally, Acerenza was in my sights, "perched on high like a nest," just as Horace had written epochs earlier. At 833 meters (2,733 feet) above sea level, the natural fortress was more imposing than I had imagined. In its heyday Acerenza had clearly been a substantial community. Today, the town's prominence has been reduced to one of Italy's *"Borghi più belli"* or most beautiful villages, nothing to sneeze at, mind you. However, clearly the intentions of its founding fathers had been anything but quaint. The Roman historian Titus Livy pronounced it a battle fortress, and due to its strategic location the Eastern Orthodox and Roman churches wrestled for its control.

I would worry about which religious faction had the upper hand after I found a place to put the car. The principal streets were so narrow that the only way in and out of the old town was on a one-way loop. I managed to come upon the free spaces next to the cathedral at an optimum moment of availability and that's where my car stayed for a couple of days. That night, I wandered the tidy streets lined with old stone houses, some with simple wooden doorways and others fronted by imposing portals adorned with family crests. Although late spring, there was a nip to the air that I warmed with a comforting bowl of *pasta e fagioli* (pasta and beans) in a local restaurant.

On the following morning I met an enthusiastic young man from the Acerenza *pro loco*, which is an organization found in communities all over Italy with the mission to promote the location and its events. I would discover that he was in the minority around town as his name wasn't Canio. Yes, Acerenza is a beautiful village with a surprising number of male citizens possessing this uncommon name, that of their patron saint. San Canio (Saint Canius) was a third-century bishop and martyr of the Catholic Church, whose body was brought to Acerenza around the year 800. In 1080 during construction of a new cathedral, the saint's remains were uncovered, and St. Canius would become the protector of the church and diocese. As Acerenza had recently been elevated to Metropolitan Archdiocese with dominion over a newly formed ecclesiastical province that reached from Potenza to Matera and from Gravina in Puglia all the way down to Oriolo in Calabria, the *Cattedrale di Santa Maria Assunta e San Canio* (Cathedral of the Assumption of

Mary and Saint Canius) was designed on a grand scale. And it is believed that this monumental basilica, constructed by the Normans over the ruins of an Early Christian Church, which had been built over a Roman temple, inspired the name of the region, Basilicata.

The cathedral's roots go deep, and its walls incorporate physical reminders of earlier structures. My guide presented Acerenza's history as he highlighted details of the church's exterior: pieces of Roman sarcophagi with busts draped in togas, marble columns from the ciborium of the Early Christian Church, a Knights Templar cross, coats of arms of prominent families and allegoric sculptures. The splendid Romanesque structure in the shape of the Latin cross impressed with both its architectural grandeur as well as its intricate particulars. In 1456 the cathedral suffered severe damage in a devastating earthquake that destroyed the city, and the facade and bell tower were rebuilt in the following century.

The interior, a long sanctuary with three naves, is decidedly unembellished, almost contemporary in its minimalism. In great contrast, the magnificent crypt under the chancel features evocative Renaissance frescos by 16th-century Lucanian painter Giovanni Todisco. Entering the richly decorated space feels just like what it must have been for those gaining access to the noble family's crypt back when it was consecrated in 1524.

Another interesting characteristic of the cathedral is the ambulatory, or circular walking space around the apse, off of which is St. Canius' chapel. His remains were hidden for protection from Saracen invaders a long time ago and their exact location has since been forgotten. His walking stick, however, can be spied through a small hole in his altar. The knotty piece of wood, smooth at the top from the saint's grip, is, by many accounts, magical. Every so often, the pastoral staff moves on its own. The most remarkable documented levitation occurred on the 30th of May in 1799, when the simple cane remained suspended in air for an entire night. Either you believe or you don't. I can only say that there are a lot of people with the name Canio in Acerenza.

Numerous valuable objects connected with the church as well as ancient, pre-Christian pieces, are on display in the Diocesan Museum, housed in the former castle. My tour ended in the center of town at the *casa contadina* (peasant house). A visit to Acerenza wouldn't be complete without seeing how the other half lived. The traditional, two-room home in the center of the village faithfully presents a time when man and animals shared close quarters: the kitchen and stall in the first room, the bedroom and chicken coop in the second.

As I was leaving town the following morning, I passed a small old woman dressed in black. Her hand was held out, palm up with an orange in it. My car windows were open, not just for air circulation, but to ask those I passed for help in tight spots. Can I fit? Am I going to scrape up against anything? On narrow streets, passing people in the car felt a bit like being on foot for a *passeggiata*, so I greeted the old woman as I inched past. She immediately began to chat. I braked. Where was I from? She spoke in *acheruntino*, the language of her village; I responded in Italian. We seemed to have all the time in the world; no one was behind me on that sunny morning. She said that her son had places to rent. Thank you, but I'm on my way out of your lovely town. The individual words were difficult to decipher, yet everything she said seemed quite clear, all the time with the orange in her outstretched palm.

The old woman played a part, no matter how small, in Acerenza's grandiose story. She was a descendent, a bridge between the old and new worlds. In the town of Ripacandida, I would discover another *gioiello*, a small church that has been named both a national monument and a UNESCO monument of culture and peace. Its religious and cultural significance has given rise to the community's nickname, *Piccola Assisi Lucana* or Little Lucanian Assisi. The house of worship was first documented in 1152 and is dedicated to St. Donato (Donatus), a local saint from later in the century. If I hadn't known the church was there, I might have passed by the unassuming facade without a thought. However, pilgrims have sought out the Sanctuary of San Donato for centuries.

The crowning glory of the Romanesque church is what is referred to as the *Bibbia di Ripacandida*. This "bible" fills the cross-vault ceiling and pillars in 16th-century technicolor glory. The images jumped out and greeted me as I crossed the threshold. There was an immediate sense of joy and of movement, like being in a child's Sunday school class with colorful Bible images coming one right after the other. My guide from the Ripacandida *pro loco* hadn't been exaggerating one iota as we walked through the monastery's gardens, today a public park, on our approach to the church. His passion was justified, the Sanctuary of San Donato with its church of a single nave and simple wooden benches is a jewel.

The frescos are divided into three themes: Genesis and the Saints, attributed to Nicola da Novi, and the life and Passion of Christ by Antonello Palumbo, artists of the Giotto school. Individual scenes in painted frames, from rectangular to whatever shape fit on the pillars and in the vaulted ceiling, illustrate the Bible stories in a very approachable manner. The characters are dressed in clothes of the period. The images are simple yet detailed. I was particularly drawn to the stories from the Old Testament, such as the building of Noah's ark, in which the workers wear tunics, tights and headwear of the late Renaissance, wield axes, push and pull a two-person saw, and hammer nails into the roof. I can imagine the faithful, from earlier periods through today, marveling at Eve who literally emerges from Adam's rib, knee-deep, pulled out by the hand of God.

The many Franciscan saints portrayed on the pillars leave little doubt that the paintings were designed for a Franciscan order. Today, Franciscan nuns live in the monastery and take care of the sanctuary. St. Francis, himself, is depicted receiving the stigmata as he looks up at a Christ-angel, feet crossed as on the crucifix and enveloped with over-sized red wings. Many of the frescos seem as vivid today as when originally painted; others have suffered gravely over time. A lovely Baroque organ, previously located above the main church entry, sits in the middle of the left wall. An original card with the 1735 date of construction and the name of its Neapolitan builder Leonardo Carella is glued to the wood above the single keyboard. My guide encouraged me to try it out, so I sat on the bench, pulled a couple of stops and one mellifluous chord led to the next. The instrument's pure, fluty tones unobtrusively filled the sanctuary with an old-world intimacy. One could pass a pleasant Sunday morning gazing at the frescos while listening to the organ. For further meditation, just outside the church was a tranquil garden with boxwoods and a California sequoia over 200 years old. That day, I mulled it all over with a nice lunch of spaghetti with shellfish in a tomato sauce and a plate of fried calamari. I was reminded that the coastline of Puglia was not far at all, but I stuck with the local Aglianico del Vulture to wash it down.

About a half hour to the south of Ripacandida, the chapel in the Castle of Lagopesole exudes a completely different ambience. The austere Romanesque church, constructed by Frederick II in the middle of the 13th century, is unique amongst the Hohenstaufen Emperor's many castles. While the main entrance is off the courtyard, I went in from a side door with my ticket to the castle's small historical museum. What a surprise! I hadn't expected the large chapel, a long, rectangular, unadorned sanctuary with a ceiling of cathedral heights. I could almost hear the distant clip-clop of horse hooves and envision valiant crusaders swinging off their horses out in the courtyard. The church was bare of images, except for a few faded paintings on the stone wall of the semicircular apse, such as those of a kneeling knight in full regalia with hands together in prayer and a large shield with a white cross. A silence pervaded the chapel's stone walls, between which were narrow staircases and passageways that led up to the emperor's private viewing room and that of his men at arms. The chapel was the stuff of legend.

In addition to the history museum, the Lagopesole fortification houses a very interesting emigration museum and an elaborate video presentation that evokes the world of Frederick II on the walls of the castle chambers to immerse the visitor in the life of his court. Personally, I was already thrown back with Frederick and his medieval posse at first site of the stone ramparts. To soak up that atmosphere a bit more, I picked up a sandwich at a small grocery store to eat on one of the benches just outside the walls. The man at the deli counter made me a panino of *pancetta coppata* (pancetta wrapped around capocollo) and *caciocavallo* (a stretched curd cheese) on sourdough bread. I brought the sandwich with a half-liter bottle of water to the checkout and the cash register rang up 1.75 Euros. The woman must not have seen the items clearly. Have you added the water? *"Sì, noi siamo onesti!"* (Yes, we're honest!) I looked at the receipt: *panino* 1.50, *acqua minerale* 0.25—not only was she honest, but she had a crazy-low profit margin. I exclaimed over the price and took a picture of the sandwich, water and fiscal receipt. We had a nice chat, and I said goodbye to a happy, proud, honest Lucanian. I enjoyed that sandwich as I basked in the castle's majestic beauty.

V.

CHALLENGES

Craco

14. BRIGANDAGE

The brigand is like a snake, if you don't provoke it,
it doesn't bite you.

Carmine Crocco in *Voices from Life In Prison*

HEN I ENTERED the *Museo del Brigantaggio* or the Brigandage Museum, housed in a former prison in Rionero in Vulture, I came face-to-face with a giant golden bust of Carmine Crocco. The small Trilby hat, cocked at an angle on top of his head, made the somewhat benevolent visage of the General of the Brigands all that much larger. Similar images of the humbly but respectfully dressed legend clad in a lapeled jacket and button-down vest of wool can be seen throughout Basilicata. Folk hero to some, notorious outlaw to others, Carmine Crocco (1830-1905), known as Donatello, was born in Rionero and would become its most famous citizen. His words were written over the doorway of one of the museum's cells. As a brigand, he did what he had to do. The *Generalissimo* reacted to provocation. Snakes should be left well-enough alone.

I've yet to read a positive definition of the word brigand, in English or Italian: a member of a gang that ambushes and robs people in forests and mountains. *Webster* doesn't allow for provocation or social justification. Even Robin Hood, the brigand with a social conscience, is commonly defined as an outlaw, albeit a friendly bandit suitable for children.

In Southern Italy, however, the word *brigante* is generally viewed as positive, despite the arrest records, court transcripts, legal documentation and newspaper reports to the contrary. The seemingly incontestable evidence of hardcore criminal intent ignores the fact that the accused rarely had an opportunity to speak, other than a few last words. So in many ways, Crocco spoke not only for himself but for those who were unable to do so. Ironically, some of the famous brigand's best-known quotations were conserved for posterity in an interview with Salvatore

Ottolenghi, a medical doctor and criminologist of the discredited Lambroso school of anthropological criminology, which advocated guilt by birth, often used to condemn Southern Italians by lineage. Crocco's interview was published in *Voci dall'ergastolo*, quoted above.

Another doctor and criminologist of the same ilk as Cesare Lambroso, Pasquale Penta examined Crocco in prison. In his monthly magazine of forensic psychiatry of 1901, Penta reported his observations of a man with a rather tranquil disposition, a model prisoner, respectful of authority and of women, and a hard worker, who was generous with the poor. His list of crimes was long, but as a person, even someone who founded a museum that was stocked with brigands' skulls and who was predisposed to condemn Crocco from birth, judged him to be a nice guy.

In another statement on the museum wall, excerpted from *Voices from Life In Prison*, the general of the brigands admitted, "Without a doubt, I have done harm to society, but I did it in defense of my life, for which I would have set fire to the whole world." Despite the accusation of 67 homicides, 7 attempted homicides, 4 attacks on public order, 5 revolts, 20 extortions, 15 acts of arson to houses and stacks of grain with damages of more than 1,200,000 lire, and his conviction on numerous homicides, armed robbery, kidnapping, the formation of an army and revolt, the *New York Times* published an article in 1872 with the title "Italian Brigandage: The Story of Crocco—The Hero of One Hundred and Thirty Crimes." The phenomenon of the brigand-hero had caught the attention of an international audience and the paper sought an explanation or at least posed a question:

> Persevering and intelligent, it is easy to see that under better influences, Crocco, the brigand, might have been an honest, industrious citizen.... Though the trial of Crocco is over, and all its interest may be supposed to have passed away, some of the features of the examination appear to me worthy of notice. Monster as Crocco is, he has been, perhaps, the victim of social institutions and social omissions, and Italy and other countries have much to learn from a trial which has occupied the public attention for so long a time.

Brigandage was certainly not a new concept on Italian territory. In 1799, however, political brigandry emerged with the resistance to the Napoleon conquest. After unification, brigandage not only increased, but took on the characteristics of a popular uprising against the Savoys and the newly formed country. The brigands were mostly humble people, but also counted former soldiers and common criminals in their numbers. They were encouraged and aided by the Bourbons in exile as well as the Catholic Church. To distinguish the movement from ordinary banditry, this Southern Italian revolt between 1861 and 1865 is referred to as the *Grande Brigantaggio* or the Great Brigandage. Motivations included deteriorating economic conditions, the augmentation of taxes, an increase in the price of basic goods, an exacerbated situation with regard to land due to the opportunism of rich landowners, as well as the new rulers' indifference and lack of understanding.

Francesco Saverio Nitti, Italian politician from Melfi, reflected on the popular view of brigands within their sphere of operation in *Eroi e Briganti* (Heroes and Brigands) of 1899:

> For common southerners the brigand was often an avenger and benefactor, sometimes justice itself. The brigand revolts, consciously or unconsciously, in most cases took on the character of true, primitive proletarian revolts. This explains that which others and I have corroborated: the people of the southern countryside often don't even know the names of the founders of Italian unification, but they remember with admiration the names of Abbot Cesare and Angelo Duca and others, more contemporary, like them.

Cesare was a 17th-century brigand, and Angelo Duca (1734-84) has been described as the most benevolent brigand of them all, lauded by the likes of writer Alexandre Dumas and the philosopher Benedetto Croce for his efforts to help the poor. Nevertheless, this Italian Robin Hood was hanged, dismembered and his head exhibited on a stake like a savage criminal. Such was the practice of discouragement. Many laws were passed to stamp out brigandage over the years. The newly formed

Kingdom of Italy instituted harsh measures, such as banning the seasonal migration of herds, which devastated poor farmers, and the introduction of the concept of collective responsibility, which punished families and even whole communities in an effort to stop the aiding and abetting of the brigands. Massive military reinforcements were needed to squelch the rebellion, and Italy was criticized internationally for its brutal methods of suppressing the brigands.

In Basilicata, the people initially backed the "liberation" movement of Garibaldi with the hope of a better life, but were quickly disillusioned. Following the reneged promises of the abolishment of large estates and the redistribution of state lands, the Lucanian poor began to revolt. The insurrection was set in motion in Matera with the killing of Count Francesco Gattini in August 1860 and the unrest in various localities the following October during the referendum that formalized the annexation of the Kingdom of the Two Sicilies by the Kingdom of Sardinia, which would become the Kingdom of Italy.

Basilicata was a hotbed of brigandage up until 1870. The mountainous territory, particularly the forested areas of the Vulture, lent itself to guerrilla tactics. Carmine Crocco assumed leadership of the insurgents and was assisted by Bourbon representatives and a cadre of deputies as heads of individual bands. In April 1861, the brigands quickly took control of the entire Vulture territory. Crocco's bands, commonly referred to as an army, continued their occupation of other Lucanian towns, gathering reinforcements while setting their sites for Potenza. The exiled Bourbon government even engaged the Spanish General José Borges to work with Crocco. Although the brigand army had initial success throughout Basilicata, Potenza remained unattainable and with the drastic "Pica" laws set in motion in 1863, the tide turned in favor of the newly formed state. Cruel punishment or execution often without a trial, the assumption of guilt by virtue of not denouncing brigand activity, being related to a brigand or through collaboration of any kind, and clemency in exchange for information broke the back of the movement. However, brigandage lived on in folk culture as observed by Carlo Levi sixty-five years later in the remote town of Aliano:

When I talked to the peasants I could be sure that, whatever was the subject of our conversation, we should in one way or another slip into mention of the brigands…. The peasants, with a few exceptions, were all on the side of the brigands and, with the passing of time, the deeds which so struck their fancy became bound up with the familiar sites of the village, entered into their everyday speech with the same ease as animals and spirits, grew into legends and took on the absolute truth of a myth.

Although Crocco opposed unwarranted cruelty and pillaging, there was undoubtedly a certain amount of unjustified criminal activity on the part of the brigands. Such circumstances would have been unavoidable. One of Crocco's most devoted lieutenants, nicknamed Ninco Nanco, for example, had a reputation for a detached brutality. However, stories of his generosity also persist and he is remembered by popular culture with fondness.

His reputation even made it to an adventure story for boys, *Ninco Nanco, The Neapolitan Brigand* written by the English writer William Henry Giles Kingston in 1867. Assuring his young readers that the protagonist (who was actually from Avigliano, Basilicata) wasn't born a brigand, Kingston opens the tale with a description that reflected the popular perception of traveling through Southern Italy at the time:

Who has not heard of Ninco Nanco, the daring cut-purse, and sometimes cut-throat, of the Apennines, who, with his band of fifty chosen men, has long kept in awe the district of Basilicata in the once kingdom of Naples? Certainly, those who have travelled from the Adriatic to the Bay of Naples, across that mountainous region which in the map looks very like Italy's ankle-bone, will retain a vivid recollection of the curiosity with which they examined every dry stick projecting from a bush or rock, lest it should prove the barrel of one of his followers' rifles; and the respect which they felt for every shepherd they saw feeding his flocks on the mountain side, lest the said peaceable-avocation-following gentleman should suddenly jump down, joined by many more from among the rocks, who could salute them in the choicest Neapolitan with words, which may be freely translated, "Stand and deliver! Your money or your life!"

Kingston left the ruthlessness to members of Ninco Nanco's band. The story's hero, himself, had established such a terror of his name that all he had to do was write a letter with a request of money, horses or supplies, and his demand would usually be met.

Such sympathetic views of the brigands were not recorded by the new government. However, since that time, the history has been revisited, revealing a complicated situation that has yet to be resolved. The figure of Crocco often plays prominently in the retelling of the story. In fact, numerous films, songs and documentaries over the years have featured this and other famous brigands. In Basilicata, the town of Brindisi Montagna in the Province of Potenza presents an outdoor multimedia extravaganza every summer that tells the story of brigandage with a cast of 300 and a host of animals in a large, natural amphitheater surrounded by mountains and embellished with water features, cinematographic elements and pyrotechnic effects. The spectacular's park setting immerses the visitor in nature, history and traditions, with everything from falconry displays to food demonstrations and from historic military encampments to exhibitions of rural folklife. The legend of brigandage comes alive in the pastoral environment.

In Rionero, the Museum of Brigandage is housed in a sturdy stone building that was originally the granary of an abbey. The structure was abandoned and then repurposed as a jail by the Bourbons. The small prison housed local ne'er-do-wells and then those who took up arms during the period of the Great Brigandage. Ironically, Crocco grew up right across the street. By all accounts, he didn't have an easy childhood. His father was a shepherd and his mother, a housewife. Early in his life, Crocco witnessed his mother beaten by a local landowner to the point of losing her unborn child, and his father, unjustly sent to prison for a crime he didn't commit. An uncle taught him to read and write on a basic level, but he was forced to earn a living from a very young age. His intelligence and grit led him to command an army, the tactics of which were admired by friend and foe. He fought for survival, both personal and for a cause. Upon capture and a well-publicized trial, Crocco was sentenced to death. The brigand who spent much of his life under the stars would spend his last 29 years behind bars on a commuted sentence, far away from his home. Born and died without a penny to his name, he had become an important personage for whom a reprieve was granted, which has been attributed to political diplomacy on an international level.

One of the former prison cells in the museum was dedicated to Crocco. Another cell was arranged with displays relating to the *brigantesse* or female brigands. Guns and a rifle hung over a box of jewelry. Some *brigantesse* were women of the *briganti*—girlfriends, wives, sisters, who filled useful roles as cooks and nurses. And there were also true *brigantesse* who shot rifles and were quick with knives. Several women also became popular folk heroes, such as Ninco-Nanco's companion, Maria Lucia Di Nella, whose youth and beauty fueled the fascination. Carlo Levi heard about her legendary adventures many years later from a grave digger in Aliano and recorded them in his book.

Amazingly, the brigands were not only popular locally, but back at the time, their photos were circulated on souvenir cards, which were in demand, not only with Italians, but with foreigners, as well. Many of the photos were taken after capture, posed dead or alive, and were used as anti-brigand propaganda.

The knowledgeable docent at the museum presented the material with enthusiasm. In addition to the *brigantesse*, what made the biggest impression on me that day was the prisoners' graffiti. Yes, there were plenty of initials etched into the brick and stone walls, but there were also many crosses and rough outlines of churches. These were regular people, religious even. One had incised, *"Io innocenti dei furti di Rionero"* (I innocent of the thefts in Rionero), in capital letters into a brick. The guilty always say they're innocent in court. However, the careful way this message was scratched into the wall for future generations, I think he really needed an affirmation. He wanted a record, somewhere, that he was innocent, whoever he was. I believed him.

Are there brigands in Basilicata today? This question is surely going through the minds of many a reader. All I can say is that you won't run into one on the high road, but they are certainly there in spirit.

15. VIGGIANO: THE BLACK MADONNA AND BLACK GOLD

I PASSED A LOT of green before arriving to the town known for its black. I had made a wrong turn on my way to Viggiano and it ended up taking twice as long as it should have. I hadn't stuck to the major state roads and highways. How far could it be, I asked myself as I glanced at the map. The lines didn't look all that squiggly. I was traveling through beautiful countryside, mountainous, woodsy and then every so often, a settlement. I'd see a sign for the next town or one further along and thought that the road I was on must be the most direct route until I started winding up and then down and then up again and what seemed like circles several more times.

I was driving in the *Parco Nazionale Appennino Lucano Val D'Agri Lagonegrese*, and the road I was on was not only the most direct but was the only one between where I was and where I wanted to be. The park links parts of the Lucanian Apennines and the Agri River Valley as it extends south to the area around the town of Lagonegro, and on the way incorporates 29 towns over almost 70,000 hectares (173,000 acres). Its territory loosely forms a bridge between the Cilento Park in Campania and the Pollino Park that straddles Basilicata and Calabria within Italy's National Park system.

I should have kept a little closer behind the scores of big rig drivers who did the route every day. Truck drivers? How many do they need to bring Basilicata's famous cheese from the town of Moliterno to the rest of the world? I would learn that all the oversized vehicles on the area's highways were not for the transportation of *Canestrato di Moliterno*, the cheese made, literally, by hands that press the sheep milk curds into cane baskets *(canestri)*, nor were they for the beans from nearby

Sarconi. On my circuitous route to Viggiano I found myself winding up to and back down from Moliterno, and I couldn't help but admire the impressive medieval castle that was silhouetted on its signature cheese rind. Going around the mountains and taking state road 598 that ran along the bottom of the Agri Valley would have gotten me there quicker that day, but then I wouldn't have been able to stop and smell the pecorino cheese.

I started to worry a bit as evening approached. I wasn't a fan of driving unfamiliar, twisty roads at night. When my phone finally registered a signal, I sought out the closest hotels to my location and Viggiano popped up at only a half-hour distance, so I called its nearest accommodation and spoke with a lovely young woman who assured me I wasn't far away at all. I was in a rural area right up until I pulled into the parking lot, making the turn with a couple tractor trailers coming from the opposite direction. A large industrial building loomed over the fence. But it wasn't until I stepped out of the car that it hit me. The sulfur smell practically knocked me over. In the lobby, apart from the heavy percentage of men in work clothes, everything appeared normal. There was even a family with small children.

The black dog was upon me and I hadn't seen him coming, the six-legged, fire-breathing animal, a stealthy creature, the metaphoric logo of ENI, the Italian multinational oil and gas company. Beware its strike! Even the hair of its own dog is permanently stuck up on the back of its neck. But to be fair, ENI only owns 61% of the rights to the *Val d'Agri* Oil Center in Viggiano. Shell has the rest. Other area oil rights have been divvied up between ENI, Total, Shell and Mitsui.

I had spent the afternoon driving through a national park and at its core had come upon the largest oil field on the European continent. I was in the *Val d'Agri*, what is referred to as the *Texas d'Italia*. This Valley of the Agri River also features a long, narrow artificial lake, *Lago del Pertusillo*, that was created at the end of the 1950s through a damn project for irrigation and land development in Basilicata and Puglia. Apart from the lake, much of the valley's bottom, the flat, wide area where the petroleum activity takes place doesn't fall within the park, (although there are seven well stations that do). In Viggiano, serious extraction began in 1996, but the exploration and initial exploitation of Basilicata's *Val d'Agri* went in phases throughout the 20th century. I had heard reports of the region's elevated incidence of cancer and other diseases. However, government numbers didn't demonstrate higher rates for Basilicata compared with other regions, and oil companies claimed complete compliance with environmental regulations and posted facts and figures within the "norm."

ENI boasts the results of its tests for all sorts of chemicals in the air and even has *nasi elettronici* placed in various locations throughout the valley to monitor smells. Personally, I don't need any electronic noses to tell me if something stinks. My sniffer is more than capable, and in the *zona industriale* or industrial zone, the odiferous atmosphere goes way beyond any "norm" I could ever imagine, and I grew up in New Jersey. And irony of ironies, one of the locations for monitoring air quality goes by the name *Masseria Puzzolente* or Stinking Farm.

I'm not saying you can get used to it, but life goes on, and after a long day of driving, I was hungry. So aromas aside, I took advantage of the 10-Euro dinner offered in the hotel restaurant where my entrance set in motion a wave of turning heads. I'm sure the percentage of female workers in the oil fields is also within the norm. The family I had seen earlier must have already eaten or had other plans. Apart from a couple of unassuming waitresses, I was the only woman in the place. The meal plan was quite generous with a few choices for first and second courses, wine, water and dessert. The food was very decent, nothing fancy but tasty, with white tablecloths and respectable flatware. I recall a basic pasta with tomato sauce and a pork cutlet one evening, and a bean soup and meaty fried anchovies another. The bed was comfortable and before I knew it, morning was upon me and I was on my way to Grumentum, one of the reasons for my stay in the area.

Grumentum was an ancient Roman city founded in the 3rd-century BC. I've seen tourist materials that call it the Little Pompeii of Basilicata, which is perhaps a bit overstated, but the remains are quite extensive and include several large structures, such as an amphitheater, a smaller theater, a couple of temples, a patrician house with floor mosaics and a forum area. I enjoyed wandering through the archeological park on that beautiful spring day. Colorful wildflowers popped up all around the open fields of long grass and amongst the ruins that once accommodated a thriving Roman community in this lush, verdant area. After the fall of Rome and as a result of centuries of Saracen invasions, the inhabitants settled on the hilltops throughout the surrounding Agri Valley and founded the communities in existence today. A lovely view of the ancient town's namesake, Grumento Nova, can be seen from the park. The nearby Grumentum National Archeological Museum documents the area settlements dating back to prehistoric times with an emphasis on the Roman period.

Culture feeds the mind. The Sanctuary of the Black Madonna was on my program for the afternoon, so my soul was covered. I just needed to find a little nourishment for the body. Searching out a bit of local ambience, I followed signs that led from the archeological park to an *agriturismo* in the vicinity. It was closed, so I crossed the valley floor in the direction of the sanctuary and came across another large Viggiano hotel, probably one with more stars than mine. First things first, the property's environs had no apparent smell, although I don't know what the *nasi elettronici* would have had to report. The dining room, with dimensions and amenities to accommodate a substantial Italian wedding party or a gala luncheon for oil executives and their staffs, was completely empty. Well-maintained and looking out over a large pool with a view of the surrounding hills, the restaurant was poised for the next big event or noteworthy influx of tourists. That day, however, the chef whipped up a modest lunch for one, just a simple first course to fortify myself with a few carbs before hiking up the *Sacro Monte* (Sacred Mountain) of Viggiano. The flavorful bowl of homemade pasta was presented with crushed *peperoni cruschi* and breadcrumbs, and topped with generous shavings of pecorino from Moliterno. I was ready to make the ascent.

The Sanctuary of the *Madonna Nera* or Black Madonna is about twelve kilometers (7.5 miles) from Viggiano's historic center on top of Mount Viggiano at 1,725 meters (5,660 feet). This mountain also dou-

bles as a ski slope in the winter, one of three in the national park together with neighboring Monte Volturino (1,836 meters or 6,024 ft.)
and Sellata-Pierfaone, Basilicata's premier ski center in Abriola twenty
kilometers from Potenza. I was visiting in the spring, however, when at
lower altitudes the deciduous trees were aglow with fresh bright leaves.
Winding up from the valley floor, I passed the ski station, and further
up through secluded woods the road widened to a broad open space
and the end of vehicular traffic. This natural piazza overlooking the valley hosts Masses and serves as one of the resting places for the Madonna and her followers during pilgrimages. Twice a year the devoted make
the long journey on foot, bringing the Madonna up from the Minor
Basilica in Viggiano on the first Sunday of May and back down from the
sanctuary on the first Sunday of September.

Legend has it that the worship of this image goes back to Grumentum and the dawn of Christianity. The Black Madonna herself is closely
connected with the Byzantine presence dating from the 6th century. As
the story goes, when the Saracens destroyed the ancient city, the statue
was hidden in a hole on top of Mt. Viggiano and discovered many centuries later by shepherds who noticed a mysterious flame on the mount.
The sanctuary was erected on the spot in the 14th century. Another tradition tells of the Madonna's miraculous movement from the mount
to the historic center of Viggiano, which prompted construction of the
mother church. She then returned to the sanctuary on her own accord.
The twice-yearly pilgrimages thus carry out her will.

On the day of my visit, the Madonna had already ascended to her
sanctuary and the multitude had returned to their routines. Although
I had missed taking part in the procession with its compelling cultural
and religious elements, camaraderie, colorful folk music and impromptu repasts, I had the mountain to myself on that glorious spring day
and I walked the final distance in complete tranquility. The path was
steep and I couldn't imagine having done the entire itinerary that also
included night vigils, fascinating as they surely would have been. After a
while, the walkway left the cool shade of the woods and emerged above
the tree-line from where I was able to get an excellent lay of the land.

The wide valley floor was a rich farmland divided into irregular check-erboard patterns. The center of Viggiano sat on a ridge. The narrow lake, like a wide river could be seen further away, and the industrial zone didn't look all that foreboding. Foothills and taller mountains with large swathes of dark green forests rolled out on the other side of the valley.

The path was neatly laid in attractive slate paving stones with low sidewalls. It zigged and zagged through the grassy knoll embedded with weathered rock. From the flat walkway, I spied the ancient trail of a more direct, even steeper route. Eventually, I reached the top. A simple, single-nave stone church with a more recent bell tower stood on the very crest of the mount. A prominent sign next to the door enumerated all the things I wasn't supposed to do inside. I entered. The Madonna's gold vestments shone brilliantly in the bare surroundings.

The *Madonna Nera* sits in a glass case atop a stone pillar with Baby Jesus perched on her lap. Only their faces, hands and Jesus' bare feet reveal the wooden sculpture and the dark brown skin tone reminiscent of ancient Byzantine icons. Their bodies are clothed in elegant gold garments. Bright golden crowns rest on their heads adorned with curls, also of pure gold. Both hold globes in their outstretched hands; on hers, Italy with its islands of Sicily and Sardinia are clearly outlined. I sat alone in the chilly church, despite the warmer outside temperature. Yes, I was resting from the hike, but I also felt a spiritual presence on the top of the Sacred Mount. Perhaps it was just the simple beauty.

The *Madonna Nera di Viggiano* was crowned Patron Saint and Queen of Lucania by Pope Leo XIII in 1890; Pope Paul VI confirmed the honor in 1965; and Pope John Paul II re-crowned her in 1991. In *Christ Stopped at Eboli* in which Carlo Levi tells of his mid-1930s ex-periences in a remote Lucanian village, he remarks on the Madonna's importance for the local population: "To the peasants the Black Ma-donna was beyond good and evil. She dried up the crops and let them wither away, but at the same time she dispensed food and protection and demanded worship. In every household, tacked up on the wall above the bed, the image of the Black Madonna of Viggiano looked on with expressionless eyes at all the acts of daily life."

So even though I had the full 360-degree view at the top of the mount practically to myself that day, it didn't mean I had the Madonna's undivided attention.

The only other person I saw that afternoon was the custodian, who had just finished repairing a section of the pathway and was putting up ropes and a sign indicating not to cross. The Sacred Mount was full of things I shouldn't be doing, and just one pertaining to what I should do. It was taped to the bathroom wall: "Only use toilet paper." No problem, as it was supplied at the entranceway—two rolls over a lockbox marked, *"Offerta Grazie."* Its location forced me to take more paper than I would ever have needed, and I sensed the Madonna was watching. In retrospect, I'm not sure I gave my offering accordingly.

The view on the way down was perhaps even better than going up, as I didn't have to turn around to take in the panorama of the *Città di Maria.* This appellation was proudly announced on the welcome sign at the trailhead. I was in Mary's City and on my way to its historic center, where I was greeted with another sign, *Benvenuti a Viggiano, Paese dell'arpa e della musica* (Welcome to Viggiano, Town of the Harp and Music). For a town of about 3,400 people, they appeared to have a lot going on. I had read of their historical connection with music and hoped to learn more about their harp-toting minstrels on my visit. To that end, I had been calling the phone numbers posted on the Internet for the *Museo delle tradizioni locali* (Museum of Local Traditions), but to no avail, so my plan was to show up on the odd chance it would be open.

Symbols of the harp and the Black Madonna popped up all over town, most notably on the heavy bronze reliefs embellishing the doors of the Minor Basilica. From the church, there's an expansive view of the fertile valley that is unfortunately interrupted by the industrial zone, which isn't pretty, but still relatively unthreatening compared with the up-close-and-personal perspective. The grandeur of Mother Nature has a way of improving things when seen in a larger context. I was still looking for the museum, though, which I had read was located in the St. Anthony convent on the edge of town. After a few passes and assistance from a couple of locals, I was finally able to follow the signs that led to the parking lot. I pulled into a space and shut off the car.

"You can't be here!" A uniformed security guard had come running over and his authoritatively disdainful tone rattled me. I said that I just wanted to try and visit the museum. "You can't be here!" I thought—I'm in Italy, the country that invented parking on sidewalks and this lot is practically empty. And then I noticed signs that said "for guests of ENI," but ENI clearly didn't have any guests that day. Before pulling into that lot, I hadn't dug deep with regard to the relationship between ENI and Viggiano, but in that moment I got a bad feeling. There wasn't any reasoning with the guy and in South Italy you can reason with most everyone. This security guard had his orders. So in a country where policemen have recommended that I just double park for a couple of minutes when asking where I could put the car to run into a store for a loaf of bread, I couldn't park in an empty lot for two minutes while I ran down the steps to see if there was any information on the door of a museum that shared the same building? Another case for which I did not need the assistance of an electronic nose.

I moved the car. The museum was closed, but there was a cellphone number on the door and I arranged a visit for the following morning. Back at the hotel, the maid had once again closed my windows up tight, choking me with the scented air freshener as I entered the room. She was also following her orders, but there wasn't any masking that smell. A shame, really. Except for the sulfur odor, the hotel was pleasant and the employees with whom I came in contact at the front desk and in the restaurant were very courteous and personable. In conversation with one of the young women, I broached the subject of the area's rumored health issues and asked her if she had a fear of getting cancer. It's a sensitive subject and I eased into it. I had read conflicting newspaper stories and wanted to hear directly from someone living and working in that environment. She was born and raised in Viggiano. And yes, she was afraid, but she was also in favor of the petroleum extraction because she said it gave people work. Although there had been a recent flash in the news about a possible leakage with a mandated pause in extraction, the young woman hadn't noticed any change in activity level. The hotel dining room was full again that evening—Calabrians at the table to my left and Sicilians to the right. They were truck drivers and they weren't hauling cheese.

The next morning I returned to St. Anthony's former convent that housed the seats of ENI and the local museum. I made sure that my parking didn't interfere with oil executives and their guests. An enthusiastic young man was already waiting for me inside the building's basement that was dedicated to the museum. The displays were a collaboration between the community administration and the public schools, and portrayed Viggiano's past through a simple arrangement of everyday items from work and home. My docent for the morning had opened up the museum just for me and was an excellent guide, putting it all together with an engaging presentation of the agricultural tools and domestic objects to tell the story of the lives of ordinary working people.

We talked for a couple of hours and our discussion worked its way to contemporary life, including the petroleum industry, jobs and health. I inquired whether he had a fear of getting cancer and he responded immediately, "Yes." Mentioning the smell in the industrial zone, I asked if the cancer was concentrated in that area. "No, it's in the entire town." He also lamented that the sacrifice wasn't worth the jobs as very few locals were employed by the oil companies and emphasized that most of the people who worked in the industrial zone came from outside. I looked at this well-spoken, amiable young man (so many throughout the region and all of Southern Italy), who didn't have much hope for his future, short of going elsewhere. Oil drilling was certainly not the fix, although some money was brought in with residuals. Viggiano had a brand-new swimming pool complex, a summer music festival with international artists and a sign boasting a past of which a trace was difficult to find.

The museum had a little display about the procession of the Black Madonna, but I was very surprised and a little disappointed that there weren't any particulars with regard to Viggiano's history of music. My guide said the administration was in the process of remedying that and a few months later the museum would inaugurate a photo display together with an interactive component in the form of a downloadable app. Until then, I had to content myself with the large sign welcoming me to the City of Harps.

Perhaps the disappearance of musicians in a town once famed the world over for their presence begins to explain the museum's initial difficulties in presenting a subject that was formerly such an important element in the fabric of Viggiano society. Incredibly, this small town, which in the 19th century was almost twice its present size, produced a proliferation of musicians who subsequently spread throughout the world. The harp was the centerpiece of this musical phenomenon, and harp players needed harps. Historically, the town had a strong tradition of woodworking out of which grew the craft of harp making. Anchored by a celebrated craftsman who produced concert harps for the stage, Viggiano's workshops also constructed smaller, less-expensive harps with soundboards made from local, uncultivated pear trees. Called *arpicedda*, these portable, diatonic harps were the instruments of the town's itinerant musicians, who at first traveled to Naples at Christmastime and then eventually throughout Europe and the world. These musical groups from Viggiano can be viewed in the historical nativity scenes in the collection at the Museum of San Martino in Naples.

In 1884 when the Italian poet Giovanni Pascoli visited Viggiano, he remarked that harp playing was ubiquitous and compared the town to the ancient Greek city Antissa, the birthplace of the lyre. The musicians mixed folkloristic and classical elements, and their repertoire included tarantellas, ballads, love songs, strophic choruses, Christmas carols, Neapolitan songs and Italian opera arias. Other prominent instruments were the flute and violin. Eventually, many musicians with roots in Viggiano moved from the street to the concert stage, where they filled principal positions in major symphony orchestras. As for the town of origin, Viggiano has opened up a harp school in recent years in an effort to bring a tradition that lasted 200 years back to life.

Historically, as well-known as Viggiano was for its musicians, agriculture was still the principal occupation of the area. Today, oil companies claim to bring jobs, so I was surprised to read the numbers proudly stated on ENI's website. In 2018, ENI had 316 employees in all of Basilicata of whom only 64% resided in Basilicata. Perhaps a few more workers might have helped to fix oil tank leaks that had been actively hidden by the company for five years and discovered in early 2018— at least 400 tons of crude seeped into the earth between the plant and the underlying water layer in that incident. Add this finding to other environmental issues, questions about the lake water and health problems of Agri Valley residents.

The same week Basilicata was honored by the *New York Times* on their yearly list of 52 places to visit. Well deserved, but interestingly, the short description cited, "a dearth of organized crime" as one of the positives along with beautiful beaches and ancient towns. I ask myself, just what is organized crime? And how much space is there in ENI's parking lot?

The City of the Black Madonna, the black gold that brought the black dog, the lost harp and not to forget the water of the Agri River. A beautiful area full of contradictions. Rich in oil, water, agriculture, religion and culture, but the future path? It seems to me that the people need to dig deep and find another harp, something unique. There's an electric bike factory in Grumento Nova's industrial area. All of the company's electrical energy comes from solar panels on the roof of the factory. Just for the record, I'm not a tree-hugger, but such an enterprise leans in the right direction.

My final lunch was in a restaurant on the outskirts of town. There were a number of petroleum workers with two Brits in jumpsuits struggling to understand the menu at the next table. Jobs they couldn't have trained a local to do? Okay, enough with the politics. In Italy, it's complicated. The valley is beautiful and their DOC red wine, the *Terre dell'Alta Val d'Agri*, is good.

Note to ENI: Spring for the toilet paper at the Sanctuary of the Black Madonna. Thank you.

16. LUCANIAN EMIGRATION

Lucanians roam the world in great numbers, but nobody sees them,
they aren't exhibitionists.
The Lucanian, more than any other, lives well in the shadows.
He nests where he lands, he doesn't disturb his neighbor with threats
nor with a ruckus of demands. He is of few words.
    Leonardo Sinisgalli, *Un disegno di Scipione e altri racconti*

W HEN I FIRST came across Sinisgalli's words, it dawned on me that I hadn't ever met anyone from Basilicata outside of the region. Or more likely, I was unaware of the fact. Not so with those whose forebears hailed from, say Sicily, Calabria or Naples and its surroundings. Clearly, Basilicata is a smaller region and I wouldn't expect to have run into the same numbers, but as Sinisgalli says, perhaps they really do know how to live in the shadows.

The Lucanians are definitely out there, as Sinisgalli assures his readers in the very first line of his ode to the people of Lucania: *"Girano tanti lucani per il mondo."* He would have known of Lucanians roving the world, as the poet was a *lucano* himself. When he was very young, his father emigrated to the Americas where he worked as a tailor for many years before returning with his savings to buy a house in his hometown. The family was from Montemurro in the Agri River Valley, one of many towns in Basilicata plagued with the devastating combination of earthquakes and landslides, and topped off with persistent emigration.

Who knew the offspring of a humble tailor and grape farmer would become one of Basilicata's honored sons? A short biography of Leonardo Sinisgalli (1908-1981) would describe him as a poet with a background in mathematics and engineering. Digging deeper into his creative output reveals a wide range of interests that embraced writing, art, design, publicity and radio. His activities put him in important positions with major Italian firms, such as Olivetti, Pirelli and ENI, and a life away from his village would be his destiny. However, he always remembered who he was and where he came from. Continuing with the poetic reflection dedicated to the Lucanians in the world, Sinisgalli goes on to say, *"Lucano si nasce e si resta."* One who is born a Lucanian, remains a Lucanian.

Perhaps this strong love of homeland comes from the Lucanian's state of perpetual emigration. The *Museo dell'Emigrazione Lucana* in the castle of Lagopesole calls Basilicata the *"terra d'emigranti"* or the land of emigrants. This concept is explored through a multimedia presentation that gives the visitor an experience mimicking as close as possible the events in the lives of those who left the region to settle elsewhere. But the museum begins the story further back in time, before the period of mass emigration from the Italian south, and puts forth the idea that the region's exceptionally mountainous terrain had always made Basilicata a land of emigrants. The Lucanians were either pulled towards the agricultural land of Puglia to the east or drawn by the appeals of the larger Neapolitan cities to the north. Thus, from time immemorial farmers and artisans sought their fortunes outside Basilicata. Many of these workers were seasonal or temporary and returned on a migratory path that would become a way of life.

In the 19th century the routes began to expand past Naples to northern Italian soil, Europe and across the Atlantic. The musicians of Viggiano, for example, traveled far and wide in order to make enough money to improve their social standing back in Basilicata, and in the process became famous throughout the world. In 1838 the Neapolitan poet Pietro Paolo Parzanese was inspired by the songs of itinerant musicians from Viggiano to write his own book of "songs," *I Canti del Viggianese.* The first stanza of *"Il Viggianese"* is as follows:

Ho l'arpa al collo, son viggianese;
Tutta la terra è il mio paese.
Come la rondine che lascia il nido,
passo cantando di lido in lido:
e fin che in seno mi batte il cor
dirò canzoni d'armi e d'amor.

With harp on my neck, I'm from Viggiano;
The whole world is my home.
Like the swallow who leaves his nest,
I sing, passing from beach to beach:
And until in my chest my heart no longer beats
I will sing songs of love and war.

These traveling musicians were also said to be the muses for the French writer Hector Malot. In 1878, he penned *Sans famille* (Without Family), the tale of Rémi, an orphan boy adopted by an Italian street musician, who taught him to play the harp. (*Nobody's Boy* was the original English title.) His adventures have since been made into movies and several animated television series, which have been seen all over the world. The Lucanians really do get around!

The life of the traveling musician became more difficult after the 1848 uprisings in Italy. Their itinerant nature was viewed as suspicious and they were treated as possible spies, which resulted in the denial of travel passports. Another issue was the growing sensitivity to child labor beginning in the 1860s, when young street performers were regarded as victims of a white slave trade. The French kicked large numbers of the children and their masters out of their country. In the United States, several of the children's *padroni*, as they were called, were prosecuted. The Italian Embassies saw the matter as an embarrassment. And worse, many of these Lucanian musicians, both adults and children struggling to make a living, were subject to the new racist theories of criminal anthropology proposed by the Italian criminologist Cesare Lombroso. His bigoted views of Southern Italians criminalized an entire population merely by birth, which subsequently compounded the unfavorable image of the street musicians.

However, despite the negativity in the years following Italian Unification, the musicians from Viggiano and the area of the Agri River Valley were on the forefront of the great emigration. Many transformed from street musicians to those of the theater and concert hall, most notably the flutist Leonardo De Lorenzo (1875-1962), who was an esteemed performer and educator in the United States, and Victor Salvi

(1920-2015) and his family, who have roots in Viggiano and were well-known harpists and luthiers, and continue to produce world-class Salvi Harps today.

Before Italy's unification in 1861, emigration varied amongst the Italian states. The northern regions of Liguria, the Veneto, Lombardy, Piedmont and Tuscany had a heavy overseas flow. From the south, emigration was more limited and tended to involve identifiable groups such as the musicians from Viggiano. However, after 1861, southern emigration from the former Kingdom of the Two Sicilies grew to be an epidemic. The destination of choice was the Americas. The new Savoy government was not in favor of emigration and together with large landowners wanted to hold onto its abundant source of cheap labor. However, in 1888, the Kingdom of Italy recognized the need for the poor to have what was referred to as a *valvola di sfogo* (relief valve) in order to escape from their intolerable situation. Moving abroad was a way out for the impoverished without any hope or prospects in Italy, but restrictions were put into place to ensure young men weren't emigrating in order to dodge their military obligation. In 1901 the liberty of the individual to emigrate was acknowledged, and measures to protect this right and to safeguard passage were instituted. The numbers rose proportionately.

By 1885, over 10,000 Lucanians emigrated every year. Figures continued to rise, and the maximum flow occurred between 1901 and 1913, with a peak of over 18,000 in 1906. The First World War interrupted what was called the *"Grande Emigrazione"* or the Great Emigration, which resumed after the war, although to a lesser extent. Following the Second World War, the direction changed and Lucanians headed for the mines of Belgium, France and Germany and the farms of Australia. Emigration increased in the 1960s due to the stark economic differences between northern Italy, which was experiencing a period of growth, and the southern regions still in serious difficulty. Only in the 1980s did the departure numbers begin to decrease.

The Museum of Emigration immerses the visitor in this extraordinary exodus. The individual stories of these highly determined people are moving. Their grit and resilience are admirable. Interestingly, the exhibit also considers the local population. We tend to center our attention on those who picked up and started a life far, far away, but the museum doesn't forget those left behind. How did they feel and how do they continue to feel in the face of this mass emigration? The museum strives to keep alive the memory of the region's emigrants, their sacrifices and their accomplishments, also because the emigration continues today.

The exhibits focus on the emigrant's journey up through the first half of the 20th century. At the entrance, each museum guest receives the identity of a Lucanian emigrant, a passport, if you will. Mine was of Filomena Iacovino from Grassano, a mid-sized community in the Province of Matera that today has about 5,000 residents. I once met a policeman from Grassano who boasted that the grandmother of the current mayor of New York City Bill de Blasio had emigrated from his town. In addition, the municipality was the first place in Basilicata where Carlo Levi was confined. He would write favorably of the hospitality he received as well as of the beauty of its landscape. "Grassano, like all the villages hereabouts, is a streak of white at the summit of a bare hill, a sort of miniature imaginary Jerusalem in the solitude of the desert."

Born in 1927, Filomena Iacovino would have been a young child in 1935 when the political prisoner arrived in her town. Her father had already passed away and her official schooling lasted just three years. She learned to cook, sew and embroider at her mother's side. Had Levi, by chance, seen her working in the fields alongside her sisters? Filomena met Pasquale Amato in 1946, just back from Australia where he had been sent to work on a farm as a prisoner of war. They married and in 1949 decided to seek their fortunes in Australia, making the long journey from Grassano by cart to the town's railroad station, followed by the train to Naples, then a seven-week voyage to Fremantle, in southwestern Australia, and ending up raising sheep for wool in Gnowangerup, a town of 500. A move to Katanning and with four children in tow, they opened a café with Filomena in the kitchen; a couple more relocations and the family established a cheese factory, and finally in the 1970s near Perth, a winery. A full life.

At the museum, I scan my "passport" to be immersed in Filomena's experience via videos, such as at the prefect's office where she goes for her travel documents and in her family home where a discussion is in progress about her imminent departure followed by goodbyes. The presentation is effective. The displays then show the makeshift baggage and a donkey cart on which the visitor can perch. Next comes the train, the ship's long voyage and the interrogation upon arrival at the entry point of the new land. The museum follows the life of other individuals, as well, several of whom end up at New York's Ellis Island.

Basilicata didn't say her goodbyes lightly, and the emigrants didn't forget, either. In 1926, *La Basilicata del Mondo* claimed to be "the most widespread Italian magazine in the world" with monthly editions reaching 10,000 copies each in the Americas alone. Many of these Lucanians made permanent homes in their adopted countries, others went back. Carlo Levi talks about how important the image of the United States was for so many in the town of Aliano, where he spent most of his confinement in 1935-36. On the walls over the beds in the peasants' homes were tacked two cheap prints, he says, the Black Madonna of Viggiano and Franklin Delano Roosevelt. And occasionally, a dollar bill was added to make up the trinity. He goes on to explain that Rome was the capital for the gentry and Naples was the capital for the poor, who flocked there only to get on a ship headed elsewhere.

Earlier in the century, Basilicata's dire conditions came to the attention of the country's Prime Minister Giuseppe Zanardelli, who toured the region in 1902. He was equally moved by the warm welcome he received and the pitiful state of the territory. He noted a complete lack of infrastructure with regard to roads, the railroad, bridges and the ability to travel and communicate between the towns; a malaria epidemic in the valleys; a population reduced to old people, women and children due to the mass emigration; a deforesting that resulted in dry, impoverished soil; and a medieval agricultural system due to lack of funds. He spoke with citizens that ranged from high government officials down to small landowners, artisans and poor farmers. The images of his journey made a deep impression on him and his reports would be fundamental in the creation of a law instituting provisions to address the situation, which was one of the first attempts to reduce the gap between the north and south that had been created by Italian unification.

As represented by the dollar bill Levi saw on the walls of homes, sometimes money was sent back and at other times the emigrants returned themselves. Often, families were split on either side of the ocean. Levi observed, "The women wove on ancient looms, but they cut their thread with shiny scissors from Pittsburgh.... They simply took gladly whatever came to them from New York, just as they would take gladly whatever might come from Rome. But from Rome came nothing. Nothing had ever come but the tax collector and speeches over the radio."

The figure of the *"Americano"* features prominently in Levi's writings of the village. These transplanted individuals were commonly referred to as "American" upon their return, a few of whom were changed by the experience, but many, seemingly not at all. Continuing in his ode to the people of Basilicata, Sinisgalli speaks to this inclination of the temporary emigrant, notwithstanding scores of years away from home:

> The emigrants who return from Colombia or Brazil, from Argentina or Australia, from Venezuela or the United States, after forty years of absence, don't ever say anything about their lives passed as exiles.
>
> They fall back into the daily village routine, they are happy, in hovels or grottos, to chew on fennel or a lettuce leaf, to watch the pot that boils, to listen to the fire that prattles on.

Today, Basilicata would not be easily recognized by Levi or Sinisgalli, as so much has changed. However, the issue of emigration continues into the 21st century. Unemployment throughout Italy, particularly in the south, is very high, especially amongst young people. Italians are on the move again, and the migratory path flows heavily towards other European countries and South America. According to the official government numbers of the *Anagrafe degli Italiani Residenti all'Estero* or the Office of Vital Statistics for Italians Residing Abroad, in 2019 there were 130,719 Lucanians living in foreign countries or 23% of the population, whereas nationally, Italians residing outside Italy came to 8.8%.

Will they stay or will they return? And what will the stories of their offspring be? When Francis Ford Coppola (b. 1939), the famous American filmmaker whose grandfather hailed from Basilicata, returned to the town of his Lucanian heritage and transformed a 19th-century mansion into a luxury hotel, he said, "The Palazzo Margherita for me is a dream come true." He had come home, and he had renovated this palazzo in the historic center of Bernalda to create a sense of family, for him as well as the guests of the boutique property. Agostino Coppola left the town of his birth at the height of the Great Emigration and his descendants prospered in America. Many years later, Bernalda made his grandson an honorary citizen.

While Palazzo Margherita is not for every budget, I decided to check out the hotel's Cinecittà Bar when I was in the area. I'm not one to gawk at the lifestyles of the rich and famous, but oddly enough, the Lucanians seemed to expect that I would have an interest in a fellow American. After all, Coppola was my *paesano*. I was surprised that the Palazzo Margherita wasn't all that easy to find. People who vacation in luxury properties like their privacy, so even though the hotel was smack in the middle of the main street in the center of town, there wasn't the least indication out front. Apparently, there are plans to install an interpretive sign by the historic palazzo. Nevertheless, with a couple of passes, I managed to locate the discreet, two-story patrician structure with harmonizing blue-gray doors and shutters. The entrance to the Cinecittà Bar was on the right side of the building. As to be imagined of a café named after Italy's Hollywood, the walls were lined with black and white glossies of cinematic stars. Lina Wertmüller, the unabashed-glasses-wearing writer and director, smiled out at me as only she can. Coincidentally, her father was Lucanian.

The focus of the bistro was the wooden bar at its center. A vaulted ceiling, original marble flooring and simple café tables completed the casual atmosphere. The other clients for lunch were an older Italian gentleman from the neighborhood seated at his usual table by the

French doors and a pair of Americans who looked as if they had carefully dressed and rehearsed for their lunch at the celebrated director's café. They were slim and attractive with accents so flat that I wondered if they weren't Brits overacting a young midwestern couple attending a regatta on the Thames. "Is *he* here?" I heard her ask the waiter in a stage whisper from across the room. No, the director was not in residence. And a little while later they learned from the same waiter that the hotel was not available for tours. But how they enjoyed their meal! And truth be told, the food was excellent.

I had a delicious lamb chop stew with tomatoes, potatoes and *lampascioni*, also known as *lampagioni*. This very particular bulb presents itself like a small, bitter onion, but is actually a type of hyacinth and is a traditional food in Basilicata. The bulb's strong flavor with delicate aftertaste lends an interesting character to dishes. Often *lampascioni* are preserved and eaten in oil. When fried with numerous cuts to the bulb, they create quite a show as the layers open out to look like a flower and the subtle crunch is appealing.

The restaurant featured seasonal organic ingredients from Basilicata. Even the yeast for the bread was made using local apples, and the naturalness shone through. So could I have gotten any closer to the source with the plate of seasonal fruit from Metaponto for dessert? (Bernalda is one of the hill towns in the area called the Metapontino Plain.) Cantaloupe melon, kiwis, oranges, cherries—all were exquisite, and the *pezzo forte* or the pièce de résistance or the jewel in the crown were the strawberries. I hadn't had a strawberry that sweet and flavorful from back in the day when fruit was sweet and flavorful. And those local strawberries didn't have a speck of sugar on them.

A little while later, I'm out on the street and I get a call from an acquaintance who works for the tourism board. "Where are you?" "I'm in Bernalda." "Do you want to see Coppola's place?" I was feeling quite satisfied with the stew and fruit, but I'm not inclined to turn down a peek at a beautifully restored historic building. So she made a phone call and I was escorted behind the blue-gray doors. I was immediately struck by the sense of oasis. I hadn't expected such tranquility right in the center of town. I noted the familial tone set in the large eat-in kitchen, which I thought could have been interesting for guests to have the opportunity to observe dishes being prepared. But I had to smile as I went up to the second floor and heard the Love Theme from the Godfather surging with its distinctive poignancy. I was told that Coppola didn't originally want to project his own films in the elegant salon that doubles as a movie theater, but that's what many guests wanted.

Before leaving town, I combed the streets for Coppola's strawberry guy, Dino il Contadino. No luck, Dino The Farmer wasn't at his usual spot. He was probably still reposing after lunch. I would have to search out Basilicata's succulent Candonga strawberries on the road elsewhere. Looking back, I wonder if Dino or his family ever spent time in a foreign land or in Naples, for that matter, but I would like to think that he had found a certain contentment in his existence. He certainly was able to enjoy exceptional fruit. And such fruit brings to mind Coppola's heartfelt description of the beloved land of his forebears: "When you see Basilicata, you see fields, you see grapes, you see beautiful country, you see the earth as it was intended to be."

17. CRACO: A GHOST TOWN

ITALIAN VILLAGES are getting smaller, and the dwindling of a population is sad. Whether the reason be lack of opportunity for young people, a change in lifestyle, or agricultural competition from poorer countries, the diminution occurs gradually. Normally, older folks are still around to talk about the way things were. Catastrophic events, however, are sadder, especially when it would seem that there's no turning back. The abrupt disruption changes the community and the lives of its inhabitants forever.

Ghost towns are not uncommon in America's Wild West. A sign along the side of a dusty road points the way to gunfights on Main Street and saloons with swinging doors. Such flash-in-the-pan places grew up overnight with populations that soared quickly into the thousands at the hint of gold or other such valuable commodity. A good fifty-year run and people moved on.

Craco isn't like that. Evidence of settlement goes back to ancient tombs from Greek times. Byzantine monks broadened its agricultural potential. Even its name, derived from Graculum in Latin, means small, tilled field. Up until the tragic abandonment, Craco was known as the *paese del grano* (town of wheat). And as with any place that has been around for so long, the community has had its ups and downs. Emigration was common after unification. Many immigrants settled in New York City. They worked hard and carved out niches for themselves, such as in the paper stock business, what we would call recycling today. These *crachesi* (people from Craco) who dealt in waste paper were known as the Cracotan paper stock men. Their impact on Manhattan, a city of skyscrapers, is noteworthy, considering the rural town from whence they came. At the end of the 19th century Craco had roughly 2,000 inhabitants. That population would drop by half into the early 20th century and then build itself back up before disaster struck.

What happened? Many sources simply state *frana* or landslide as the cause of Craco's demise. We imagine a big rain, the earth becomes soft and houses start to slide down the hill, but the story is more complicated than that. The town was built on a slope made up of different layers of clay and while it had experienced shifting earth in earlier periods, the medieval structures had held their ground, so to speak. The first documented movement occurred in 1888 as a result of the building of a new bridge with deep pylons erected in the valley below the old town. In 1931 repairs to said bridge triggered another geological activity. In 1954 the construction of a soccer field over the unstable zone provoked a greater precariousness, which reached its breaking point in 1959 with an extremely heavy rainfall that brought about the destruction of the new playing field, the shifting of the bridge and the initial cracking of buildings. The abandonment of homes began in 1963.

The last straw came in 1971 with the construction of a new containment wall. That "straw" was made of reinforced concrete and the camel's back couldn't take it. No sooner had the work been finished when the village collapsed. Perhaps the Italian expression, *la goccia che fa traboccare il vaso* (the drop that makes the vase brim over) would be equally appropriate in Craco's case, as studies also point to a faulty water supply network as a contributing factor to the landslides. In the end, the hill of clay couldn't support indiscriminate modern technology. And a town that had flourished for over a thousand years was destroyed by 20th-century progress. Many residents left the area for good and others settled in Craco Peschiera, a new housing district in the valley for the displaced *crachesi*. Today, fewer than 800 people live in the modern town and historic Craco appears frozen in time.

Located 58 kilometers (36 miles) south of Matera, the *paese fantasma* (ghost town) is a popular day trip or stop-off for tourists passing through the area. And like Matera, Craco is sought out by movie directors, who can't resist the abandoned medieval village in its austere surroundings. Italian director Francesco Rosi chose Craco as the town site of Carlo Levi's exile in his film version of *Christ Stopped at Eboli* (1979). A quarter of a century later, Mel Gibson selected the location for Judas' hanging in *The Passion of the Christ*. Craco definitely has its own brand of allure. Halfway between the mountains and the sea, the hilly landscape exudes an eerie beauty with its pale, dry *calanchi* (badlands). The village can be seen for miles around, up on a crest with a bed of olive trees at its base. As all over the region, the high point was chosen for surveillance. In Craco's case, the 390-meter (1280-feet) altitude is crowned with a square Norman tower that stands to one side above the medieval settlement. Stopping the car to photograph the panorama is instinctive. The emptiness can be felt from a distance: the windowless windows, the dark, vacant doorways, the stone pillars pointing out from the bottom of the rock mound. The old town appears to have morphed from the landscape.

My visit of the *paese fantasma* began with the obligatory donning of a bright yellow hardhat over a throwaway gauze head covering. Italians wouldn't think of letting their head touch the inside of a communal helmet. The historic center was fenced in and although the area hadn't

shown any recent movement, the head protection lent the appropriate air of unpredictability to the proceedings. Walking along the road
leading into the old town, I noticed a satellite dish on a second-sto-
ry balcony. One of the French doors was partially open and six pairs
of socks, 4 white athletic and two black, were hanging on the rusted
wrought iron railing. Perhaps they were the last to dry as the laundry
line above was empty, its old wooden clothespins hanging limply on the
rope. The building's paint was faded and chipped. To the right of the
balcony protruded a rectangular addition, one of several throughout
the old town. The guide said they were bathrooms. Their small, square
windows would have afforded pleasant views over the valley. Several
arched doorways of brick were blocked with masonry to discourage
any thoughts of entering the old stone buildings. I heard the ringing
of sheep bells in the distance. Clearly, everyone hadn't wanted to leave.

We proceeded through the locked gate as the young guide spoke
passionately of Craco. He and his people had been displaced, casualties
of their environment, both physical and political. I trod the old paving
stones that had been meticulously placed. Cars once rolled into town
over the smooth stones. At the time of the disaster, donkeys would have
lumbered alongside the more modern means of transport. Many small
businesses thrived and there was even a movie theater. Wild grass and
other vegetation have taken over the collapsed area; the bright green
contrasted with the beige ruins, whitish stones, larger boulders and ce-
ment rubble. The guide led us up a solid stairway made of irregular
river stones and past the remains of modest dwellings as well as noble
homes from the Renaissance. Weeds sprouted from the maiolica tiles
that adorned the mother church's cupola.

Up in the Norman tower at the top of the village, I peered down
into roofless houses and gazed out over rolling hills all the way to nearby towns, perched on their own distant ridges. The sun was setting as
our tour wound down. I had heard braying earlier, and two donkeys
appeared in the evening light as if on cue. They contentedly grazed on
the vegetation strewn with stones from the historic buildings that reflected a golden hue.

The voices of children are no longer heard bouncing off the walls, men are not chatting in the piazzas, and women are preparing their evening meals elsewhere. Craco is a ghost town, immortalized in film and populated by tourists, and one *paesano* with clean socks.

VI.
SOCIAL JUSTICE

Detail of "Lucania 1961" Mural by Carlo Levi

18. ALIANO: CARLO LEVI AND
HIS LUCANIAN CONFINEMENT

They have gentle hearts and patient souls; centuries of resignation
weigh on their shoulders, together with a feeling of the vanity of
all things and of the overbearing power of fate.

Carlo Levi, *Christ Stopped at Eboli*

I'M ALWAYS SURPRISED when I hear someone say he wants to learn Italian in order to read Dante Alighieri. Although I can appreciate the challenge, I would personally recommend a goal within easier reach. Trust me, the *Divina Commedia* is extremely difficult, not only for the archaic Italian, but also with regard to the vast historical knowledge needed to fully understand the meaning of the poetry. On the other hand, *Cristo si è fermato a Eboli*, Carlo Levi's story of his time in Basilicata, is quite approachable, as it is written in an appealingly straightforward modern Italian. But despite the 20th-century setting, the social context feels rooted in a far more distant past. Levi, himself, had trouble reconciling the Lucanian world of his exile with that of his northern-Italian city life.

Carlo Levi (1902-1975) came from a well-to-do Turin family. He studied medicine and after finishing his degree, continued in medical research. However, his interests gradually turned more towards the arts, and he decided to pursue an artistic career. As a painter, he engaged in a freedom of expression that resisted the Futurist style advanced by the Fascist regime; and his ongoing antifascist activities led to arrest and banishment to Basilicata, the far-flung region whose name Mussolini had changed to Lucania in order to reflect its days of glory. While in exile, he painted regularly, but was also pressed into service as a physician by the residents of Aliano, who were desperately in need of a doctor. (In the book, Aliano becomes Gagliano in imitation of the local pronunciation.) His confinement was originally set for three years, but he hadn't yet finished his first when he became one of many political prisoners granted amnesty in celebration of Italy's Ethiopian victory in 1936. Levi wrote *Christ Stopped at Eboli* between 1943 and 1944, and it was published in 1945. Translated into thirty-seven languages and more recently into the Aliano dialect, the book was his greatest success. He continued writing, painting and his involvement with politics throughout his life.

The exile of the Fascist period is an interesting phenomenon. Political prisoners were sent off to what was considered the back of beyond and were forbidden to engage in political activity, but the detainees were free to move about the town of confinement and associate with the locals. Levi was sent to the Province of Matera, originally to Grassano, a community of over 7,000 at the time, and then abruptly transferred to Aliano, a town with almost 2,000 inhabitants during his period of residence. He couldn't travel outside the municipality and was obliged to sign-in with the local authorities, once a week in Grassano and every day in Aliano. But other than the systematic censoring of letters and adherence to a somewhat flexible curfew, he was able to live in the far-removed land according to his means. Levi was a gentleman in his life outside of confinement and he was treated as such as a prisoner. Aliano had a dozen political prisoners during his time there.

Because of his work as a physician, Levi became well acquainted with Aliano's poor. His experiences made a deep impression on him, and his book is a condemnation of the peasants' living conditions and the system that created and perpetuated them: "The State cannot solve the problem of the South, because the problem which we call by this name is none other than the problem of the State itself." Exile clearly didn't stop the wheels in Levi's head from turning. Meticulous observation, evocative description and insightful analysis immerse the reader in the sociological reality of the world of his confinement. His firsthand account of peasant life is as shocking today as when it was first published, and the government's historic incapacity to understand or deal with the problem is made clear. The book had immediate impact and brought the woeful state of Southern Italy to the attention of Italy and the world.

Literarily, *Christ Stopped at Eboli* is difficult to categorize. A memoir, an essay, a novel—on which shelf does it belong? The book has long been popular with travelers, especially since so little has been written about Basilicata. Travel writers have taken a particular interest. Who wouldn't want to write a book with such depth and significance? The well-known travel writer and novelist Paul Theroux includes *Christ Stopped at Eboli* whenever asked about his favorite travel books. On his hurried tour around the Mediterranean, chronicled in *Pillars of Hercules: A Grand Tour of the Mediterranean*, he paid homage to Levi with an inland detour to Aliano. Theroux admired Levi's strong sense of place and sixty years later hastily confirmed that life in the town hadn't changed much. I repeat, hastily. British travel writer David Yeadon characterized pilgrimages to Aliano as the "lure of Levy." He and his wife were so moved by *Christ Stopped at Eboli* that they relocated to Aliano for a year. Yeadon's memoir *Seasons in Basilicata* is based on their experiences.

Today, bus tours roll into Aliano in the warmer months. Carlo Levi's words have transformed a 20th-century backwater into a 21st-century tourist attraction, what is packaged as the *Parco Letterario Carlo Levi*. This "literary park" consists of the house Levi lived in, a gallery of his paintings, his gravestone in the local cemetery and a museum of rural culture. Sign me up.

I was staying in Matera and hired a car and driver to take me the 86 kilometers (53 miles) southwest through the wide valley past Ferrandina and Pisticci, home of the region's celebrated liquor, the Amaro Lucano. I probably would have rented a car if there had been an automatic available, but the upside was I could relax, take in the scenery and chat with a local on the hour and a half drive. The driver turned out to be from just over the border in Puglia, although as is the case with many a Southern Italian, he grew up in Switzerland where his parents had found work and spent summers back in his homeland.

Eroded hills of clay flanked the roadside. These were the region's famous *calanchi* or badlands. Imprints of rivulets that had long since run their course remained down the length of the weathered, irregular mounds. The white clayey dunes dominated the sparsely vegetated landscape. Yeadon described the Dakota-like topography as lending a "mood of utter barren wilderness." Levi said, "Christ never came, just as the Romans never came, content to garrison the highways without penetrating the mountains and forests, nor the Greeks, who flourished beside the Gulf of Taranto." Poetic, but then he wouldn't have had the opportunity to visit the Archeological Museum in nearby Policoro, which was inaugurated in 1969. Aliano and its Alianello district that Levi also mentions in his book are both well represented with sophisticated, 7-6th-century-BC Greek artifacts found in area tombs.

The car wove up through hill country that was a patchwork of white clay and Mediterranean green, clumps of bushes as well as cultivated fields of olive, peach and citrus trees. The local economy is still based on agriculture and pastoral animal husbandry. The population is half of what it was in Levi's time when "the peasants got up while it was still dark to travel three or four hours to their fields, in the direction of the malarial banks of the Agri and the Sauro or the slopes of the faraway hills." Aliano sits at 555 meters (1,820 feet), precariously perched on a bed of clay, which has at times slid and been shaken out from under its inhabitants.

We pulled into the center of town and got out of the car with the usual complement of *vecchietti* (little old men) watching our every move from their sidewalk chairs. Walking down the street, my eyes were drawn to the steep-sided gorges surrounding the historic center, "the island among the ravines," as characterized by Levi. The dramatic canyon to the west is noted for the demise of a *bersagliere* from the Piedmont area. The incident occurred following one of the major military episodes of *brigantaggio* or brigandism just after Italian unification in 1861. According to legend, this infantryman of the type renowned for quick steps and fancy-plumed hats was the last survivor of the Battle of Acinello between the *briganti*, led by Carmine Crocco and José Borjes with soldiers of the former Kingdom of the Two Sicilies, and the Italian army. Upon discovering the *bersagliere*, the people of Aliano took him in; however, he is said to have repaid their kindness with the sort of interest in local women not appreciated by the townsfolk and

124

was made to take a tumble down the ravine. The Bersagliere's Grave is one of the few Aliano landmarks that doesn't bear Levi's name. A bust of the writer sits proudly in a narrow park that overlooks this *Fossa del Bersagliere*. The inscription reads, "From Turin with his love for the people of the south."

After breathing in the ruggedly picturesque landscape, we located the tourist office to begin our exploration of the Land of Levi. My driver was also curious as this was a new route for him. In the small office we found two women, who sold us our tickets and had us sign their book. We would have to wait a half hour or so for a tour, so we walked briefly around the town, admiring several of the older houses made of rough clay bricks. A particularly handsome facade across from the town hall caught my eye. The features of the house outlined a delightful face, with small square windows for eyes, a long narrow chimney up the center for a nose and the large, arched entranceway, a wide-open mouth. This was folk art at its very best.

A row of grottos carved into the rock cliff on the opposite ravine piqued my interest and I filed away the question for later. We returned to the information office at the appointed time and both women accompanied us on our rounds of the various buildings that made up the Literary Park. They unlocked doors and waited. We quickly realized that information was not forthcoming. The women clearly weren't tour guides. We wondered why they had closed the office and hazarded that perhaps one was the custodian of the key while the other was the security officer, as they weren't talking amongst themselves, either. I made small talk as best I could and then asked about the grottos I had seen, to which one of the women indignantly replied, "I've lived in Milan!" She wanted me to know that she wasn't a rube; she had seen the world. However, I had in no way implied that she or her forbears had resided in caves. I just asked if she could tell me something about the grottos, but her response reflected how at least some of the locals felt about Levi's characterizations and the visitors who came for the Levi experience. I later read that today the grottos were used for winemaking and as shelter for animals.

As I was writing this chapter, I came across an analogous story in H. V. Morton's *A Traveller in Southern Italy* (1969). The British journalist and travel writer stopped in Grassano on his journey through Basilicata and asked a "member of the gentry," whom he passed on the street, if he remembered Carlo Levi. Morton realized that, "This question was a mistake," as he had "touched an exposed nerve.... The man replied with indignation: 'Christ stopped at Eboli! Such wickedness!' He spread out his arms. 'Christ is *everywhere!*'" The man then turned and continued on his way.

And we, nevertheless, proceeded with our tour of Aliano, which included a Via Carlo Levi and even a street mural of the artist's face together with the local landscape that had been painted on a wall by the students of the Carlo Levi Artistic High School of Matera. The town's small *pinacoteca* or art gallery featured numerous of Levi's oil paintings and lithographs. "Essential naturalism" was how he characterized his artistic vision, nature's visceral impulse translated to the canvas. From the many portraits of himself to those of the peasants, his work confronted and transmitted melancholy and suffering. He also painted landscapes and still lifes. During his time in exile, he produced at least seventy paintings, although on my visit to Aliano, the museum exhibited more work from later in his life. Despite the fact that he was a political prisoner and deeply felt the confinement, when his sentence ended, Levi wasn't ready to leave Aliano and stayed on an additional ten days.

His apartment was on view just down the street, three simple rooms on the second floor of a building overlooking the *calanchi*. The living quarters were left empty to let the visitor's imagination fill in the space. The smoke-stained, narrow brick fireplace and worn floor tiles hinted at the rudimentary circumstances of his time there. But climbing the outside steps to the panoramic terrace, I could imagine the artist's contentment with both the solitude and its grand vista. Levi wrote: "The fiery streaks of the sunset lingered for hours over the mountains of Calabria and the air was filled with bats and crows. From my terrace the sky seemed immense, covered with constantly changing clouds; I felt as if I were on the roof of the world or on the deck of a ship anchored in a petrified ocean."

Underneath his apartment was an olive oil mill that shook the whole building when in function, but the crop was small that year so Levi was spared any significant disturbance. The oil press is now part of the *Museo della civiltà contadina* on the ground floor. This Rural Culture Museum has a collection of farm tools, milking and cheese-making implements, domestic objects and a corner set up like a typical peasant's room with a large bed in the center. As described by Levi, animals would have occupied the space underneath the bed and a suspended cradle swung above. A yellowed print of the Black Madonna of Viggiano hung on the wall.

Nearby, a good-sized patrician house had been renovated to accommodate a museum dedicated to the American abstract expressionist Paul Russotto (1944-2014), whose mother hailed from Aliano. The museum was founded with sixty of his donated works. A long list of museums was being planned at the time of my visit, to be dedicated to archeology, ethnographic masks, photography, hydrogeological risk, and not surprising, Carlo Levi. Quite ambitious. We popped into the church and drove to the cemetery, which was Levi's outer limit as a prisoner and one of his preferred painting locations. He enjoyed frequent walks to the edge of town.

When Levi left Aliano in 1936, he vowed to return. He kept that promise and his last visit was less than a month before his death. The writer was buried in the graveyard, a pleasantly shaded spot with a good view back over the town. I was surprised at Levi's tombstone, though. I don't know what I expected but certainly not the starkness of two brick walls facing one other with a large slab on the ground between them. Just his name and dates left room for the many stones placed on his tomb in keeping with the Jewish tradition. The other graves had traditional headstones, many with photos of the deceased and most all with flowers in vases and pots clustered around the grave markers. Perhaps the brick walls represented his confinement, an internment with open sides and a view.

Heading back to the center of town for lunch, we passed *"La casa dell'Americano."* Levi wrote of the emigrants who had gone to America and returned, several with the crash of the stock market in 1929. Families were divided after that year, he noted, when they stayed on whichever side of the ocean they found themselves. This "House of the American" was built a couple years before Levi entered the scene and was turned into a bed and breakfast by the great-nephew of the *americano* who built it with the money he had saved working twenty years in New York. A stately archway framed the elegantly carved double doors with brass knockers that led into the substantial two-story structure. The present owner was actually born in Buenos Aires as his parents had also emigrated to make their way in the world. However, they, too, returned to their homeland, and the house they inherited plays its part in presenting the Carlo Levi story of Aliano.

Our story that day continued with lunch, nothing like the meagre rations of the poverty-stricken farmers a century ago: "As for the poor, they ate plain bread the whole year around, spiced occasionally with a carefully crushed raw tomato, or a little garlic and oil, or a Spanish pepper with such a devilish bite to it that it is known as a *diavolesco*." Unlike in Levi's time, the bread on our table almost seemed like an afterthought amidst the bountiful repast. Levi reminisced: "The bread was of the characteristic black variety made of hard wheat in great loaves weighing five or ten pounds. They lasted a whole week, the mainstay of rich and poor alike, round like the sun or like a Mexican calendar-stone."

The country-style restaurant around the corner from the church didn't have a written bill of fare, but offered an inexpensive tourist menu of antipasti, pasta and meat, all served family style. The string of appetizers consisted of a plate of cold cuts (prosciutto, salami and capocollo), mozzarella and black olives, *frittelle* (rings of fried dough), baked eggplant, fried zucchini flowers, a potato soufflé, stuffed zucchini and string beans with such large, lean chunks of pancetta, the dish could practically have been considered a meat course. Homemade fettuccini in a mushroom sauce and slices of pot roast with a green salad followed. I'm a good eater, but the driver was a better one, so our plates were clean. And as we sat down, I realized another plus side of having a driver. I could have wine with lunch!

But when I compare such abundance with the general poverty found by Levi, the Aliano of today seems as far from the 1930s as Levi's Aliano must have seemed to his world: "These two civilizations could have no communication except by a miracle." For Levi, he had been sent further afield than India or China. Words and laws didn't have the same meaning in such distinctly different universes.

Thinking ahead to the spring and mosquitoes, Levi hoped to counteract Aliano's battle against malaria with the development of a land reclamation plan and a malarial prevention project. He submitted his proposal to officials in Matera. Many of the precautions were compulsory by law. Shortly thereafter, he received formal notice that, under threat of prison, he was forbidden to practice medicine in Aliano. I can only imagine what may have been behind such a decision, which could have only hurt those who had no one to turn to—the intransigent wheels of bureaucracy, greedy interests, innocent negligence, malicious criminality… Levi summed up the futility through his observation of a local priest: "After a few days of acquaintance with the village gentry, with their feuds and rivalries, and the scorn they displayed toward the poor benighted peasants, he understood that there was little he could do to combat the network of established interests built up on the impunity of one class and the passivity of the other."

Christ Stopped at Eboli shocked the nation in the name of basic human decency. Levi's descriptions of the squalid living conditions in the provincial capital of Matera and in the towns of his confinement didn't fall on deaf ears, but the special interests didn't magically go away, either. Political gears advance in fits and starts, when they do. And at what cost to the rural traditions that had so captured Levi's imagination? Fusing the ancient culture with what is called progress is an ongoing challenge and perhaps that is at the heart of Levi's success. Only by appreciating, studying and even admiring the old customs and rituals can worlds so different truly meet.

19. TRICARICO: ON WRITERS, A MAYOR AND MASKS

JUST AS ALIANO inspired Carlo Levi to create his fictionalized Gagliano of *Christ Stopped at Eboli* fame, Tricarico moved the American writer, Ann Cornelisen (1926-2003) to share her experiences of life in a Southern Italian town in her narrative *Torregreca*. Levi had been banished to Aliano, but Cornelisen chose to live in a place she described as "waiting, unchanged over the centuries ... a stage set." By way of happenstance and a humanitarian inclination, she worked for a British charitable organization under whose auspices she assisted nurseries and infant care centers throughout the Italian south. As head of a project to build a nursery training center in Basilicata, she lived in Tricarico, a good-sized community in a mountainous area halfway between Potenza and Matera. Her residency began in 1959 and lasted three years, but she would go back often and eventually turned her experiences into a book, which was published in 1969. She changed the name Tricarico to Torregreca, to give the town and its people anonymity but also, to create an "Every Village" of Southern Italy.

From the observations of Levi to those of Cornelisen, the suffering of the poor Lucanians remained constant in the decades before and after the Second World War. The two outsiders from different backgrounds and with unrelated motivations found the same destitution fostered by an eternal exploitation. Both felt little camaraderie with the middle and upper classes in general, as they assigned much culpability on the local level to their systematic perpetuation of the status quo. Rulers past and present squeezed without mercy and Cornelisen, in particular, put much of the blame on the Catholic Church. She assessed living conditions with the cool eye of a social worker, which perhaps make her descriptions of the gloomy, cramped, unsanitary hovels all that much more potent, and a single-room home with a neatly swept dirt floor and just two chairs for six people and 5 chickens all the more heartrending.

A local perspective from the period can be found in the poetry of Rocco Scotellaro (1923-53), one of Tricarico's own, a writer and politician who spoke for the poor. He was the voice of his people.

"Full moon"

The full moon fills our beds,
the mules trot on soft iron
and dogs gnaw bones.
You hear the donkey under the stairs,
its shivers, its scratching against the wall.
Under another staircase
my mother has slept for sixty years.

This short poem extracted from *The Dawn Is Always New: Selected Poetry of Rocco Scotellaro* (translated by Ruth Feldman and Brian Swann) is just one brief example of the poet's ability of expressing strong images and emotions with few words. Unlike other writers and poets who came from the outside and could only observe, Scotellaro was born into the world of the *contadino* or peasant, which was not the bucolic existence seen in the smiling faces of the happy farmer on pasta sauce labels.

Scotellaro's father was a cobbler, his mother, a homemaker and *scrivana del vicinato* or neighborhood scribe. Due to the high illiteracy rate, there was a great need for someone who knew how to read and write close to home, whether to deal with official correspondence or to be able to communicate with relatives who had emigrated overseas. Often these scribes would set up a little wooden desk on the street and the clients paid in whatever way they could, some cheese, a few eggs. And like so many Lucanians, Scotellaro's father was also forced to emigrate for work opportunities; he went to the United States where he lived in Paterson, New Jersey.

Excerpt from "There was America"

The America of my twenty-year-old father
was beautiful, far away.
It managed to break his heart.
America here, America there,
where is it now, my father's America?

After his studies in various cities away from Tricarico, Scotellaro
returned to his hometown to organize the working classes with the
aim of bringing dignity, employment and a modicum of justice to his
people. He founded a branch of the Italian Socialist Party and in 1946
Scotellaro, at just 23 years old, was elected mayor of Tricarico, a town
of close to 10,000 inhabitants at the time. He opened a hospital, fought
for agrarian reform and promoted education. After four years, he was
stopped in his tracts. Accused of malfeasance, he was sent to a prison in
Matera where it is said he read aloud from *Christ Stopped at Eboli* and
Dante's *Divine Comedy* for the other prisoners. He was released after
45 days. There was no case as there was no evidence. The allegations
had been maliciously fabricated. It's no wonder that, historically, the
peasants had been apathetic with regard to protests. Scotellaro abandoned politics but continued the struggle through his writings until his
untimely death at the age of 30.

The socialist poet, honest and forever young, did not speak in vain.
Conditions would eventually improve despite the persistent imbroglios
perpetuated by Italy's thorny political machinations. The town's population has since dwindled to about 5,500, albeit a well-fed, educated
citizenry of which Scotellaro and Cornelisen would be proud. I had the
opportunity to visit Tricarico for their annual *Raduno delle Maschere
Antropologiche* that is held over the first weekend of June. This Meeting
of Anthropological Masks brings together folklore and tradition from
all over Italy as well as Europe. The masks and costumes are those of
Carnevale. In peasant culture, Carnival represents an ancient rite that
ushers in the prosperity and fertility of the life cycle and the seasons.
Basilicata's Carnival isn't like that of Venice, where participants outdo

each other with opulence. Rather, the imagery is archaic, pagan, earthy. Costumes represent animals and plants, as the participants invoke the benevolent spirits for the wellbeing of their livestock and fields. This homage to the gods welcomes good and scares away evil.

Years after his confinement Carlo Levi visited Tricarico at Carnival time to witness this marriage of the sacred and profane. He was accompanied by Rocco Scotellaro with whom he had become friends. Describing the opening of Carnival season on January 17th, the feast day of St. Anthony the Abbot, protector of animals and skin diseases, Levi wrote:

> The town was awakened, still deep in the night, by an archaic noise, by beatings of hollow, wooden instruments, like cracked bells: a noise of a primitive forest that reached into the bowels like an infinitely remote call; and everyone climbed up the mountain, people and animals, to the chapel high on the top. The animals were brought there to go around the sacred altar three times, and they came in, and they were blessed during the Mass, with a total integration of the magical, archaic ritual with that of the Catholic.

DEAFENING! The bellringing could wake the dead. This ritualistic observance is repeated on the Sunday before Mardi Gras. Tricarico is one of seven Lucanian communities, including Aliano, Cirigliano, Montescaglioso, San Mauro Forte, Satriano di Lucania and Teana, noted for their traditional Carnivals that summon the natural world in a popular spectacle of myth and legend.

For example, the walking trees of Satriano di Lucania are particularly atmospheric. Conjuring the mystique of ancestral arboreal rites, these plant-men represent hermits and come out of the woods completely covered in shoots of ivy. They move quietly and carry a walking stick with a broom plant attached to its end that is used to rustle on doors. This subdued scraping is their hushed knock as they go from house to house requesting alms. In contrast, bear figures, dressed in sheep or goat skins with chains attached to their ankles, noisily ring small animal bells and erratically leap here and there through the streets. The third figure is called the *Quaresima*, the old Lenten widow dressed in black, who roams slowly through the village and moans in desperation over her difficult life. On her head, she carries a cradle with her child, born during the festivities and symbolizing the end of Carnival. Interestingly, both men and women act out the *Quaresima*. And to complete the picture of Satriano's surreal Carnival traditions, there is even a wedding ceremony with a man acting the role of the bride and a woman, the groom.

Each town features its own characteristic customs and costumes. In *Christ Stopped at Eboli* Levi wrote that the peasants' bond with nature was stronger than with religion. For him, the Carnival experience came on unexpectedly in 1930s Aliano: "They were jumping and shouting like maddened beasts, drunk with their own hue and cry.... They carried dried sheepskins in their hands, rolled up like sticks, which they brandished threateningly and brought down about the head and shoulders of anyone who failed to get out of their way."

By the time David Yeadon came on the scene at the turn of the 21st century, the festival was anticipated with great joy and in his *Seasons in Basilicata* describes "the villagers' irrepressible spirit of mischief, fun and pride" in their heritage: "They were everywhere. Frighteningly bedecked in garish, devil-like masks, with enormous horns and swirling *cappelloni* (head-dresses) of colored ribbons, hundreds of them to each mask, they tore around the piazza and Via Roma, chasing the villagers with sticks and whips, all the way down the *corso* and into Piazza Garibaldi. Shouting and screaming like the mad animals they were, they threatened everyone with fiendish clubs."

Other nearby towns celebrated in their own ways. Yeadon continues: "Cirigliano offered to its proudly insular villagers a mysteriously intimate, alley-by-alley procession of musicians, oddly dressed characters reflecting village legends and folktales, frantic dancing to accordions, drums, and flutes, and feasting on time-treasured culinary oddities such as sheep's head, pig trotters and tripe."

Several communities also feature more contemporary Carnivals complete with elaborate floats parodying politics and popular culture. My trip to Tricarico, however, focused on those of yesteryear. As the publicity materials boasted, "A people's wealth lies in its roots."

I was to meet the 500 participants very much in touch with their roots in a large warehouse outside of town. Groups were coming from great distances and as to be expected, there were delays. Luckily, just as I was about to faint from hunger, a local volunteer pulled his home-made cheese and salami out of one jacket pocket and a knife from the other. As I bit down on the flavorful cured meat, an ensemble of three costumed musicians from Bergamo serenaded into the building with a dancing masked man in a cape. The former physicist and electrotechnology researcher turned shaman whirled round and round, attempting to manipulate his own energy in an effort to achieve the perfect trance. His path and roots marched to their own drummer. The other participants stuck closer to their European heritage.

Organizing an event of this size took a village, and Tricarico's citizenry busily funneled bulk wine from large plastic jugs into recycled liter water bottles, laid the tables with paper place settings and went about serving hundreds of people out of the back of a truck in a building without a drop of running water, except for the roof leaking from the morning's rainstorm. Groups gradually arrived, some in costume and others in travel clothes, excited for the weekend's events.

The highlight of the afternoon was the parade of children from Tricarico. They were miniature versions of their parents who would be taking part in the official spectacle the next day. The clanging of brass bells and buzz of high voices bounced off the stone streets and walls, like a herd of young animals was being led through town. And that is just what they represented. Walking along in their two separate lines, they weren't schoolchildren separated from their buddies, but they personified a herd of cows in *transumanza*, transhumance or seasonal migration. The "cow" wears a wide-brimmed hat with a scarf and veil attached from which long, multi-colored ribbons cascade down to its ankles. More scarves and ribbons are tied around its neck, waist and arms under which is simply a pair of long johns. The "bull" is similarly attired except all in black with a few red ribbons. Cowbells of different shapes and sizes are rung incessantly, and the costumed townsfolk mimic the gait and maneuvering of the animals. The herder keeps the creatures in line with a handmade shepherd's crook, and gentry ride along in a carriage.

Bands played, flags thrown, meats grilled in the piazza, and I didn't stay around to find out what an anthropological DJ was, but he apparently took the revelry past midnight. The following day, Carnival's diverse pastoral images, their significances and the connection to the church were discussed at a conference. While these rituals may have emerged organically, in Italy there always seems to be a table of intellectuals with microphones ready to analyze and discuss them. St. Anthony the Abbot, in particular, received a good deal of attention in his role as the hermit monk who cured skin afflictions, such as shingles, with pig fat. And I now can recognize him in paintings and statues as I learned that he's the saint with a bell hanging from his walking stick.

The conference was held at the ducal palace in the center of one of Basilicata's best-preserved medieval towns. Interestingly, Tricarico bills itself as an Arab-Norman city. The Arab comes from the urban layout of neighborhoods constructed between the 9th and 10th centuries when the area was under Arab control. Terraced gardens also remain from those years. The Norman refers to the period in which the town's large round tower was completed. This imposing Norman tower dominates the skyline, visually anchoring Tricarico's old town. Taking a walk through the narrow lanes past several notable churches, I arrived at the tower and as I was taking a picture, someone shouted down from the entrance gate, "Do you want to take a tour?" Of course I do. He was waving from the door of a massive structure built on top of natural rock.

As he launched into a detailed explanation, a group of Lucanians from a nearby town with Kiwi relatives in tow walked up. They clearly weren't interested in learning about the 27-meter (89-foot) tall tower with 5-meter (16-foot) thick walls or the history of the attached castle that had been donated to the Order of St. Clare to become a monastery in the 14th century. The guide was speaking so enthusiastically, I wondered how the interest of this familial unit wasn't even mildly piqued, which both dumbfounded and disappointed the docent, who took the approach: you have to eat your vegetables if you want the dessert.

When we finally climbed up the four-storied tower all the way to the top from where you could see clear to Puglia, everyone was happy. The euphoria didn't last long, though, as they insisted on descending immediately so as not to miss the parade. Not a chance. A local with the keys to the castle knows exactly when the festivities will begin no matter what the posted starting time says. They ran off as I was viewing the photographic exhibit of Rocco Scotellaro *con calma* (leisurely), after which the guide drove me down the hill to the start of the parade, past the policeman who pushed a barrier aside and waved us onto the route lined with the expectant crowd. I felt as though I should have been smiling, turning and waving as part of the pageantry.

The parade participants came from as far away as Greece, Slovenia and the Basque region. Basilicata and the rest of Italy were well represented. The spectacle featured far-out folk apparel, the ringing of bells from those of the smallest kid to the largest bull, dancing and even a group on stilts. My guide stuck with me for the duration, pulling aside his costumed friends for colorful selfies. The scene was original in every sense of the word, a contemporary celebration of ancestral traditions.

In her experience and analysis of the local culture, Ann Cornelisen observed that, "in Southern Italy life is reversed; the simplest thing becomes the most complex." Viewing the fantastical diversity before me, I thought, would the reverse be true as well?

VII

ITALY'S LARGEST NATIONAL PARK

Festival of the *Madonna della Stella*, San Costantino Albanese

20. THE ALBANIAN POLLINO

I WANTED TO SEE the exploding heads—I won't deny it. I could have visited San Costantino Albanese any time of the year, but I didn't want to miss the life-sized figures spinning and whirling until they burst on center stage of the piazza. Italy boasts countless festivals, but this spectacle is unique. And not unlike other happenings of a folkloristic nature, the extravaganza takes place as part of a religious festival. In San Costantino Albanese, the patron saint of the day is the *Madonna della Stella* and her celebration falls on the second Sunday of May, a perfect time of year to enjoy the beautiful wildflowers on the journey there.

Nestled in the hills of the Pollino National Park, San Costantino Albanese has historical roots that have shaped and continue to define the community. The approximately 700 inhabitants descend from Albanians who fled from Albania and the Peloponnese after the Ottoman invasion and founded both this as well as the neighboring village of San Paolo Albanese in 1534. These refugees were welcomed by the King of Naples and were even exempt from taxes for a little over a hundred years in recognition of the Albanians' valiant efforts in the fight against the Turks. Amazingly, the residents still speak their original language, an ancient Albanian called Arbëresh. South Italy counts fifty historically Albanian or Arbëreshë communities that have maintained their language, customs and religion. Calabria has the greatest number, while Basilicata has just five: San Costantino Albanese (Shën Kostandini) and San Paolo Albanese (Shën Pali) in the Pollino Mountains and Barile (Barilli), Ginestra (Zhura) and Maschito (Mashqiti) in the Vulture area.

San Costantino Albanese welcomes visitors with a colorful, dual language billboard at the entrance to the town. Suffice it to say, Arbëresh looks quite foreign to the English or Italian speaker, and it sounds equally exotic. I didn't understand a word of it, and perhaps in comparison, the Italian was crystal clear. I arrived on the Saturday afternoon before the main event as the street vendors were closing up for lunch. The road was lined with their booths, which left considerably less space than what I perceived to be the width of my car. I inched along, people stared, I missed the merchandise by centimeters, but no one batted an eyelash. I was hungry and there was a food truck, so I parked in what clearly was not a space and downed a delicious panino of *porchetta pizzaiola*. The chef manning the large pot of pork meat in a rich, somewhat complex tomato sauce with just a hint of spice assured me the recipe was local. It boded well.

The town was in repose and I took a brief stroll around its center, up and down lanes with street signs in the two languages. The main street, Corso Scanderbeg memorialized the 15th-century Albanian military leader who led the Christian resistance against the Ottomans. Old houses, some with rustic stone and others with plastered facades crowded the narrow lanes. Several buildings had exterior staircases leading to the second floor. I wasn't able to secure accommodations in the village but was lucky to have found a place nearby. While I wasn't traveling in what would be considered the high season, for San Costantino Albanese, it didn't get any higher than the *Festa della Madonna della Stella*. I was staying in an *agriturismo* (agricultural tourism restaurant with lodging) in Martorino, a *frazione* or district of the town. The four curvy miles felt like a solid thirty. And although I was tired from my morning's drive and my stomach was weighted down by a pork sandwich, I couldn't help but stop and snap a few pictures along the way, particularly of the lush fields of deep pink wildflowers waving gently under the billowy clouds floating overhead.

A little rest and a short walk, and as the Italians say: *"L'aria di montagna fa venire la fame."* Mountain air makes you hungry. I had the opportunity to preview my dinner as the *agriturismo* was a working farm with a vegetable garden and lots of pigs, even a variety crossbred with a boar. I was happy to see the animals had large fields adorned with bright yellow tufts of scotch broom in which to root around. And if scientific studies weren't proof enough that animals with a stress-free life produced healthier, tastier meat, the pork I consumed that weekend was all the empirical evidence I needed. The siblings of those carefree

140

organically raised swine made a fine presentation that evening and at the next day's festive lunch. I ate copiously and I noticed that it wasn't just the smokers who occasionally stepped outside for a breath of that mountain air before diving into the next plate.

The appetizers kept coming and I couldn't say which dish was served when, as the plates and meals have since merged in my head. The *salumi* (cured meats) were exquisite. On the top of my list would be the thinly sliced *guanciale* or jowl bacon that looked as incredible as it tasted. Striped like an inviting candy cane with a thicker white alternating with a tempting natural red, the raw *guanciale* glistened atop slices of toasted bread and literally melted in my mouth. Yes, like butter, but with an ever so delicate pork flavor. The bruschetta with ricotta and *ciccioli* or soft cubes of pork renderings (not to be confused with crispy versions in other parts) was also noteworthy, as were the *capocollo*, a cold cut made from the pig's neck, and the *culatello*, which comes from the animal's posterior region (*culo* in Italian) and is thus tender and lean with an intense red color. Italians talk of eating at *"chilometro zero"* and at literally zero kilometers, this was as locally sourced as it gets. Dishes of sautéed chard, green beans and eggs, potatoes with *peperoni cruschi*, an earthy pecorino cheese and a simple bruschetta topped with chopped tomatoes balanced the meat. And then there were the first and second courses. Big chunks of porcini mushrooms were featured in a plate of *scialatelli* pasta (thick, medium-length homemade noodles). For the meat course, the house pork and the neighbor's lamb were charcoal grilled to succulence. And to top it off, the strawberry cake for dessert brought back memories of my grandmother's.

This *agriturismo* was a small family operation with the proprietor wearing many hats—owner, farmer and chef. His wife, sons and relatives filled out the rest. The same people fed and butchered the pigs, prepared the meats and sausages, took care of the garden, hunted for mushrooms, cooked the food and made liquors from local fruits and herbs gathered by hand—the original "farm to table" experience. Clearly, there was more to San Costantino Albanese than the exploding heads or even the *Volo dell'aquila*, a large four-person hang glider attached to a stainless-steel cable that takes its passengers on a short, panoramic ride over the valley. I would save the "flight of the eagle" for another time, definitely before lunch.

On festival day, strolling musicians set a convivial tone with their earnest renditions of simple folksongs played on various sizes of *surdulina* (bagpipe) and *ciaramelle* (shawms). I joined a guided visit of the museum and cultural center that had been organized for a couple of Italian tour buses. I called ahead and not only did the friendly local guide look out for me the entire time, she gave me a book about the Arbëreshë in San Costantino Albanese. I suppose she didn't want the lone American trampled by a mass of Italian day trippers on her watch. Just the opposite of getting lost in the crowd, as I traveled around Basilicata to places that saw few foreign visitors, the locals tended to reach out and welcome me.

At the town's *Etnomuseo della Cultura Arbëreshe,* the knowledgeable guide, who I would discover was a volunteer, enthusiastically immersed us in her culture. She was proud of her Arbëreshe history and traditions. The ethnic museum houses a library of Albanian culture, icons painted by Josif Droboniku, a well-known Albanian artist who also painted the interior of the main church, a delightful Arbëresh nativity scene and a display of traditional objects, crafts and clothing from the area. The nearby *Casa Parco* presents a collection of plants historically important for the community, musical instruments made in San Costantino as well as neighboring Terranova di Pollino, and an exhibit pertaining to the festival and its fascinating theatrical manifestations.

San Costantino's main square is dominated by its Mother Church, which follows the Greek-Byzantine rite with the Mass sung almost entirely in the Albanian language. Dedicated to the Saints Constantine the Great and Helena, the sanctuary is preciously guarded by the local priest, who admonishes the slightest glimpse of a camera or cellphone that he is able to spot with the eyes on the back of his head. The work of the aforementioned Droboniku is impressive and his colorful icons blanketed on gold draw you in with their detail and artistry, particularly the Last Judgement that covers the entire wall above the entranceway.

With a little time before the main event was to transpire, the guide invited me to have a drink, together with her boyfriend, a Roman policeman, and her cousin, the *americano*, who turned out to be a Lucanian, recently returned from a lifetime working a maintenance job in New Jersey. Uprooted from one's homeland and then coming back after ages away is a difficult adjustment. Fitting in is a challenge in both directions, such different worlds, habits and languages. But before we knew it, the crowd was assembling in the piazza in front of the Mother Church. The stage was set with five life-size figures: a young woman, a young man, a pair of blacksmiths and the devil.

The main event is called the *Nusazit*, which literally means the betrothed couple. The razzle-dazzle takes place at the end of the late-morning Mass, when the *Madonna della Stella* in her glass-encased wooden box comes out of the church on the shoulders of parishioners. I suppose she wouldn't want to miss the spectacle. She is set down under a cloth canopy and all eyes turn towards the stage across the piazza. On my visit, the priest looked a bit exasperated by it all, seemingly peeved but resigned to the fact that the Madonna had to wait for the puppets. All he could do was hold his microphone and bide his time. The female mayor distinguished by the classic tricolor sash was positioned at his side. Her large white handbag hung from her wrist by its heavy chain straps. A man stood behind with a pair of loudspeakers on a stick. The procession was ready to begin, but first, the firing up of the *Nusazit*.

The puppets cut colorful figures. Constructed of papier-mâché over wooden frames, the characters are dressed in traditional folkloric costumes and filled with gunpowder. The female personage is decked out for a celebration in a red, yellow, white and green striped skirt, reminiscent of the pleated fabric in the traditional costumes. A lacy white blouse, fanciful belt, hat and earrings complete the outfit. The man is clad in a bright red vest, black knickers and a pointed hat. A shepherd's crook and a stick with two little baskets of ricotta divulge his profession.

The show starts with the two blacksmiths. Unceremoniously, a wheel is set spinning that brings the smithies' hammers back and forth onto the anvil until the rat-a-tat-tat of an explosion breaks the puppets apart with smoke and fire. A couple of guys with low-pressure hoses without nozzles stand by and point little streams of water in the direction of any possible hazard. Next, the shepherd is lighted, and he whirls around, faster and faster, with his ricotta swinging out to the sides. A pop here and another there, the mechanism hisses round and round. Pah-pop and then pah-pah-pop-pop-pop, the herder's body erupts, scattering in pieces, and then, BOOM goes the head! The crowd applauds.

Next, the maiden's fuse is lit, and the handler gives her wheel a spin. As she turns, so does her dress, white petticoats revealed. The contraption whirs and whizzes. She and her skirt twirl round and round, but her shoulders and head remain aloof. The workings screech and scrape as she turns. Rat-a-tat-tat and silence. She is completely intact. What does it mean? The out-of-towners search out locals for the answer. Bad luck! *Mamma mia!* Not to worry, it's much more serious if the devil's head doesn't explode. BOOM! The crowd gasps and then chuckles. Her head burst late, so she just made her bridegroom wait.

Now to the black devil who glares defiantly from his two-faced head. Four horns on top and hoofed feet at the bottom, he's equipped with the standard pitchfork and a cauldron chain. The gears rasp and spark as the devil turns, his forked tongues flap and his chain flies. The explosives pop, then splutter, his legs tear apart, a moment's hesitation, and BOOM! Off with his head to the cheer of the crowd! He bursts into flames, pieces fly about and a little boy runs up and grabs one off the ground as the devil's blazing body is hosed down.

The procession starts up and passes by the stage as smoke rises from the headless puppets. The priest begins to sing the familiar "Maria" song into his microphone and women's voices join him. The flock follows through the village streets. A number of women carry configurations of candles atop their heads. A cappella singing, bagpipes and shawms, and a band playing marches all make up the cortege that goes to the Sanctuary of the *Madonna della Stella* in the rural landscape just outside of town.

The *Nusazit* is quirky. The evening before, a manned horse-and-rider puppet prances through the streets shooting off firecrackers. And as I was looking through the book I was given, I came across an offbeat Arbëreshë folksong, another bit of lightheartedness via San Costantino Albanese. Excerpted from *Gli Arbëreshë e la "Rilindja"* edited by Pasquale Scutari, the following verses, written down in the 19th century, would have been sung by a coterie of young males in a vividly direct gibe to girls with a haughty attitude.

Nusset

Mizzòre, tunde e shcuude me ghaidhii,
Ma trimmi, cë ti mer, esht sa gnë vee.
Caa ghund si macce, dhëmbet si stighii,
E balet shtipur jà si ndranguliee.

Rin, mbaghe se jee dieli, e u t' thom ndë vesht:
Pa gghii, e thaat, e diëgur, e nghergnast,
Më ducche macce e egher shtën mbi prusht.

The Brides

Miss, you happily twirl and shake,
But the youth that you lead to the altar is like an egg,
He has the nose of a female cat, teeth of a witch,
and a flattened forehead like a snake.

Rina, you think you're the daytime star, and I'll whisper in your ear:
No breasts, skinny, dried up, irritable,
You're like a wild cat with paws up in the air.

As reflected in the significance of the *Nusazit* and the humorous Arbëreshë song, the courting rituals were an important aspect of the town's traditions. And today, wedding customs still play out as in former times. On the day of the ceremony, the groom leads a cortege from his house to that of the bride, whom he finds crying in her mother's arms. She is lured outside by a chorus of the groom and his men. The ensuing procession to the church is accompanied by more singing and the groom's brother victoriously waving a flag. The bride in a veil and crown comes behind with her family. The religious ceremony follows the Greek liturgy and concludes with the priest offering wine-soaked bread to the groom and then to the bride. Finally, three gestures are each repeated three times: the exchange of rings, the placement of crowns on the couple's heads to symbolize their new leadership roles within the family, and going around the sacred altar while holding hands, which represents the indissolubility of the marriage. After the religious ceremony, the party proceeds with traditional song to the groom's house, where the bride, surrounded by her family, visually demonstrates an aversion to entering until her new mother-in-law comes out and warmly welcomes her to her new home.

On the day following the *Nusazit*, I would learn more about Arbëreshë traditions in neighboring San Paolo Albanese, which lies across the Sarmento River on the other side of the valley. With barely 300 inhabitants, the village has the distinction of being Basilicata's smallest community, reduced to just one-fifth of its 19th-century size. I was headed for the *Museo della Cultura Arbëreshe*. When I called that morning to double check on the opening hours, the woman who responded encouraged me to arrive as soon as possible to have time for a thorough visit. I was to meet her at the town hall. Already as I was getting out of my car across the street, a man approached and asked if I was the one who had telephoned about the museum. Word had gotten around that a visitor was in town.

When the guide began to speak, I realized why I would need time. Her breadth of knowledge and passion were invigorating, and I had her all to myself for two hours. Looking in from the outside, you might scratch your head as to why this remote, sparsely populated area was so rich in museums, but these centers are the last bastions of a culture that flourished for almost five hundred years in linguistic and territorial isolation. Before the 20th century, intermarriage with Italian speakers would have been extremely rare, so socialization was limited to the Arbëreshë communities in the Pollino Mountains. The museum is thus a place to conserve, protect and promote this cultural and social identity. My docent cited language, religion and traditional clothing as the most important aspects of keeping the culture alive.

Several old stone houses in disuse were put together to create a modern museum space in the center of the village. The exhibits range from the legends and history of the Arbëresh to objects from everyday life and work with a special emphasis on the process of making textiles from Scotch broom. Amongst the museum's displays, the traditional clothing is especially attractive, in particular the women's festive costumes consisting of a white cotton blouse with elaborate lace collar and cuffs, an intricate velvet or damask bodice embroidered with heads of grain and bunches of grapes in gold or silver filigree, and lively red and gold, horizontally striped skirt adorned with precious threads and characterized by numerous pleats. Several garments of my docent's grandmother were amongst the collection.

As in San Costantino, the religion was originally orthodox, but today is catholic of the Greek-Byzantine rite. San Paolo's main festival takes place on August 16th and is dedicated to St. Rocco, the patron saint. The procession also features an ancient harvest ritual with what looks like a little house made of stalks of grain. This *himunea*, as it is called, is carried on the shoulders of several men, who also dance around with it in the *gioco del falcetto* or game of the sickle. Others dance around waving this farm implement and fistfuls of grain in representation of the struggle between good and evil.

My game in San Paolo was more of a contemporary nature, the never-ending Italian predicament of not having change. Between cash machines that spit out 50- and 100-note bills and merchants who always press for exact change, my smallest denomination was a 50 that morning. The museum admission was 2 Euros. The two-hour guided visit of the town was free. I already had a receipt for € 2,00 (Italians use a comma before the cents) from the *Comune di San Paolo Albanese* written up by the guide at the museum's front desk. She said we could get the change later. I said two twenties would do. Oh, no! "You can donate it to the museum or the church." Oh, no! She was determined to make the 2-Euro transaction and when the tour ended, told me to ask in the bar just down the street from the museum. The bar was very informal, more like just an area set up in the front room of a house. I could see that a group of four men were eating pasta in an interior room, so I had to go into what felt like a very private area and explain my situation while doing so. They looked at me like I had just dropped down from Mars. Who would interrupt an Italian eating a plate of pasta for change? I understood, but I didn't want my docent to dip into her own pocket just not to accept a tip. No one said anything, but they all pulled out their well-worn wallets amidst my abject apologies, and the oldest came up with two twenties and a ten. They turned back to their pasta as I babbled my most heartfelt thanks. A colleague at the town hall came up with the *spiccioli* or small change, and I was on my way, such a rich experience for such a small price.

A few days later on San Costantino's Facebook page, I noticed a complaint from someone who had been at the *Nusazit*. The individual was disappointed that there was just one person in traditional dress. I remembered that adorable little girl in her long red-gold-and-green skirt, ornate sash and blue bodice over which flowed the large collar of her lacy white blouse. She shyly turned away from the tourists who tripped over themselves as they thrust their cameras directly in her face without any thought for her privacy or personal space. A local responded to the Facebook grumbling by saying that the Arbëresh observed traditions in their own way. Not only were the costumes very expensive, but the townspeople weren't like zoo animals to be gawked at. They were contemporary Italians and kept their heritage alive in the context of the modern world ... drinking spritzes at the bar, operating the flight apparatus of the *Volo dell'aquila* and carrying designer handbags in the procession.

21. THE POLLINO NATIONAL PARK

"*CHE BUON PROFUMO!*" What a wonderful aroma, I couldn't help but exclaim as the fragrances sprang out of the glass jars filled with teas and infusions: forest flowers, blueberries, raspberries, apples…. Just a whiff was like being transported to a blueberry patch or a secret forest. When I think of all the products on grocery store shelves full of artificial substances engineered to smell and taste like real food, and here I was in this little shop, bursting with all-natural products that no scientist, no matter how clever, would ever be able to come close to replicating. I was in San Severino Lucano, in the heart of the Pollino National Park, an area that straddles southern Basilicata and northern Calabria to form Italy's largest national park, comprising 192,565 hectares or 475,838 acres. San Severino lies on the northeast side of the Pollino massif that divides Basilicata from Calabria with several peaks exceeding 2,000 meters. The two highest are Serra Dolcedorme at 2,267 meters (7,438 feet) and Monte Pollino, which gives its name to the entire range, at 2,248 meters (7,375 feet).

The San Severino shop owner knew exactly what was in every jar and bag on his shelves, because he and other family members had gathered and prepared the fruit, vegetables, flowers and mushrooms themselves. Cheeses and meats were typical local products. In addition, the wooden objects for sale had been whittled and carved from area trees. As I sampled his delicate yet powerfully aromatic *finocchietto*, a liquor he had made from a wild fennel plant, I thought how wonderful it would have been to live and breathe such a rich wholesomeness that the good people of the Pollino Mountains experienced every day. Yet, in our brief conversation the proprietor sadly spoke of an article he had just read that reflected the region's drastic depopulation, particularly that of the interior mountainous areas. San Severino has dwindled to around 1,500 inhabitants, having lost over two-thirds of its population over the past 150 years. As in other parts of the region, the young people move away for work, and they do so in even greater numbers from isolated areas.

Back in the period following Italy's 1861 unification, the remoteness of these mountains made them strongholds for the brigandage movement. San Severino still holds harrowing memories of a Captain Gennaro Iannarelli sent by the newly formed government to squelch any and all uprisings, which he did with a ruthless violence, not just with the brigands but with the civilians as well. The area's hero was Antonio Franco (1832-65), nicknamed the *Lupo* (wolf) *del Pollino*, who hailed from nearby Francavilla in Sinni. His group was active from Sapri in the Province of Salerno all the way down to Cosenza in Calabria. Throughout the Pollino, Franco is remembered as a Robin Hood figure, robbing from the rich to help the poor. Today, hikers can follow the *Sentieri dei Briganti* or Brigands' Trails. British writer Norman Douglas dedicated three chapters to the Pollino Mountains in his classic travelogue *Old Calabria*. As an avid outdoorsman, he traversed peak and dale on foot. During his travels through the area over 100 years ago, he reflected on well-known episodes of brigandage, which would have been more palpable closer to the events. Douglas also lamented of deforestation and advocated for the preservation of these mountains. He encouraged his readers to visit as soon as possible: "Whoever wishes to see these beautiful stretches of woodland ere their disappearance from earth—let him hasten!" Luckily, the Pollino remains intact with acre upon acre of splendid forest.

In addition to the unspoiled naturalistic setting conducive to outdoor activities, San Severino's territory is well known for the Sanctuary of the Madonna of the Pollino. This religious landmark sits on a rocky slope of Monte Pollino with a wonderful view "especially towards evening, when crude daylight tints fade away and range after range of mountains reveal themselves, their crests outlined against each other in tender gradations of mauve and grey." Douglas went on to characterize the Festival of the Madonna of the Pollino as a "bacchanal" ... in a good way:

It is a vast picnic in honor of the Virgin. Two thousand persons are encamped about the chapel, amid a formidable army of donkeys and mules whose braying mingles with the pastoral music of reeds and bagpipes…. A heaving ebb and flow of humanity fills the eye; fires are flickering before extempore shelters, and an ungodly amount of food is being consumed, as traditionally prescribed for such occasions—"si mangia per devozione". [One eats out of devotion.]

Grilled goat is always a classic repast, but today, car horns replace donkey brays. The faithful come from far and wide, as historically the *Festa della Madonna del Pollino* brings together the devoted of Basilicata and Calabria every first Friday and Saturday of July.

San Severino is just one of 24 communities on the Lucanian side of the Pollino National Park. Calabria has another 32. The headquarters are housed in Basilicata's Rotonda, a town of roughly 3,500 that has held onto its population a little better than many others. I visited on a weekday in spring and the center was bustling. The churches were open and in impeccable condition, freshly painted with gleaming pews. The numerous stone doorways and arches lining the streets lent an air of prosperity—125 in all. These grand portals and many fountains were expertly carved by area craftsmen in local stone and marble.

I had read that the Pollino's Natural History Museum was in Rotonda and found it in a nondescript town administration building. Although well within the posted opening hours, the lights were off in the section dedicated to the museum. I poked my head into one of the offices and sought out an employee, who made a couple of phone calls on my behalf. They apparently hadn't expected anyone to walk in that day, but she was directed to turn the lights on. A municipal policeman who must have already given out his quota of parking tickets that morning jumped to the task and patiently manned the light switches as I moved about.

The initial impetus for this small museum came from the 1982 discovery of the fossilized skeleton of an entire ancient elephant, the *Elephas antiquus* that was unearthed in Rotonda's Mercure River Valley. This find was followed up by those of a hippopotamus, the jawbone of a rhinoceros and miscellaneous bones from several deer, all estimated to be between 300,000 and 500,000 years old. I imagine that the reconstruction of the extinct elephant next to his skeletal remains must capture the attention of the local schoolchildren who are probably the museum's most frequent visitors. Behind a locked door, there was also a laboratory full of bones waiting to be studied. Conspiratorially, the policeman opened it and gestured to the floor where he lifted a covering to reveal another ancient tusk.

On the southwestern side of the Pollino in Papasidero, Calabria, ancient human bones were discovered, much younger than these animals, but going back as far as 16,000 years. The site is called the *Grotta del Romito* (Hermit's Grotto), and the pièce de résistance of this natural cave is an 11,000-year-old petroglyph found in 1961. The prehistoric rock carving depicts an extinct bovine. Executed with a sure hand, the bull is graceful and well-proportioned, a prehistoric masterpiece. Although its beauty can be appreciated in the copy at the archeological museum in Reggio Calabria, the original image in its forest setting engenders a far greater impact.

Of a completely different nature, another of the Pollino's masterpieces is the truffle, particularly the white variety, the *tartufo bianco*. This sumptuously aromatic, delicately flavored tuber is served in generous portions in area restaurants. The *tagliata al tartufo bianco* I lapped up in Rotonda was a juicy and flavorful grilled beef that had been sliced and presented with a sauce of white truffle shavings and oil. In neighboring Viggianello I enjoyed the truffles on homemade pasta. I also had the opportunity to taste the *melanzana rossa*, a red eggplant grown in Rotonda that is a protected regional food although not native to Italy. I sampled the eggplant preserved in oil as an appetizer. The curious vegetable resembles a round tomato, but its consistency is like that of a normal eggplant. Its taste is a little sharp and slightly bitter.

The town of Viggianello encompasses a vast territory, allowing a lot of elbow room for its approximately 3,000 inhabitants in an area with one of the lowest population densities of Italy. Its historic center clings to the side of a hill with houses that appear to climb up steps, all the way to the Norman castle at the top. The imposing structure anchored by a square tower dominates the village clustered below. The castle chambers have gone from hosting the likes of the Holy Roman Emperor Frederick II to those of today's ordinary guests staying in the renovated hotel. The local economy is increasingly based on tourism with outdoor enthusiasts engaging in hiking, mushroom hunting, cross-country and downhill skiing, snowshoeing and rafting. Sparked by a brochure on display in the lobby of my bed and breakfast, I chose an excursion a bit off the beaten track in order to immerse myself in the Mercure River, whose source is in Viggianello about two kilometers from the old town. Stopping off at the spring is also well worth the quick turnoff for the gorgeous colors of the crystal clear, aqua water and rich plant life.

The Mercure spring pumps out more than 2,000 liters of water every second and is the largest in the Pollino. When the Mercure River enters Calabria, the name changes to Lao from Laos, an ancient city of Greater Greece whose territory lies in Santa Maria del Cedro on the Tyrrhenian coast. The park's numerous rivers feature tubing, rafting and canoeing, with the best known canyons on the Raganello River in Calabria. My activity, however, was calmer and dare I say, therapeutic. Called acquatrekking®, the delightful water-walking experience in the Mercure River was dreamt up by a group of young entrepreneurs who chose the clean air of their home in the Pollino over chasing after jobs elsewhere. With degrees in the sciences and a passion for the outdoors, they put their heads together and came up with an experiential tourism in their beloved Pollino and even trademarked the name of their water-walking excursion.

My guide Daniele picked me up in his jeep to take me to the adventure's starting site, a little changing cabin and a couple of picnic tables in the woods, a bit off-road. He had asked me my shoe size and had a pair of waders ready. Who knew that waterproof boots that reached all the way up to your chest could be so comfortable? But when we walked into the water and the cold water began to constrict the waterproof garment, I relished the restorative feeling. Moving around in the clear water with hanging vegetation on the banks was pure bliss. We were in a beautiful wood with just the right amount of sunlight shining through breaks in the canopy of trees. The gentle water's flow and burbling of a light cascade, the humidity rising from the plant life, the pristine air quality—this is the environment spas try to replicate. All I needed was to have a seat on the mossy bank with a couple of cucumbers on my eyes and a glass of lemon water in hand.

From the history of the Mercure Valley to its aquatic plants and tadpoles, the acquatrekking® was not only physically pleasurable, but Daniele, with a degree in geology and a lifelong passion for rivers, made it edifying, as well—what a wonderful recreation, adaptable for all ages and activity levels. Back at the starting site and changed out of the waders, which had kept me completely dry, we crunched on the *taralli* (ring-shaped cracker common in Southern Italy) and drank the bulk red wine Daniele pulled out of his backpack. He also had plastic water bottles from the San Benedetto beverage company, which captures the spring water at the Mercure's source. But I figured I could have just cupped my hands in the water, so I stuck with the wine, which went down smoothly.

Viggianello is also the starting point for many area trails. As I'm more of a walker than a hiker, my destination on the following day was the *Belvedere del Malvento* or the Panoramic Viewpoint of the Bad Wind, which was a longish drive followed by a pleasant stroll. The road from the old town did quite a bit of winding before the turnoff for even more twisting and turning. At a certain point, I thought I had probably passed it, so driving through a little settlement, I asked directions of two older women getting out of a car along the side of the road. They asked me where I was from and if I was going there by myself. *"Siete coraggiosa!"* (You're brave!) They said they wouldn't have driven there by themselves, but then again, Italians don't tend to go anywhere by themselves, particularly women.

The road was paved and had several rough spots, but nothing I needed bravery for. I was surrounded by deep green woods and large expanses of highland fields, grazing cows and a herd of wild horses against a backdrop of rolling hills and distant summits. I got out of the car at Piano Ruggio, a wide plain where I was surprised to find that the *rifugio* was closed on a beautiful day in mid-May. The shelter that also had rooms and a restaurant must have been in-between seasons, and without a reservation the doors remained locked tight. An old man in a van pulled up next to me and started to set up his handmade wooden tourist items, so I asked him my most pressing question of the moment: Where is the nearest bathroom? He recommended I quickly find a tree behind the *rifugio* as he said a tour bus would be pulling up very soon. I followed his instructions, and sure enough, while I was walking back, a bus with a group of Italians from Trieste came around the bend.

I didn't have to hustle to catch up as they were oohing and aahing over the colorful wildflowers blooming on the Alpine meadow. At first, I sort of hung back, but that was impossible. Some of them thought I was part of the group and others were curious as to who I was, so I had companionship and a guide along the lovely walk over the meadow and through the old beech forest. Numerous trees were centennials, but as Norman Douglas noted, many forests were cut down early in the 20th century. This wood's grandam was a 300-year-old tree nicknamed the "six sisters" for the unusual union of six shoots that formed its one trunk. And this was where I came in handy for the *triestini*, who lined up their cameras for me to take the group photograph under this magnificent, 28-meter (92-foot) tall tree.

The beech forest cleared at the *Belvedere del Malvento*, a natural panoramic terrace that looks out onto a wide valley with Calabria's Castrovillari far below and mountain peaks in the distance. It was hard to imagine that this overlook was once used as a cable station to transport trees down the side of the mountain. Today, it is a destination for tour buses from northern Italy that take passengers from Matera to Maratea by way of this beautiful park. From the terrace we were able to view the *pino loricato*, the symbol of the Pollino National Park. Commonly referred to as the Bosnian pine in English, the tree is native to mountainous areas of the Balkans, northern Greece and Southern Italy, specifically Basilicata and Calabria, where it grows at altitudes above 1,000 meters (3,280 feet). Hardy in the face of severe cold, wind and poor soil, the rare species holds a fascination with its windswept, sculpted appearance. Trees in areas of particularly strong winds have branches that grow out to only one side. The wood is remarkably resistant to decomposition as well as woodworms, so that even when dead, the tree remains standing, majestically silhouetted against its harsh environs. Its strength combined with a pleasant fragrance made the wood popular for the construction of the chests and trunks that Lucanian and Calabrian emigrants packed for their long journeys abroad.

I stayed behind at the Belvedere to soak up the panorama with just the forceful wind and the birds. Returning through the beech forest, I went back to see the "six sisters." Perhaps it was the light, but the ancient tree seemed to take on the character of a wise, expressively wizened old woman with multiple personalities. I quickened my pace. The tour bus was gone when I got back to the parking area. I continued on my way, and came upon another *rifugio*, where I found the bus parked out front. The group was inside eating and the same three vendors I had seen at Piano Ruggio were patiently waiting in the lot for a final sale with their assortment of local cheese, sausage, and wooden refrigerator magnets and plaques. They were confident that the group would be buying when they finished their lunch. After I used the facilities, I took a closer look at the magnets, which were quite nice. The craftsman had burnt images of Bosnian pines, mushrooms and other flora and fauna into the wood. I decided to take a couple and as I reached into my wallet for change, he proudly pulled out a little basket of Euro coins. It looked to be about a couple hundred Euros worth. I couldn't believe it. In the place I would have least expected it, a faraway mountain refuge, I finally found an Italian totally and unlimitedly prepared for that unfortunate customer left without exact change.

VIII.

MATERA

Sassi di Matera

22. INITIAL IMPRESSIONS

M Y FIRST VISIT to Matera was on a day trip from Reggio Calabria. Anyone even vaguely familiar with Southern Italian geography will wonder as to the feasibility of such a venture. I hemmed and hawed, but I really wanted to see the Sassi, and apparently so did the busload that rode six hours each way from the toe almost to the heel and back in one day. I chronicled the 18½-hour journey in the chapter "Visiting Calabria's Neighbors" that I included in my book *Calabria: The Other Italy*. After all, Matera is just an hour's drive into Basilicata from Calabria's northeastern border.

I had heard of the day trip through an email, forwarded to me by the secretary of the school where I was working. The Russian teacher who wasn't overwhelmed by the local demand for language lessons was circulating information about the excursion, and I had wanted to see Matera's ancient cave dwellings for some time. The catch, of course, was that it was all in one day. So in the wee hours of a Sunday morning in early June, I stumbled out to the bus stop, fortunately right outside my front door, at 4:35 a.m. for the 4:40 scheduled departure. I had the feeling that my fellow travelers didn't approve of what they perceived as my last-minute arrival. The Italian couple who showed up at 4:42 apologetically took their seats amidst scowls. Where was I? Who were these punctual travelers?

Vera, the tour leader, introduced our bus drivers: Antonio and Vassily "who speaks our language." The majority of the day trippers were Ukrainian, one of Italy's numerous groups of immigrant workers, many of whom clean houses and take care of the elderly. With just three very brief rest stops, we pulled into Matera's tour bus parking lot at around 10:30. Vera took the lead without hesitation, stepping out at a clip, then stopping after about five minutes and admitting to not knowing where she was going. *"Con la guida"* (with a guide), as the trip had been presented, apparently referred to her reading aloud a paragraph about the

Sassi on the bus. Her recitation went something like this: *Bushka shy-veskaza Mel Gibson dasvadanya papushka vadushka Mel Gibson djezhe zachod sashazsky chaikovsky mussoursky sayevich Monica Bellucci Mel Gibson* . . . . Clearly, Gibson's film *The Passion of the Christ* (2004) was crucial to our appreciation of the historic site.

We were wandering through the traditional, European-looking part of town. The patrician houses, churches and piazzas all looked normal, quite lovely, in fact. Perhaps for that reason, when finally coming upon one of the terraces that overlooked the Sassi, which sat at a lower level having been constructed on the slope of a ravine, the historical chasm between the two very different social realities of Matera's citizenry was all the more startling. The monochromatic jumble of modest structures blankly stared out from the gray landscape, occasionally broken by a white satellite dish of someone who had returned to live in the ancient structures, the neighborhood of which is known as the *Sassi di Matera* (literally, Stones of Matera). The houses were partially carved out of stone and partially fabricated. Blocks of high-rises poked up from the hill to the distant right. In 1952, a federal sanitation law required the evacuation of the community's 15,000 inhabitants who were relocated to new structures in the outskirts.

The clusters of dwellings and churches in Matera's Sassi districts were left abandoned for many years and their singular character attracted the attention of key figures in the film industry. To date, the Sassi have provided the backdrop for over forty movies. Signs marked the Stations of the Cross from Gibson's *The Passion of the Christ*, and tourists eagerly took pictures in front of important scene locations. Craft and gift shops occupied several buildings. A few churches and a peasant house carved out of the calcareous rock were on display. In the latter, a cutout in the floor revealed the town's ancient cistern system, canals hewn out of the stone underneath the habitations. Medieval wall paintings decorated the churches' stone interiors. The opposite hill appeared even more archaic, its ashen-green treeless slope punctuated with whitish rocks. Cave entranceways were sculpted from the larger stony formations.

On my return to the bus I discovered the main pedestrian street of Matera, a very attractive thoroughfare with many historic buildings of a different type—elegant, gentrified. When I arrived at the bus at three minutes to one, the Ukrainians were already in their seats impatiently waiting to take off. I could have lingered in the area for several days, but lunch awaited, and I knew that I would return another time.

Perhaps what stuck in my mind from that day even more than the eerie beauty of the Sassi was the great contrast of the architectural landscape. H. V. Morton articulated the dichotomy in his *A Traveller in Southern Italy* of 1969. Interestingly, he also noted that the earlier travelers who had written so beautifully of Southern Italy seemed to have passed Matera by, and it wasn't until the translation of Carlo Levi's *Christ Stopped at Eboli* that the city was addressed in a detailed, albeit frightful, manner in the English language. Morton described the city as follows:

> At first sight Matera appeared to me a normal Italian town with its Piazza Vittorio Veneto, its Via Roma, and its outskirts covered with hideous blocks of flats; then, having reached the cathedral, there opened at my feet a stupendous vista of troglodytic slums which for picturesque squalor cannot be matched in the whole of Italy.... Unlike most cities, which are ashamed of their slums, Matera, aware of their unique picturesqueness, has devised little railed-in look-out places at certain vantage points where you can get the best views of the Sassi. There is even a *Strada Panoramica dei Sassi* which skirts the whole area and, as a local guidebook says, in a rare moment of under-statement, "offers the tourist a strange experience."

Morton's words may seem harsh; however, the image of the Sassi and the feelings they evoked shortly after being emptied out of all signs of life must have been disconcerting, particularly after being lulled by the apparent "normalcy" of the rest of the town.

Earlier in the century, Carlo Levi's sister Luisa characterized the Sassi as "a schoolboy's idea of Dante's Inferno." She stopped by Matera to get her permit stamped at the police station in order to visit her brother exiled in Aliano. In his book, he described her reaction to what she witnessed there:

> Like Dante, I too began to go down from circle to circle, by a sort of mule path leading to the bottom. The narrow path wound its way down and around, passing over the roofs of the houses... They were caves, dug into the hardened clay walls of the gully, each with its own façade, some of which were quite handsome, with eighteenth-century ornamentation....
>
> Of children I saw an infinite number. They appeared from everywhere, in the dust and heat, amid the flies, stark naked or clothed in rags; I have never in all my life seen such a picture of poverty....
>
> .... a constantly swelling crowd of children followed a few steps behind me. I gave them what coins I had with me to buy candy, but that was not what they wanted; they kept on asking, with sorrowful insistence, for quinine.... The town is indeed a beautiful one, picturesque and striking, and there is a fine museum with Greek vases, statuettes, and coins found in the vicinity. While I was looking at them the children still stood out in the sun, waiting for me to bring them quinine.

How long did those children have to wait for quinine and how many didn't make it? Almost ten years would pass before the 1945 publication of *Christ Stopped at Eboli*, which catapulted Matera to the international stage. A sad story, indeed, on which I couldn't help but reflect during my first visit as I watched tourists posing in front of the cinematic landmarks. The movie industry has certainly brought the Sassi before a wide, general audience of an international scale, but I suppose that the Lucanian Film Commission will have to come up with a more upbeat storyline if it has any hopes of following in the footsteps of Salzburg's Sound of Music tours.

Mel Gibson wasn't the first director to have been drawn to Matera, and many more have come after him. Ancient Jerusalem remains a popular theme, most notably in Pier Paolo Pasolini's *Vangelo secondo Matteo* (The Gospel According to St. Matthew, 1964) and more recently in Timur Behmanbetov's 2015 remake of *Ben Hur*. Italian director Francesco Rosi selected Matera for his fairytale *C'era una volta* (More Than a Miracle, 1967) starring Sophia Loren and Omar Shariff, as well as for his interpretation of one of the few films in which the backdrop is more than a poignant stage set, *Christ Stopped at Eboli* (1979).

The Sassi's unique panorama has served as the setting for everything from historical fiction to contemporary drama, horror and even a blockbuster superhero film. But these movies don't tell the story of Matera and its Sassi. The curious visitor must delve deeper.

23. SLEEPING IN THE SASSI

EXPERIENTIAL TRAVEL is in vogue. Everyone is looking for that up-close and personal touch, feel, taste and smell of a place. So in Matera, what better way than to sleep in the Sassi? Of course, the accommodations have come a long way from when Luisa Levi peered into doorways on her brief visit. Today, a simple cave-room that would have housed a large family with their donkey and chickens is offered to tourists as a basic double room with clean, crisp sheets covering an ultra-comfortable bed in a tastefully furnished ambience straight out of *Architectural Digest*.

As anywhere, a nice hotel comes with a nice price tag. I wanted to stay in the Sassi, perhaps to have that storybook vision just outside my window or maybe to be in the center of town for ease of sightseeing or possibly because it seemed the thing to do. I had to hunt around a bit before I found what I considered a reasonably priced room and located a teensy single in a boutique hotel in Sasso Barisano. Amazing how hoteliers manage to squeeze all of their advertised amenities into a large broom closet masquerading as a single room. The traveler's overnight bag must fit over the mini-fridge, the toiletry gift basket balanced on top of the flat-screen television and everything reachable from the cozy single bed, but in this particular case, what a view out the little window! I had chosen wisely. I was part of and looked out onto one of the Sassi's hodgepodge neighborhoods crowned with Matera's stately Romanesque cathedral.

My snug cubbyhole constructed of regular blocks of stone was no doubt a later addition to the original structure, a deconsecrated church dating from around 1300. The continental breakfast was served to international travelers in the well-appointed lobby area with arched cathedral ceilings, modern furnishings and antique niches carved into the walls. The English language bounced off the ancient stone.

I had pleasant conversations with numerous guests over the course of several days, and late one morning as I was glancing through some books in the lobby, an American I had met the day before rushed out of her adjacent room in a panic. "My husband's locked in the bathroom!" The English-speaking receptionist had just stepped outside a few moments earlier, so I approached the bellhop and asked if he could assist them. The woman insisted I come along to translate, and that's when I saw how the other half lived. The multi-level suite was pure Sassi grandeur. The attendant jimmied open the bathroom door to reveal a suite in itself. The shower-cave alone was bigger than my whole room. Then there was the jacuzzi tub area and the his-and-her sink area, all chiseled out of the rock and furbished with state-of-the-art fixtures. Needless to say, the suite was striking and had it been mine, I may have been tempted to lock myself inside for my entire stay.

Some properties go further with spas and swimming pools. The word luxury has become commonplace as Matera established itself on Southern Italy's tourist circuit. Many visitors arrive in buses on organized tours. Others come on their own and visit the sites with one of the many guides in town. But when left to their own devices, they are literally *on* their devices as they wander up and down the Sassi's ancient staircases staring at their cell phones for hopes of orientation amidst the seemingly indecipherable maze of streets.

But who walked up and down those lanes, slept in the caves and worshiped in the churches before the recent gentrification? A few museums replicate life in the Sassi over the last couple of centuries. The *casa grotta* (grotto house) in Sasso Caveoso, for example, represents a typical cave house as it would have been up until the 1950s. Its inhabitants were evacuated in 1956, and as with many dwellings, the entranceway was walled off to prevent people from returning. Many features of the space, basically one large room with side chambers, made an impression on me, particularly the commonplace items. The furniture and work tools all looked familiar, typical belongings for poor people of the period. Everyday objects were placed on niches carved into the natural cave walls, and nicely framed pictures of the Madonna were lovingly hung over the bed. And here, I can say that the mattresses of the luxury hotels most certainly veer from the authenticity of the original cornhusk stuffing. The replica of the mule tied up by his trough might also give pause to the well-heeled guest. I didn't expect the tiled kitchen area nor the indoor well with the visible system of underground water canals. But as state-of-the-art as the water collection may have been when it was conceived, citizenry of the 21st-century demand über-modern plumbing and utilities.

The poor peasant, of course, no longer exists, but gone, too, are the overwhelming majority of craftspeople who once plied their trades in the Sassi. The *'u conza piott (il cucipiatti/conciapiatti* in Italian), literally the plate sewer/fixer, is no longer needed. He has been forgotten together with the ceramic platter positioned in the center of the table from which the entire family would have eaten. Now, plates are thrown out when broken, like umbrellas. So instead of having *'u mbrller (l'ombrellaio)* or the local umbrella repairman, cheap umbrellas made in China are pedaled on every street corner whenever it rains. Many jobs have dramatically changed, such as that of *'u frnèr (il fornaio)*, the baker. In the past, residents would prepare their bread dough at home and the loaves would be baked in communal wood-burning ovens, located throughout the Sassi. Other occupations, such as *'u scuarpèr (il calzolaio)*, the cobbler, and *'u faljgnem (il falegname)*, the carpenter, have all but disappeared despite the need. And what I wouldn't give for a good *l'ammlafurc (il mola forbici)*, knife sharpener! The tools of these and many other trades are on display at the *Museo-Laboratorio della Civiltà Contadina* (Museum-Workshop of Peasant Culture) in Sasso Barisano.

Gift shops in Matera offer several items that hearken back to old-world crafts, such as wooden bread stamps that were used to distinguish a family's loaf in the common oven and miniatures of the Sassi carved out of the local stone. *Il cuccù* (cuckoo), a chicken-shaped whistle, is also quite popular. In the old days these terra-cotta birds scared away evil spirits, whether placed on the fireplace or a baby's crib. The young man from whom I purchased a small *cuccù* enthusiastically espoused its traditions and said that these whistles were status symbols for children of the Sassi in the 1950s. I imagine that many a *cuccù* must have found a special place in the homes of the *materani* forced to relocate to the modern suburbs.

Some original residents, their children and grandchildren have moved back to the historic neighborhoods. Laundry can be seen hanging on lines, an umbrella leaning against an entranceway, a slot for mail on front doors and potted plants placed about, but on each of my visits I couldn't help but observe how the town had increasingly filled with tourist rather than residential enterprises: hotels, restaurants and other businesses aimed at those passing through, whether for a couple of hours or a handful of days. Clearly, the opportunity of sleeping or eating in a cave is irresistible for the out-of-town guest. The difficulty is striking a balance between the expansion of tourism and the sustained existence of a local community so that the Sassi don't run the risk of becoming an historical theme park. In fact, the Sassi are under protection as a cultural heritage site, and the law set in place for the return of its citizens mandates residential development and the reestablishment of a local population.

On my second visit to Matera, I began my exploration of the city's history at *Casa Noha* in the Civita section of the old town. Civita is located on a strip of higher ground that extends between Sasso Barisano to the north and Sasso Caveoso to the south. When viewed from Civita, the Sassi districts appear as valleys on the edge of a ravine. Civita, the city's oldest institutional settlement, was once surrounded by a protective wall, the arched gateways of which can still be seen amongst the more conventional architecture of its historically more affluent residents. *Casa Noha* was constructed by a noble family between the 15th and 17th centuries. Today, its rather simple rooms are filled with thousands of years of history, as Matera's challenges and successes are projected for visitors on its walls. I had understood that the Sassi were overcrowded many times over. However, what struck me watching the brief documentary video was that many of those caves were never meant for people at all.

A few pieces of the puzzle fell into place for me that day. While Carlo Levi's *Christ Stopped at Eboli* was important in calling attention to the desperate living conditions and associated politics of the time, one book cannot possibly afford a complete picture of the road that led to the grave difficulties nor of an understanding as to what the Sassi represent. Matera's history is long and unique, and the casual observer can get distracted with elements of popular culture superimposed on the Sassi. While a director's framing of a scene might be considered brilliant cinematography, it can in no way compare to the dedication and achievement of the *materani* themselves, who over thousands of years chiseled away at rock to not only form the Sassi that we see but also to excavate the amazing underground network that we don't see.

24. OUR LADY OF THE WATER

I HAD ANOTHER EPIPHANY on my third visit to the area. I was on a guided tour with a young architect who had been recommended to me by my hotel. This time, as I had already experienced sleeping in the Sassi, I opted for an accommodation on the edge of the old town where I could park my rental car right outside the door. Those Sassi stairs are irregular and steep, and bouncing up and down the steps with the best of carry-on rollers is a challenge.

Upon check-in, the pleasant desk clerk told me that the tourist information office at the bottom of their driveway would give me a bigger map and a complimentary *"gadget."* She was speaking in Italian and I wondered what sort of gadget they could possibly be giving away: a keychain, a mini-flashlight or a shoehorn with an image of the Sassi? I would discover that as with many word appropriations, Italians have their own meaning of the word gadget. I showed up at the shop and to my surprise was presented with a choice of postcards, which were quite lovely, photographs of frescos from the ancient rupestrian churches; however, not your classic mechanical or electronic device. It turns out that *un gadget*, Italian style, is a little promotional gift or novelty item.

I chose a photo of a 13th-century fresco of the Archangel Michael from Santa Lucia alle Malve church, which I would learn was the first female monastic settlement of the Benedictine Order. I had signed up with *Oltre L'Arte*, the tourist office with the *gadget*. The organization turned out to be a cooperative focused on the advancement of Matera's religious heritage. They reopened and manage several rupestrian churches, each with its own fascinating history. Santa Lucia alle Malve, for instance, is an excellent example of how Sassi caves have been subject to a repurposing over many centuries, and my visit to this rupestrian church put a few more pieces into the Matera puzzle for me.

The monastic community of Santa Lucia dates back to the 8th century and parallels Matera's urban development. The rock church is situated in a panoramic location overlooking the canyon and opposite hillside in what is today Sasso Caveoso. As Matera grew, the monastic center moved up to the Civita and then to the Piano neighborhood. One section of the original Sassi church, however, has remained open as a place of worship for over a thousand years, and a Mass for St. Lucia is celebrated there every year on her feast day of December 13th. (Santa Lucia alle Malve or of the mallow refers to an herbal plant that proliferates in the area.)

From the outside, the church is unassuming with various entranceways carved into the rock face that lead into the three-nave interior. The right door, framed with blocks of the local stone and a decorative arch, opens into the nave that has remained a functioning church. The other two naves were deconsecrated and turned into living and warehouse space, a very common transformation of Sassi churches beginning in the 18th century when new houses of worship were built in the burgeoning Piano district. The interior is considerably larger than it would seem from the outside and has been brought back to the form of the original structure to the extent possible. Elements of the Eastern rite, such as the remains of iconostasis screens and Byzantine-style paintings can be seen. Frescos date between the 11th and 17th centuries. Perhaps the most unexpected detail is the corner kitchen that testifies to the period in which the cave served as a home. How the residents survived the visible green mold and dense, musty air for any protracted length of time is remarkable.

Other must-see Sassi churches are Santa Maria de Idris and San Giovanni in Monterrone, both excavated from the outcropping that dominates Sasso Caveoso on the edge of the ravine. This rock spur is one of the Sassi's most characteristic images and the panorama is as compelling when facing the formation as it is gazing out in all directions from the rock itself. Interestingly, the two ancient churches were connected in the 19th century by an underground passageway. San Giovanni is the older of the two, dating from the 12th century, and has an evocative, frescoed interior. Santa Maria de Idris has a rather simple sanctuary and its modest church facade made of excavated stone blocks is hidden from most angles except when approached from the northwest. The church even has a belfry jutting out of the dramatic rock formation.

My guide was quite thorough in her presentation and as she began to point out particulars of the frescos in Santa Maria de Idris, I made a connection that hadn't clicked into place on previous visits. This humble house of worship, dug out of the striking rock that has attracted the eyes of everyone from the ancients to contemporary film directors, is truly the symbol of Matera. And with its dedication to Maria of Idris, it's as if it had been planned. Derived from the Greek *Hodegetria*, the name means "she who leads the way." Many sources add "or Maria of the water" when explaining the origins, but in Matera, that would hardly seem necessary, as water *is* the way. The Madonna leads her people to water. To dispel any doubt, not only does the church have a cistern, but the fresco of Santa Maria above the church's only altar features water jugs in the image. Without the system of water collection and vast underground network of canals and reservoirs, Matera could never have developed as a city. The *materani* knew to whom to pray and who to thank. Our Lady of the Water holds a position of honor in the center of the Sassi.

Visiting these rupestrian churches, one needs to employ a bit of imagination, as age, humidity, abandonment, theft and vandalism have taken their toll on the Sassi. However, judging by the frescos on display in the local Museum of Medieval and Modern Art of Basilicata, the plain rock walls of Santa Maria de Idris once dazzled with colorful paintings. These works were removed and restored for preservation sake.

The largest rupestrian church is San Pietro Barisano, originally excavated in the 12th century and subsequently enlarged and modified up through the 18th. Today, attendants don't even allow photos, but in the 1960s and 70s when the church was left unprotected following the evacuation of the Sassi, many works of art were stolen or damaged. The church is still interesting to explore with its partially frescoed side aisles and underground passageways complete with niches for the draining of corpses before burial. Already in 1903, the parish was moved to a nearby church because of excessive dampness. How must have San Pietro Barisano and the other rupestrian churches appeared in their heyday?

In the period of the Sassi's decline and decreed removal, their patrimony was not only threatened by thieves and vandals, but by time and memory. Many of the caves had been forgotten, and with the loss of this ancient culture came the loss of pride. The Sassi and those connected with its heritage were at rock bottom…

25. SONS AND DAUGHTERS OF HISTORY

THE *VERGOGNA NAZIONALE* was what the Sassi were called, the national shame. This condemnation was handed down by Palmiro Togliatti, head of the Italian Communist Party on his visit to Matera in 1948, three years after the publication of *Christ Stopped at Eboli*. The name stuck. In 1950 Prime Minister Alcide De Gasperi visited Matera and seconded the pronouncement. He set the political wheels in motion. Better late than never. The infant mortality rate was four times higher than the national average, and politicians could no longer ignore the abominable sanitation. The government responded to the humanitarian crisis.

Reports and images spread. To avoid embarrassment when asked where they were from, many *materani* would respond, "a town near Bari." *Hollow City* (2012), a moving minidocumentary directed by Andrea De Sica (grandson of Vittorio De Sica), recorded this and other reflections of Raffaello De Ruggieri, who would eventually become mayor of Matera. He went on to say that in the minds of its residents the Sassi were *"testimonianza della loro subalternità e quindi anche della loro miseria"*—proof of their inferiority and therefore also of their extreme poverty. They wanted an escape.

Prominent intellectuals weighed in on what was to be done. Adriano Olivetti, industrialist of the well-known Olivetti typewriter family, was a driving force in the study to understand the needs of Sassi citizens and to come up with a solution to transfer them to newly built districts without breaking down the social structure of family and community. The 1952 law for the evacuation of the Sassi provided for the construction of public housing that was suitable for agricultural workers, other manual laborers and craftspeople. New residences were built in the Piano district and further outside the city with the assistance of funds from the Marshall Plan. The evacuation took place over a twenty-year period with the first fifty families moving into their new homes in 1953.

The transfer was disconcerting for many of the elderly, who were used to the conditions and style of life in the grottos. However, the new accommodations were welcomed by large families who suffered in the humid, overcrowded cave dwellings that they shared with their animals, if they were lucky enough to possess a donkey and a few chickens. I asked one of my guides how the Sassi residents and their children felt or how they feel looking back on that period. Was or is there anger, resentment, a desire for reparations? She said that her feeling was that people put that difficult time of their lives behind them, that they looked forward not backwards. Her father had grown up in the Sassi, but he didn't talk much about it. He recalled taking weekly showers at a communal bathhouse outside the neighborhood. He was happy to put the nagging hunger in the pit of his stomach behind him. The *materani* didn't want to be the *vergogna nazionale*.

In *Hollow City*, De Ruggieri recounts a meaningful encounter he had with Umberto Zanotti Bianco, philanthropist, archeologist and environmentalist who dedicated much of his life to Southern Italy. The young man had spoken of Matera with bitterness and Zanotti Bianco responded by asking him how well he really knew his hometown. This chance meeting prompted a soul searching by De Ruggieri and his friends. "Who are we? Are we the sons of misery as everyone says or are we the sons of history like Umberto Zanotti Bianco, Adriano Olivetti and Rocco Mazzarone were telling us?" (Mazzarone was a doctor and *meridionalista* from Tricarico, Basilicata.) So in 1959, a group of young professionals, office workers, students and housewives dedicated themselves to the exploration of their history. They called their club La Scaletta as they met in a basement room at the bottom of a small staircase.

Every Sunday they went on the hunt for grottos, identifying known caves and finding new ones, from prehistoric through medieval times. The members of La Scaletta applied themselves with scientific diligence and documented about 150 cave churches; they also restored grottos, studied socio-economic issues, published papers and books, and organized art exhibitions and conferences. The group of young volunteers went against the prevailing notion of what the Sassi represented and their efforts were instrumental in turning the Sassi from a *vergogna nazionale* to an international wonder. Clearly, there was more to the story than overcrowding and problematic sanitation.

Strolling through the Sassi's narrow lanes is an immersion in history, and gazing across to the other side of the canyon is like traveling even further back in time. People have lived on this land for 10,000 years. Artifacts from the Paleolithic through the Medieval Periods are on display at the city's *Museo Archeologico Nazionale "Domenico Ridola,"* Basilicata's oldest archeological museum that was named after the local medical doctor, politician and archeologist whose donated collection of ancient objects founded the museum. Ridola conducted digs in the Murge, a high plateau covering a large area of central Puglia and eastern Basilicata. In Matera, this bleak, rocky, grayish landscape is called the Murgia Materana, and with the discovery of its many rupestrian churches, a regional park was established. Within its territory is the Gravina di Matera, the canyon along which Matera and neighboring Montescaglioso are situated. Its water course eventually flows into the Bradano River and out to the Ionian Sea. Numerous entrenched Neolithic villages have also been discovered on the eastern cliff of the Gravina di Matera. With the development of metal tools, dwellings were dug out of the gorge's porous limestone, often generically referred to as tufa, and a community sprouted on the opposite bank, where the Sassi sit today.

Numerous historians have concluded that Matera had close connections with Metaponto, a Greek colony along the coast. During Roman times it functioned as a way station and supply post near the Appian Way. After the fall of Rome, the Lombards, Byzantines and Saracens fought for control of the area. Peace came with the Normans around the year 1000, and the Civita developed within the city walls. Meanwhile, monastic communities had been arriving from the east beginning in the 8th century. Basilian and Benedictine monks settled in the grottos and contributed to both the spiritual life and the area's urbanization. The vast number of churches and the history of over a thousand years of their excavation, decoration, enlargement, repurposing and refurbishment are mind-boggling for the tourist trying to wrap his or her brain around the basics. Structures range from small, one-nave chapels to larger two and three-nave churches with foyers, multi-level configurations, hermit-size grottos, complexes for an entire monastic community, and pastoral religious centers. The walls of many rupestrian churches still have the original Byzantine-style frescos. Surely, the spiritual impact of worshiping in such locations must have been powerful.

A walk in the Murgia Materano Park with an expert guide from the *Centro di educazione ambientale* (Center for Environmental Education) gave me a sense of the rugged canyon landscape and those who have called it home. Starting out from the "Jazzo Gattini" Park Headquarters in a restructured 19th-century sheep farm, the tour included entrance to several caves, such as the early San Falcione complex that dates from the 9th century. The monastic community cleverly excavated their church in a spot where the earth had already been cut away. In addition to faded frescos, the guide pointed out subsequent uses of the grotto space, such as very old beehive niches for the production of honey and wax, as well as animal troughs. The entire compound was enclosed by a 19th-century wall built for the containment of sheep.

The park also encompasses the remains of Neolithic villages, which were initially studied by Domenico Ridola and documented in the local archeological museum. The occasional tomb and cistern dug out of tufa can be seen along the path leading to the park's panoramic viewpoint. This *Belvedere* affords an expansive, unobstructed vista of the Sassi from across the canyon. The picture-postcard spot is especially popular at twilight. To our modern sensibilities, the vision is otherworldly, an ancient nativity scene. As the city grew and more and more lights twinkled, what must the shepherds have thought?

Many of the rupestrian churches were excavated near ancient paths and in the vicinity of rural settlements. Atmospheric elements, abandonment and repurposing have taken their toll on the rupestrian communities over the centuries. One particularly beautiful church, the Madonna delle Tre Porte, however, was transformed overnight by a deliberate act of vandalism that shone an international spotlight on Matera, its worth and the need for preservation. I felt a sinking in the pit of my own stomach when I listened to members of La Scaletta describe the 1962 incident in *Hollow City*. The Madonna delle Tre Porte was so named for the three-arched entranceway corresponding to its three interior chapels, although one has since collapsed due to erosion. The church was richly decorated with medieval frescos. Enthusiasm turned to shock shortly after its discovery when the young explorers returned one day to find that the faces of several paintings were gone. Broken bits and pieces of the frescos were on the ground where they had crumbled, and intriguingly, together with a pile of German cigarette butts.

Just a few questions led quickly to the culprit. A shepherd had noticed a red car in the area for a couple of days. A red Volkswagen was
reportedly seen outside one of Matera's two hotels, and when ques-
tioned, its proprietor complained of dirt all over the lodgings. But who
would have expected such behavior of a German university professor,
whose name was clearly written in the registry? With the help of La
Scaletta the Italian police and Interpol quickly caught up with the art
thief, although only one of his two young assistants was ever identified.
Of the 24 images stolen from 5 rupestrian churches, 17 were returned
to Matera in 90 days and an additional image another 50 years later
when it was discovered amongst the works of an unknowing collector.
The perpetrator Rudolf Kubesch was sentenced to six months in prison
and a 25,000 Lire fine at a time when a Fiat 500 cost about 500,000 Lire.
The "esteemed" archeology professor justified his actions by saying that
he was saving the frescoes from abandonment and deterioration. His
credentials quickly lost their luster.

Although most of the stolen fresco pieces were recovered, the brutal manner in which they had been ripped from the walls didn't allow
for their return to the churches and the individual images are displayed
in the museum in Palazzo Lanfranchi. Ironically, it has been said that
the unfortunate case of the stolen frescos had a positive collateral effect,
as the incident brought the value of art and archeology of the Murgia
Materana to both the government and the public at large. The territory
became a regional park in 1990.

26. WORLD HERITAGE

ONCE THE WORD began to get out, international recognition followed closely behind. In 1993, fewer than fifty years after Matera
was labeled the *vergogna d'Italia*, UNESCO designated the Sassi and
the Park of the Rupestrian Churches of Matera a World Heritage Site.
This esteemed cultural agency of the United Nations crowned Matera,

"the most outstanding, intact example of a troglodyte settlement in the Mediterranean region, perfectly adapted to its terrain and ecosystem." Selection considerations focused on the over two millennia of continuous settlement, the evidence of various historical stages and "the evolution of a culture which has maintained a harmonious relationship with its natural environment over time."

Simply put, Matera has what UNESCO characterizes as "outstanding universal value." The European Union seconded this sentiment when honoring Matera as the European Capital of Culture for 2019. Criteria for this recognition also took into account the potential for socio-economic development and cultural transformation through a long-term growth strategy. Matera chose "Open Future" (in English) as its motto and its program was packed with 21st-century buzz-phrases such as interdisciplinary experimentation, capacity building and change makers. Five cutting-edge themes anchored the year's cultural program: ancient futures, utopias and dystopias, continuity and disruptions, roots and routes, reflections and connection. The state-of-the-art verbiage would prove to be as complicated as the city's underground network of tunnels and caves.

Did the *materani* go a bit overboard in an effort to counterbalance the "troglodyte" label? The negative connotations aren't easily overcome with a little whitewash and a vegan restaurant. Matera's transformation is not a simple tale of neighborhood rehabilitation. The story is one of adaptation, innovation and tradition that dates back through a 2,000-year thread of life in the historic Sassi district. Although ofttimes not readily visible, the culture had always been there, lingering below the surface, and today, what was formerly considered the *vergogna d'Italia* is hailed as a masterpiece of architecture and engineering. In this semi-arid Mediterranean climate with limited and intermittent availability of water and rainfall accumulations that vary greatly from year to year, the *materani* came up with an ingenious system of collecting and storing this precious resource. They were pioneers in conservancy.

In addition to excavating living quarters, the *materani* also dug a sophisticated matrix of cisterns and conduits that branched like tree roots beneath the entire community. Many homes in the Sassi had their own cistern, others shared a neighborhood reservoir. They collected rainwater and funneled water from the spring by Castle Tramontano, as well as directed watercourses for drainage and sewage. To purify the rainwater, channels passed through decantation cisterns. And interestingly, the condensation of nocturnal humidity was also captured and utilized. The entire system is estimated to have 2,039 small cisterns with a capacity of approximately 10 cubic meters or 10,000 liters each, 170 of medium size with 50 cubic meter volumes that were shared between neighbors, and two extensive storage containments of 5,000 and 1,300 cubic meters. The largest reservoir within the system, the Palombaro Lungo has a 5-million-liter capacity. This massive, underground cistern was constructed in the 19th century by the linking and expansion of existing grotto-tanks. Palombaro Lungo supplied water for the Piano district, the Baroque section of the old town. Today, tours descend to this large reservoir directly below Piazza Vittorio Veneto.

Cistern network diagrams and layouts of the dwellings need a three-dimensional perspective to comprehend. Socially, the architectural design of the Sassi fostered communal interaction as homes faced onto small squares, many with shared cisterns and ovens. Numerous houses were designed with a lower-level cave serving as a warehouse and residential quarters fashioned out of the excavated rock on the floors above. In the 17th century, however, living conditions began to decline. As the population increased, more and more people were forced to live in a space not able to satisfactorily accommodate them. Many were compelled to take up residence in grotto churches, animal shelters, storage caves and even cisterns.

A visit to the Rupestrian Complex of the Madonna delle Virtù in Sasso Barisano gives a good idea as to the variety of excavated space and the maze of passageways involved. As a matter of fact, the Madonna delle Virtù was the first rupestrian church restored by La Scaletta. During the renovation, a monastery that had started out as a crypt in the 9th century was discovered under the three-nave Romanesque church. After the underground structure was abandoned by the religious community, it was used by farmers to store hay, mill grain, as well as to make and keep wine. And incredibly, above the Madonna delle Virtù is yet one more church, which is dedicated to San Nicola dei Greci. The visitor can also twist and turn through a series of grotto houses in this Rupestrian Complex.

Back in 1978, La Scaletta presented the Sassi's first art display in the sculpted space of the Madonna delle Virtù complex. The ancient caves proved to be an evocative venue, and other exhibitions followed and continue to be held today. The MUSMA Museum of Contemporary Sculpture is another immersion in the dichotomy of contemporary art in the excavated caves. Moreover, the visitor gets a glimpse of a privileged life in the Sassi, as the works by sculptors of international repute are displayed in Palazzo Pomarici, a 17th-century noble house. The premises extend through a network of grottos that started out as a Dominican convent. In addition to the exhibition in the main house that has an enviable view onto the Sassi, sculptures are placed throughout the caves that branch out from central courtyards and resemble long, irregular fingers reaching into the bowels of the stony earth. The Pomarici family used the rupestrian chambers to store grain and coal, to produce wine, and as stalls for animals. At the beginning of the 20th century, the descendants moved elsewhere, and the house and caves were divided up and rented out to numerous families.

As throughout the Sassi, the residents of Palazzo Pomarici were forced to evacuate in the 1950s and this particular property remained empty for over thirty years. Many other caves in the area had long been forgotten and belonged to that unknown Matera, waiting to be discovered and eventually celebrated as an important part of Italy's *patrimonio culturale*. That cultural heritage would include what has come to be known as the Sistine Chapel of rupestrian art, a splendid cave church, once again brought to light by La Scaletta. The first mention of the chapel was happenstance, a chance conversation with an old man, who as a young shepherd boy remembered *"la grotta dei 100 santi"* (the grotto of the 100 saints). In 1963, the group found the cave in a rural area 14 kilometers (9 miles) outside the town center. Its most recent use was as a place of refuge for shepherds and their flocks.

Renowned for its beautiful frescos from the 8-9th century, this magnificent cave has been christened the *Cripta del Peccato Originale* or the Crypt of the Original Sin and was the church of a nearby Benedictine monastery. The exquisite images in Byzantine style cover 41 square meters (441 square feet) on two of the four walls. These surviving paintings are incredibly vibrant considering the age and the atmospheric damage to several walls of the crypt. A beautiful and unique feature is the curvilinear floral motif that surrounds and unifies the biblical portrayals. Art historians have dubbed the fresco's anonymous creator, the Flower Painter of Matera. The lively red flower in question is the rockrose, a Mediterranean shrub typically found in the area. The materials for the fresco's colors came from both local sources as well as those far away, such as the precious lapis lazuli powder from the Orient.

What a joyful atmosphere the Flower Painter created! To have been a medieval worshiper surrounded by such a brilliant cave-world must have been a truly religious experience. The early churchgoer would have had time to appreciate the Biblical stories. On a guided tour, the experience is brief, a short introduction with a guide who indicates the step or rock with a flashlight where each visitor should sit. Then, a recorded presentation coordinated with lights that focus on the various paintings discussed. A few minutes to mill about and you are kindly asked to exit the cave. The images were meant for a people who had more time.

The left wall features three apses with representations of, amongst others, the Madonna and Child, and the Saints Peter and Michael Archangel, both of whom, curiously, have six fingers. Scenes from Genesis are depicted on the main wall. Interestingly, in the temptation of the Garden of Eden, the fruit of the original sin is not an apple, but a fig. Few artists have chosen the fig as the tree of the knowledge of good and evil, but the Flower Painter of Matera is in good company. Michelangelo would paint his fig tree on the ceiling of the Sistine Chapel over 500 years later. The Bible doesn't actually specify which fruit is forbidden.

Back outside the church, the natural light shines brightly on the whitish rocks. The sanctuary is perfectly hidden beneath an overhang. Other cave-like openings can be spied in the rock across the ravine, and a concrete railroad trestle stands in great contrast to the natural landscape. Rows and rows of olive trees line the chalky, pebbly road. Rock, water and light—a seemingly inhospitable landscape comes alive when people live in harmony with their natural environment. Like the Flower Painter of Matera, generating joy from a simple, yet dynamic flowerbed.

27. ENCOUNTERS

L ARGE, IRREGULAR, CREVICED and with a hard outer crust: the landscape? Yes, but also the bread. The *pane di Matera* is distinctive and significant amongst many memorable encounters in the City of the Sassi. The traditional shape is immediately recognizable with its unusual, crownlike top made by three cuts to the dough that represent the Holy Trinity. The "bread of life" takes on new meaning as the faith of Matera slices to the fundamental core. Awarded the European Union's IGP designation (*Indicazione geografica protetta*, Protected Geographical Indication), the loaf must be made with a local durum wheat semolina from historical grain varieties, weigh one to two kilos and have a dark, crisp crust with a thickness of at least three millimeters.

Baskets of this flavorful bread grace every table. The yellowish interior is characterized by an irregularly holed texture produced by a yeast starter of fermented fruit from the area. This hearty bread can support a load of fresh, chopped tomatoes, as served atop the bruschetta. Slightly more unusual is the *polpetta di pane*, a ball of bread made from the *mollica* or soft interior. Mixed with eggs, cheese, parsley and a pinch of salt, this meatball without meat is fried in olive oil and makes for a tasty, economical appetizer, eaten plain or in tomato sauce.

If you want to strike up a conversation with diners at nearby tables, either order an uncommon, local specialty or comment on the one your neighbors are eating. In Matera, there are several choices. The black chickpea is one of them. This misshapen legume has ancient origins and is particularly rich in iron and fiber. Preparation requires up to two days of soaking and at least two hours of cooking time to soften the tough, wrinkled skin. The dark *ceci neri* definitely make an impression on the plate, as a side dish, in a salad, pasta or soup. A modest crock of *zuppa di ceci neri* or black chickpea soup, served with a few slices of grilled bread, will fill you up and warm your bones on a cold winter's night. And a simple chickpea puree will counterbalance the rich fat oozing from a sausage hot off the grill.

The presentation of the *pignata*, however, will turn heads, and you'll be able to see how many people in the restaurant are not native *materani*. Taking its name from the traditional terra cotta vessel in which it is baked, the dish is carried to the table in glazed earthenware and served tableside. The *pignata* is basically a lamb stew with potatoes, celery, onions, tomatoes and *soppressata* (a Southern Italian pork salami) or sausage. Despite the heavier ingredients, the recipe is not necessarily a winter meal, although the addition of wild chicory and mushrooms, for example, might put it into that category. Traditionally, such a dish would have been inspired by the accidental injury of a sheep. The restaurant where I sampled the *pignata* covered the cooking vessel with a pizza-like dough that puffed grandly and made quite a show. I had Italians from Torino inviting me to their table for a coffee and a couple from the Emilia-Romagna region offering me an after-dinner drink. The latter meeting was particularly fortuitous as the following night when I entered a different restaurant with no-room-at-the-inn, the same hospitable couple, who were already seated, waved me over and asked the waiter to find another chair.

That evening I had the most succulent *capocollo di suino nero con insalata di arance di Tursi e crusco di Senise*. Usually, *capocollo* indicates a cold cut made from the neck of the pig. This dish, however, was the neck meat of the black pig, grilled and served with a salad of oranges from nearby Tursi and *peperoni cruschi* from Senise, the home of this dried-fried pepper. The fatty meat balanced by the sweet orange, both as juicy as could be, with the crunch of the crumbled *peperone crusco* was immensely satisfying with regard to both taste and texture. Accompanied by local wine, the meal was capped off by a dark bitter appropriately named *Amaro dei Sassi* and followed by an after-dinner *passeggiata*. At the close of a day filled with the up-and-down of Sassi staircases, a classic, Italian-style evening stroll through the flatter streets of the Civita and Piano districts was just what the doctor ordered. Social media demanded a selfie, or better yet a group selfie, with the twinkling lights of the Sassi behind.

Visitors who only expect to see the Biblical starkness of the Sasso Caveoso neighborhood crowned by its evocative rock church dedicated to Maria de Idris are often surprised by Matera's resplendent European architecture spanning from Romanesque to the Baroque. Ambling along the beautiful stone streets that glistened in the evening lights, I encountered this completely different world. Although the media and tourism focus on the Caveoso and Barisano districts, this higher ground was the site of the original settlement. One of my walking tours even began with an extended explanation of the layout of the old town's upper level. The magnificent cathedral holds a position of importance in the central Civita district between the Caveoso and Barisano Sassi; its tower dominates the skyline. Dedicated to the Madonna of Bruna and St. Eustace, the *Cattedrale della Madonna della Bruna e di Sant'Eustachio* was constructed in the 13th century, a few years after Matera was elevated to the status of archdiocese together with Acerenza. It was built over a Benedictine monastery as evidenced by the frescoed remains of two underground chapels discovered during recent renovations.

The cathedral's elegant facade retains its original Romanesque style, but the interior has been subsequently adorned. Highlights include colorful medieval frescos and a chapel with a large Renaissance nativity scene carved out of stone. The cathedral is only one of many exquisite edifices in the Civita and Piano districts. Two other jewels not to be missed are the Church of San Giovanni Battista, the first to be built outside the original city walls and the Church of Purgatorio that admonishes with skulls and skeletons.

The stately Romanesque cathedral, however, is the city's focal point both visually and spiritually, as it is home to Matera's patron saint, the Madonna of Bruna, whose festival is celebrated on July 2nd every year. As the legend goes, Bruna was a young pauper who miraculously turned into a statue of the Virgin. In this festival with an over 600-year tradition, the Madonna of Bruna is carried in an elaborate cart made of *carta pesta* (papier-mâché). Each year the *materani* must construct a new triumphal float, because in keeping with tradition, it is ripped apart in a frenzied euphoria of faith in a much-anticipated conclusion of the procession.

Creation of the elaborate float is quite involved, with a theme selected by the archbishop, a collaborative master plan and highly skilled artisans executing the work. In fact, Matera is historically known for its papier-mâché craftsmen. The interest of the Spanish painter and sculptor José Ortega (1921-1990) serves as an excellent modern example. Fascinated by the area and the local art of *carta pesta*, he bought an abandoned property in Sasso Barisano in the 1970s and created numerous works with the assistance of *materani* artisans, who helped him discover a three-dimensionality in his painting. These vivid pieces are on display at his former home *Casa di Ortega*, the 17th-century house that his heirs donated to this project.

It is curious that the *materani* perfected a skill as a result of deliberate destruction. A couple of legends are associated with the ceremonial demolition of the *carta pesta* chariot. One narrative accounts for the annual wreckage as a way to keep valued possessions out of the hands of Saracen attackers. Another story relates that Count Tramontano, builder of the city's unfinished castle of the same name, promised a new float every year in order to pacify the population during the festival. To make sure he kept his word, the townspeople methodically destroyed the processional cart. Tramontano was infamous for the heavy tax burden he imposed on his subjects and in 1514 was assassinated coming out of the cathedral. Perhaps he should have thrown himself into the fray and taken a piece of that *carta pesta* wagon home to the castle for protection throughout the year.

Another important rebellion in Piazza Duomo (cathedral square) focused on Palazzo Gattini, a grand noble home established in the late 15th century. In 1860 during a period of significant unrest, a peasant protest demanding the redistribution of land from large estates spun out of control in the piazza. Amidst the turmoil, Count Gattini was dragged out of his palazzo and down the street to his death in Piazza del Sedile, in early times the market area, then the government center and today, an attractive square anchored by the city's conservatory.

Carlo Levi would show the faces of the impoverished masses in his large mural entitled *Lucania 1961*, which was commissioned for Italy's centennial celebrations. The painting depicts various scenes that feature the difficult lives of the poor during the period of his exile in the region, as well as intellectuals, politicians and poets of the day, principally Levi's friend Rocco Scotellaro from Tricarico. The mural is part of the Medieval and Modern Art Museum housed in the historic 17th-century Palazzo Lanfranchi, originally built as a seminary and a prime example of Matera's period of expansion beyond the Sassi.

The visitor encounters history around every corner, and although difficult times tend to be emphasized, Matera appears a normal, bustling city. The capital of the province of the same name, Matera is the second largest community in Basilicata and its approximately 60,000 inhabitants are joined by innumerable tourists walking the streets of the old town and sipping coffee in fashionable cafes. Proud moments can be found throughout its history, such as during the Second World War, when the *materani* distinguished themselves as the first southern city to rise up against the Nazi occupation. As a result, the Germans retreated and the Sassi were spared Allied bombardment.

The beautiful old town is now a museum in itself; the *materani*, however, live in the present. Ancient caves with medieval frescos host contemporary art exhibits. Old traditions blend with the new. The *Festa della Bruna* thrives alongside what has blossomed to be the largest Christmas *presepe vivente* (live nativity) in the world. Matera is both a testament to survival and a manifestation of human achievement. People come from all over the world to admire the architecture and art, to enjoy traditional food, to learn about and to soak up the unique atmosphere. They wander up, down, through and around the maze of streets. By day, the sun bounces off the bright white walls, and voices fill the streets as they have for millennia. At night, the Sassi sparkle like a life-size nativity scene, not just at Christmastime, but every day of the year.

IX.

COAST TO COAST

Maratea on the Tyrrhenian Sea

28. MARATEA

SPECTACULAR SCENERY, stray cats and a colossal statue of Christ the Redeemer — these are the images, not necessarily in that order, that welcomed me to Maratea, the region's westernmost community that bridges the gap between Campania and Calabria. Maratea is Basilicata's 32-kilometer (20-mile) access to the Tyrrhenian Sea, a mountainous land that meets the coastal waters in a dramatic, take-your-breath-away panorama, a view that can be had for a song, particularly on the off season.

My first vision of Maratea, however, was that of cats, lots of them milling around the train station, decidedly more cats than humans. I was getting off at Marina di Maratea, the southerly of the community's three depots. Six or so of the felines skulked around the station's side door, along with several brooms and a mop. A black cat sprang up onto the outdoor pizza oven, perhaps to get a glimpse of the sea far below, the Gulf of Policastro that extends from the town of Camerota in the Province of Salerno all the way to Scalea in the Province of Cosenza. Maratea lies in the Province of Potenza, in the middle of the broad inlet that spans the three regions. The express train doesn't stop here. Travelers in the high-speed *"frecce"* trains, the pride of Italy's Trenitalia, must transfer in Naples or Salerno, or Paola in Calabria, where the trains arrive but with the speed of a *freccia* (arrow) that has ricocheted off course. In Maratea, the cats only greet local and regional passengers, who have changed in the larger stations in order to reach this obscure cousin of a coast called Amalfi.

So on a beautiful fall day, warm and sunny, I was welcomed to Maratea by a flurry of felines and a pleasant young man from my hotel. A couple of steep zigzags in a Mini Cooper brought us up to the crest of a hill and a three-storied family establishment with potted lemon trees gracing the entranceway and garden. When I walked into my room, I would drink in the expansive seaside view that only got better as I walked out onto my balcony to a chorus of chirping birds and the very occasional passing train below. Irregular hills of whitish rock sloped towards the sea as patches of Mediterranean green foliage thickened. Perhaps the beauty lay in the panorama's continuous variation, as my eye moved from the multi-leveled cliffs down towards the water's edge with its numerous beaches, rocks and coves.

Mount San Biagio, while not the tallest of the peaks that protect the coast from northern winds, sits at the center, and is crowned by Christ the Redeemer, who both surveys the gulf and is under constant watch by all who surround. I could see the statue from my balcony and envision its arms raised to an invisible audience, as if ready to turn around and do an Olympian swan dive. That sea beckoned, so I made my way down to the waterfront where I encountered just one sunbather, a northern European for whom the season was still young. The seemingly secluded, black sand beach was framed by large, rocky outcroppings topped by prickly pear cacti and other Mediterranean plant life. Bluegreen water lapped the shore. Judging by the parking lot above, however, the seaside must surely be crowded during the summer season, I mused. Hotel minibuses shuttle passengers to the beach, a short distance as the crow flies, but far-flung when on foot with the drastic elevation change. On the return walk I had more time to contemplate, stopping to catch my breath and take in the scenery as well as a few more roadside cats, a lucky one, intently making dinner of a sizable mouse.

The next day, I head into town, to Maratea proper. Geographically, the municipality is quite spread out, and its over 5,000 residents are divided between the historic center with its many quarters, a valley area traditionally dedicated to agriculture, and nine hamlets, such as the aforementioned and largest settlement of Marina di Maratea, and Acquafredda, the northernmost, also with its own train station. The old town of Maratea, positioned on the slope of Mount San Biagio, is referred to as *il Borgo* (the village) or *Maratea inferiore* (Lower Maratea). To confuse matters further, the ancient town nucleus, called *Castello* (castle) as it was once surrounded by a walled fortification, lies at the top of Mount San Biagio. As to be imagined, the living conditions at the very peak were difficult, with limited space, maximum exposure to temporal elements and a considerable distance to arable fields; thus, Maratea Borgo developed in the late Middle Ages on land below. Today, Maratea Castello is abandoned, except for the basilica and Christ the Redeemer.

The same pleasant young man who had picked me up from the train station dropped me off at Maratea Borgo as the sky and mist were clearing after an early morning rainfall. Unlike the majority of communities that look out to the sea, Maratea's small center is hidden from the coastline, intentionally so, in order to escape the prying eyes of Saracen raiders so long ago. Narrow, winding streets and stairs branch off the main thoroughfare, which is hardly wide enough for two modest cars to pass one another. The road broadens considerably at the town hall, in front of which a contemporary mermaid fountain has been erected. As I paused to take a picture of the Annunziata Church and the column of San Biagio (St. Blaise) out front, a man in a tattered green rain poncho ducked out of my way, eloquently excusing himself for being in my photo. We smiled and went on our respective ways. I visited the church, where the patterned floor tiles sparkled in the well-maintained interior, as in the Addolorata Church a few paces away.

When I came out, the street was suddenly buzzing with activity. The handful of locals were lost in a mass influx of Italians from parts further north. Shops were full and a guide with a microphone was talking in front of the San Biagio statue. A tour bus, either on its way to or from Christ the Redeemer, had stopped to let its passengers look around the main village. The little gift shop with a window display featuring local food, handcrafts and a cake stenciled with Christ the Redeemer in powdered sugar was a Mecca. I, too, popped my head in to check out the area specialties. I was surprised to hear the Italian tourists exclaiming over the bergamot and citron products made from the remarkable citruses of Southern Italy, specifically the bergamot from the Province of Reggio Calabria way down in Italy's toe and the Diamante citron from northwestern Calabria, just south of Maratea. Basilicata's mountain divide fosters such association with neighboring regions and the tourists were undoubtedly pleased with the shop's offerings.

Back outside, as I was attempting to decipher a sign hanging at the end of the street, the man in the light green poncho suddenly popped up again. Was I interested in the museum? It was probably closed, but he'd lead me to it. Salt and pepper hair, a friendly, bearded face with twinkling eyes, he was a local *personaggio* or character. On closer inspection, his rain gear was either a thin, green plastic bag called into service in an unexpected downpour or a one-time-use poncho that he had been wearing for years. The clogs and the absence of pant legs sticking out beneath what appeared to be a plastic dress completed the image. "We have 44 churches." "Yes, I just read that number this morning." I didn't actually see anywhere near that many, but there were several churches in Maratea's historic center and with the innumerable outlying districts, they obviously added up.

This cicerone of Maratea was well spoken and knowledgeable about his town. The cats? "I feed them!" He had an infectious laugh. He was also a devotee of historic preservation and I imagine his letters denouncing abusive building practices must have been known throughout the province. On some of the narrow lanes, the old houses were built right into the rock. He zealously showed me a monstrosity of a contemporary steel and glass bay window that looked as though it grew straight out of an ancient stone staircase in complete disregard for historic district guidelines, not to mention taste. He was a man with a mission, this Maratea native who had a grandfather descended from French royalty by way of a marriage in Switzerland, if I understood correctly. The *chiesa madre?* He wanted me to see the *borgo*'s mother church that he said wouldn't be open, so we climbed up to the top of the town to confirm that it was closed tight with a heavy chain and padlock. He shook his head, knowingly.

When we returned to the center of town, he abruptly turned to me and extended his hand. "I'm Giorgio," he said as he vigorously shook mine. "What's your name?" I barely finished uttering mine and with a genteel, "*Un piacere,*" he disappeared into thin air. A pleasure, no doubt, although I might not have remembered his name correctly. I figured it was about time for lunch, so perhaps he had a few hundred cats to feed.

I would return another day when Maratea's modest museum, housed in the 18th-century Palazzo De Lieto, was open. Its ancient anchors and amphoras found in local waters have been around from the Roman period, patiently biding their time off the coast, mostly around the Santo Janni Island. Christ the Redeemer, however, couldn't wait and was always ready to welcome visitors with outstretched arms, even on the off season. No need to phone ahead. Finding a ride was a little tricky, but the *tabaccaio* (owner of the tobacco/catch-all shop) made a few calls and a comfortable BMW with a driver and his girlfriend pulled up shortly thereafter. As I said, the lunch hour was imminent, so dallying over the statue wasn't in the cards that morning. The young couple was quite friendly, but how long can a family wait to *buttare la pasta* (throw the pasta in the water)?

Maratea's *Cristo Redentore*, as the statue is called in Italian, is impressive. On another visit to Maratea, I would meet an American couple living in Europe who had seen photographs and planned a trip to Italy just to see the sculpture. It's understandable. Can it compare to its counterpart in Rio de Janeiro? I haven't seen it, but bigger isn't always better. Maratea's statue, for all its grandeur, is accessible. And as with the Brazilian *Cristo*, the setting is everything. The view from the peak of Mount San Biagio is *mozzafiato*, simply breathtaking.

As for Jesus, notwithstanding his short hair and well-manicured beard, he looks like he's posing for a curtain call in a production of *Jesus Christ Superstar*, barefoot and all. Despite the enormity of the statue that measures 21 meters (69 feet), the sculpture feels approachable as *Cristo* stands directly on the ground without a pedestal. The toes of the left foot emerge naturally from under his tunic. His arms are outstretched and palms turned upward, but his face looks down to his flock, not out to the sea or up to the sky. His sleeves, the garment's only embellishment, are reminiscent of wings. Clean, simple lines render a grace to the slender white figure that is composed of concrete mixed with shavings of Carrara marble. The 400-ton sculpture is supported by a steel framework that extends far down into the rock. It was completed in 1965 and has since become the symbol of Maratea.

Bruno Innocenti, the Florentine artist and sculptor of the statue, intended his *Cristo* to represent rebirth and a new hope revealed by the risen Christ. This *Cristo Redentore* isn't concerned with the splendid view behind him. Rather, he looks towards the basilica and the mountainous hinterland beyond. The ancient town that flourished on top of the mountain for centuries is gone. The old city walls that held back 15th-century attackers fell to the French in 1806 and the *Castello* has been a ruin ever since. Only the *Basilica Pontificia di San Biagio* or the Basilica of St. Blaise remains. This church is the religious heart of Maratea's Catholic community and houses the relics of St. Blaise, their patron saint.

The 4th-century martyr is the patron of choking, problems of the throat, shepherds and wool combers, amongst other protectorships. Maratea celebrates the saint's official feast day on February 3rd, when the benediction of the throats is given. However, a grander festival commemorates the city's association with St. Blaise's holy remains, which have been in Maratea ever since the year 732 when the ship on which they were being transported to Rome was forced ashore in a storm, in May according to traditional lore. The faithful of the area promptly took custody of the sacred marble urn and its contents, and placed them in the basilica on the mount.

I returned to Maratea for the *Festa della traslazione delle reliquie di San Biagio* or the Festival of the Transfer of St. Blaise's Relics that begins on the first Saturday of May with the procession, *"San Biagio va per la terra"* or St. Blaise walks on the earth. A highly polished silver bust of the saint is taken out of the basilica and carried around the *Castello* area on the shoulders of a group of men dressed in white and red cassocks. Originally, the festival took place just in this upper village, where today the *Cristo Redentore* reigns. Understandably however, the growing *Borgo* below wanted to be included, and so a procession from the upper parish to the lower one was instituted in 1695. Then in 1781, as the result of an argument between the two parishes that went all the way to Naples for a resolution, a royal decree abolished the official exchange between the districts. So to continue with the transfer but in a less formal manner, the bust was to be hidden with a bright red cloth cover that represented the saint's martyrdom and accompanied by a priest without his sacred vestments.

This colorful procession survives till the present day and is the centerpiece of a weeklong festival. St. Blaise's descent from the castle occurs on a Thursday and attracts large crowds. On my visit, just like everyone else, I tried to arrive early enough to get a decent parking space without waiting too long for the saint's arrival to Capo Casale, the location where the disrobing would take place. You can't have everything. I did find a good spot alongside the winding road.

The crowd was small at first. A *carabiniere* (policeman) with his plumed hat tucked under his arm stood guard of the pedestal, a permanent fixture that patiently awaited St. Blaise's celebrated annual appearance. His sword and a small wooden ladder leaned up against the plinth, upon whose base also rested a well-dressed old woman. Gradually, people of all ages began to arrive. Balloon salesmen set up shop and it seemed that every small child, particularly those being pushed in carriages, had a Disney character bobbing and weaving above his or her head. I thought that when a car pulled up to drop off a young priest, the procession was upon us, but he just paced around in his neatly pressed garb with a microphone loosely gripped in his hand. A man carrying a loudspeaker on a pole followed in his wake. The arrival of the politicos a good half hour later was a better sign. In Italy, there isn't any guesswork regarding which guy in the suit is the mayor, as he (or every so often, she) proudly wears a large green, white and red sash at all official occasions. At this event, however, the mayor would have a very important role.

St. Blaise was making his way down the historic path the inhabitants of the upper village had used for centuries, and he wasn't coming quietly. A marching band decked out in matching red button-down shirts preceded him with traditional band fare. The police did their best to make room where there wasn't any, and the red-clothed bust wobbled down a staircase out of the woods and up to its place on the expectant pedestal, at which point the purpose of the small wooden ladder became clear. When the band finished its tune, a priest climbed up the handful of steps to remove the red covering.

Interestingly, the mantle is quite close fitting with no attempt to hide the saint's identity. His head crowned with a miter, the distinctive shepherd's staff sticking high out of his left hand and his right raised in benediction are all silhouetted under the red cover. Thus, the unveiling was lengthier than most had the patience to capture in one uninterrupted cellphone video. The crowd was respectfully subdued with an undertone of a unison choral recitation and a smattering of applause as each stage of the removal was completed. The mayor then took to the little ladder. His cobalt blue suit set off the mayoral tricolor sash as he raised the keys to the city high above his head in an authoritative gesture that delighted the crowd. He then tied the pair of long skeleton keys with a red ribbon to the saint's raised right wrist.

Once the transfer was complete, the procession continued, led off by a pair of *carabinieri* whose tall, red- and blue-feathered dress hats stood out above the throng. St. Blaise shone, even on the hazy day. On one side, the keys swung independently as he teetered, and on the other, the shepherd's staff remained in its fixed position, rocking together with the bust and the prominent silver cording comb that I hadn't previously noticed. The devoted kissed their fingers and reached out to touch the statue's base. Many fervently crossed themselves as he passed and followed the procession to the mother church, which was waiting to receive the saint for the numerous masses to be held during the festivities. Others hustled to their cars. Events were planned throughout the week: concerts, a procession along the streets of the *Borgo* and another to return to the basilica the following Sunday. In the end, everything wrapped up with fireworks, obligatory at the conclusion of Italian festivals, and sometimes just for birthday parties.

That day, I went up to see *Cristo Redentore* again, this time driving myself. Wow! Engineers had to put the road somewhere and I'll just say that it's not for the faint of heart. The support posts reach down to infinity as the road loops up and up over a lot of air. And incredibly, there were actually cars still randomly parked along the side of the treacherous curves, vehicles of those who had participated in the morning Mass and procession but weren't able to squeeze into the upper parking lot. (Perhaps on this particular stretch of road, the driver would do better to invoke St. Christopher rather than the protector of the throat, shepherds and wool carders.) I inwardly thanked the woman controlling traffic earlier that morning for not letting me drive up any further as I might have panicked amidst the perilous jockeying that surely took place.

The *Cristo Redentore* didn't look any worse for wear that day. Maratea doesn't have many days in which he plays second fiddle. After reacquainting myself with the sculpture and vista, I got a bite to eat, a plate of delicious sausage and pork patty made from the meat of black pigs at a trattoria amongst the gift shops on the top of the mount. The air was fresh, the view was superb, the repast was tasty. What must it have been like for the inhabitants centuries ago?

The *Castello* was founded after the fall of Rome when the Saracen invaders pushed the population inland; however, evidence of human settlement in the grottos near the sea goes back 40,000 years. In fact, Maratea has a wealth of grottos, 132 between the sea caves and subterranean caverns. One of the underground grottos in Marina di Maratea can even be visited. *La Grotta delle Meraviglie* was discovered by road workers about 100 years ago and is another example of the biggest not always being the best. This small Grotto of the Wonders holds its own with a beautiful variety of stalactites dripping down to their hungry stalagmites, and the best part is that you don't have to get all bundled up to see it. The cave maintains a rather comfortable 15-18-degree Celsius temperature (59-64 F). After all, Maratea is the "pearl of the Mediterranean," as promoted by the Basilicata tourist board.

Back above ground, the long, twisty coastline boasts a different picture postcard at every turn, although for the driver, it's a little tough not being able to simply sit back and enjoy the scenery, particularly with crazy Italians passing on the curves. Down at the small port nestled between the hills, luxury boats fill the slips and tourists sip cocktails in the locales and take short walks along the shore while gazing up at the *Cristo Redentore*.

Due to Maratea's geography, seafood dishes stand alongside those of the land. I've enjoyed its excellent *casereccio* (down-home) cooking, from basic ricotta-filled ravioli served with a simple tomato sauce to *lagane e ceci* (wide strips of egg pasta with chickpeas, a traditional dish of the area), Neapolitan-style pizzas, plates of crispy fried calamari as well as elaborate fish soups. The town even makes its own bitter, the *Amaro Maratea*, from local herbs, green walnut, sour orange, wild fennel and mint. The ping of citrus amidst the unique blend sets this amaro apart, and the artist rendition of Maratea's coastline on the label isn't bad, either.

Most visitors outside the summer high season use Maratea as a quick overnight on the way to or from Sicily. A pity. Whenever I stop in Maratea, I'm drawn to stay longer than planned.

29. METAPONTO

There is often nothing to see at all except an expanse of scrub or sandhills, with blue mountains in the distance, and at one's feet a torrent bed full of stones winding its way across the desolation to the sea. Yet such places bear high-sounding names which live only in a few stray references from Greek and Roman writers. This is Magna Graecia; this is a country for scholars. Only those who remember the part played in the history of mankind by cities now ruined or vanished are able to imagine the lonely landscape as it once was, covered with streets, houses, palaces, temples and market places, and to visualize the fleets and navies of the ancient world busy in docks and harbours.

H. V. Morton, *A Traveller in Southern Italy*

I F ANCIENT METAPONTUM still existed, the names of such illustrious personages as Pythagoras, Hannibal, Spartacus and Cicero might be seen throughout the town on little plaques claiming, "X slept here." In fact, Cicero, Roman statesman and philosopher, says in his book

On Moral Ends that when he visited Metapontum (sometime before 45 BC), he wasn't able to repose in his own lodgings until he saw the spot where Pythagoras died and the very chair in which he sat over five hundred years earlier. Pythagoras is said to have spent his final days in Metapontum after being run out of Kroton, a Greek city-state across the Ionian Sea in present-day Calabria. Although his theories relating to triangles and music must have been admired, his political activities apparently rubbed some people the wrong way.

Legends associated with Metapontum are grand. Strabo, the ancient Roman historian and geographer, maintained that the city was founded by Nestor on his return from the Trojan War. If such is the case, Metapontum would have been established a second time in the 7th century BC by Greeks from Achaea as a buffer for Sybaris against Tarantum. Metapontum lay at the center of the Gulf of Taranto, the body of water under the arch of the Italian boot. Sybaris was to the southwest in what is Calabria today and Tarantum to the east in Puglia. By all accounts, Metapontum was prosperous, its affluence attributable to the fertility of the soil. Grain was an important commodity, and not only did the barley spike feature prominently on the city's coinage, but the *metapontini* donated a golden replica of the cereal to the religious sanctuary at Delphi.

In keeping with ancient lifestyles of the rich and famous, Metapontum brushed elbows with two of the most celebrated figures of the times. In 207 BC the colony offered hospitality to Hannibal and his troops, which resulted in its destruction and its becoming part of the Roman Republic. In 73-72 BC, Spartacus and his army of slaves passed through the Metapontum territory, where he rounded up volunteers and engaged in raids. Needless to say, it didn't work out for either of the two military personalities in the end. And the city of Metapontum was eventually abandoned and covered in alluvial soil.

Modern Metaponto has a National Archeological Museum full of objects that span from before the Greek colonization through the Roman period. Beautiful jewelry in bronze, amber and even gold-covered terracotta stand out amongst the many artifacts. Today, Metaponto is a district of Bernalda, whose center sits on a hill about twelve kilometers (7.5 miles) from the sea. Brushes with contemporary fame include those with the director Francis Ford Coppola, who has opened an upscale hotel in Bernalda, his ancestral hometown. In the summer, Metaponto's population swells with beachgoers taking advantage of the wide, sandy shoreline that extends 40 kilometers (25 miles) along Basilicata's southeastern coast along the Ionian Sea.

Travelers have visited Metaponto from before the days of seaside suntans, however. Armed with Latin texts recounting the glories and defeats of ancient civilizations, intrepid explorers set out to bask in the glow of philosophers and heroes. Early English travel writer Henry Swinburne visited Metaponto and was inspired to wax poetic about Pythagoras in his *Travels in the Two Sicilies* (1777-80): "This philosopher was one of the most exalted characters of antiquity; one of the few sages who did not confine their views to private and partial objects, but made their learning of use to nations at large, whom they instructed, enlightened and directed in the paths of moral virtue and real glory."

Pondering the downfall of Metapontum and the cities of Greater Greece at large, Swinburne added, "Their ruin may be attributed to the neglect of his precepts; or indeed, in some shape to the very great success attending his institutions, which raised those republics to such an uncommon pitch of prosperity, as intoxicated and finally corrupted their citizens."

One hundred years later, his compatriot George Gissing visited Metaponto and set down his musings in *By the Ionian Sea* (1901):

I passed the day in rambling and idling, and returned for a meal at the station just before train-time. The weather could not have been more enjoyable; a soft breeze and cloudless blue. For the last half-hour I lay in a hidden corner of the eucalyptus grove—trying to shape in fancy some figure of old Pythagoras. He died here (says story) in 497 BC—broken-hearted at the failure of his efforts to make mankind gentle and reasonable. In 1897 AD that hope had not come much nearer to its realization.

Alas, the plight of mankind! It's a good thing that in Metaponto there is also a tangible architectural landmark to mull over, what is referred to as the *Tavole Palatine*. Gissing was "possessed by the pathos of immemorial desolation" at the site of this ancient temple, and concluded, "Amid a silence which the voice has no power to break, nature's eternal vitality triumphs over the greatness of forgotten men."

The locals must have done their own reflecting on the *Tavole Palatine* over the years, when they weren't dragging away bits and pieces as building material. Some still refer to the structure as the School of Pythagoras although it is officially called the *Tavole Palatine*. Seeing the designation in guidebooks and on street signs as I approached the area, I couldn't help but envision the Palatine Tables as large altar-style affairs, rather than the Greek temple I knew it to be. Apparently, the name hearkens back to the period when the coastline was under constant Saracen attack. The Paladins were French cavaliers of Charlemagne's court renowned for heroism and chivalry. So perhaps these gallant knights convened at this very temple to strategize a defense.

I didn't hear any horses' hooves, but the sun shone from a deep blue sky on my visit to the Knights Tables. Purple wildflowers bloomed in the grass surrounding the 6th-century Doric temple dedicated to the goddess Hera. Its two parallel sides of five and ten fluted columns made of local limestone stood without its roof. I wouldn't see any tables or their knights, but the setting was lovely, and I certainly fared better than travel writer Richard Keppel Craven, who in *A Tour Through the Southern Provinces of the Kingdom of Naples* (1821) lamented of missing the *Tavole Palatine* altogether. The confusion that led to his self-described "mortification" was due to the aforementioned Swinburne's inadvertent mix-up of the Basento and Bradano Rivers. The Palatine Tables are near the Bradano, but thinking otherwise, Craven assumed that time and tide, or in his words, "the inundations of the stream," had buried the temple in clay and sand. What a disappointment when he later discovered the error!

Travel is so much easier today, but how many visitors, completely unaware of the temple, have sailed past those brown, tourist information signs along the side of the road without a thought? And the *Tavole Palatine* aren't the only ancient architectural reminders of Metaponto's glorious past but are certainly the most impressive. The archaic city center lies a couple miles away across the plain of plowed fields flanked by pines, eucalypti, oleander and assorted cacti. A healthy imagination, a good guide and a pair of sturdy shoes allowed me to see its urban layout: perpendicular streets, the remains of several temples and their architectural fragments, the agora and the theater. Stepping out in her delicate, Italianate footwear, my guide valiantly navigated the muddy ground as she brought the ancient public spaces and markets alive. On that occasion, she would have been better off barefoot, albeit less fashionable. Gissing had warned us that in winter the ground would become "a wilderness of mud." Those Italian heels would never be the same after their sinking encounter with Metaponto's autumn mire.

30. POLICORO AND THE METAPONTINO

Policoro has the tangled beauty of a tropical swamp. . . . and once within that verdant labyrinth, you might well fancy yourself in some primeval region of the globe, where the foot of man has never penetrated. Yet long ago it resounded with the din of battle and the trumpeting of elephants . . .

Norman Douglas, *Old Calabria*

THE BRITISH TRAVEL WRITER Norman Douglas was fascinated by the lush environment he encountered in Policoro as he made his way along Basilicata's Ionian coast at the start of the 20th century. His "plunge into the jungle" caused him to reflect on the resplendent civilizations of the ancients as well as the area's contemporary challenges regarding drainage and the partitioning of land. One hundred years later, a portion of this verdant forest has been preserved in a World Wildlife Fund oasis that is home to a rich fauna and flora, including sea turtles, monk seals and numerous migratory birds such as flamingos and swans.

This wetlands park lies in what is known as the Metapontino, a fertile territory that comprises Basilicata's only extended plains. Over the course of history, the Metapontino's particular geographical characteristics have proved challenging for its inhabitants. Five rivers, the Bradano, Basento, Cavone, Agri and Sinni, cross the plain on their way to the Ionian Sea. The positioning of the low, alluvial plain behind coastal sand dunes fosters the formation of stagnant lagoons. Back in ancient Metapontum, the Greeks dug canals to avoid a swampy urban center. Other generations did not handle the matter as well. Mosquitoes flourished and spread malaria, which continued to be a serious problem well into the last century.

To avoid infection, residents and travelers to the area sought overnight accommodations in nearby hill towns. In his *Travels in the Two Sicilies*, Henry Swinburne observed the local shepherds' method of protecting themselves when sleeping outdoors during the "bad season": "A fire is lighted, on which they put a large pot of milk. As soon as it boils, they sup up the hot liquor; custom having sufficiently hardened their throats and stomachs. This throws them into a profuse sweat; they then cover their heads with warm woolen caps, and lie down to sleep with their feet close to the fire."

Back in Swinburne's time, *"mal aria"* or "bad air" was thought to be the cause of the disease; those poor shepherds could hardly have known that human sweat attracted the parasite-infected mosquitoes. So how did the ancients pull it off? Land reclamation studies, politicians and others have repeatedly hearkened back to the success of the Greeks. And early travel writers visited the area with the glory of these ancient civilizations uppermost in their minds.

Metapontum wasn't the only flourishing city along this small stretch of the Ionian coastline. Heraclea was a neighboring Greek enclave that was established in 434 BC in the area of today's Policoro. And earlier, there existed an even older city named Siris. The trumpeting elephants to which Norman Douglas referred in the above quotation were the twenty war elephants utilized by the Greeks under the leadership of Pyrrhus in the Battle of Heraclea against the Romans in 280 BC. Interestingly, this was the first use of elephants on the battlefield, and the Romans were terrorized by the sight of the gargantuan animals they called "Lucanian oxen." Their deployment led to a Greek victory that day. Heraclea subsequently entered into an alliance with Rome. Later on, the city was conquered by Hannibal, and Spartacus also passed through. The various phases of ancient human habitation, from the Neolithic through the Greek and Roman periods, are presented through many artifacts and a modest excavated area at Policoro's archeology museum, the *Museo archeologico nazionale della Siritide*.

Policoro developed around its medieval castle about three kilometers from the sea, and today it is the largest city on the aforementioned Metapontino Plain. Encompassing approximately 800 square kilometers (over 300 square miles), this territory that was once plagued by swamps and malarial mosquitoes has come to be known as the "California of Italy" for its exceptional agricultural production. The transformation took place over many years. Initial attempts of the early 1900s floundered. The fascists fared better with the concept of a fully integrated land reclamation plan. In addition to the drainage of the swampland, the strategy included the construction of a road system, a reforestation plan, a program for the settlement of the recovered area and development of agriculture. After the Second World War, rural unrest led to protests and sit-ins by sharecroppers and field hands on the vast estates. In response, the government instituted an agrarian reform that expropriated territory from large landowners and parceled out allotments to small farmers.

As a result of the comprehensive reclamation project and reforms, the Metapontino has become an important agricultural area and produces high quality vegetables and fruit, most notably, strawberries, peaches, apricots, kiwi, grapes and citrus. The population has increased dramatically over the past 70 years, as well. Policoro, for example, had fewer than 1000 inhabitants up until the 1950s, and its numbers have recently approached 18,000. Summer tourists seek out the clear water and sandy beaches of the Ionian coast. And for those looking to combine a cultural aspect to the holiday, Matera and numerous smaller towns are a short drive away.

Close by, Tursi makes for a fascinating excursion within the Metapontino. Its origins date back before the founding of Rome. According to mythological legend, Oenotrus, father of the Oenotrian people who settled southern Campania to Calabria, was credited with the establishment of the city of Pandosia on a strategic hill overlooking the valley of the Agri and Sinni Rivers. A neighbor of Heraclea, Pandosia was destroyed during the Roman period, and the city of Anglona grew up on its ruins. During the Middle Ages, Alaric and his Visigoths attacked the city, as did the Saracens. Presently, the beautiful Sanctuary of Santa Maria Regina di Anglona is all that remains of ancient Anglona, which is located halfway between Policoro and the center of Tursi. This jewel of a church was constructed in the 11-12th centuries around a 7-8th-century chapel. The exterior of the Romanesque basilica is particularly attractive, specifically the graceful design and stonework of the apse and the arched entranceway embellished with carvings and reliefs. Frescos in the three-nave interior feature images from the Bible on the walls and of saints on the columns.

Not far away, the oldest section of Tursi reflects a different religious history. Following a period of Arabic incursions all over Southern Italy, a large part of the Metapontino plain was conquered by Islamic invaders by the year 850. The Byzantines reconquered the area in 890; however, the urban layout of narrow streets and houses of stone in Tursi's oldest and highest quarter still bears the original Arabic design as well as the name Rabatana. My guide and I were welcomed by an elderly man as we entered the medieval village streets. He was an unofficial greeter and guide, but 100% authentic. This proud local accompanied us as we strolled the stone lanes, looked into the old olive mill and took in the expansive views from the historic center that had been built on a ridge with cliffs on three sides. Our escort had seen our car approaching just as the original inhabitants would have spied strangers or enemies moving towards them. Today, most of the residents live in districts that grew up later on, lower down in the valley. Thinking of our impromptu guide and of others like him I have met on my wanderings throughout Italy, I wonder whether the role of the friendly old-timer will still be around in the future and who will greet travelers on their visits to these villages?

Nearer the sea, I made a different connection with the past in Pisticci Marina, where I was invited to lunch at a *masseria* or large farm together with a group of Swiss travelers interested in culture and tourism. The luncheon was hosted by the lovely proprietor of the estate, a marchioness with that quintessential noble grace. Her stately brick home was built by her family in the 19th century. Its ground floor was dedicated to agricultural production, while the aristocratic family lived on the upper level. The marchioness lives there to the present, but instead of sharing the space with farmhands and produce, the *masseria* is used for weddings and events. The agricultural business continues, however, with a 370-acre organic farm that surrounds the residence with citrus and olive groves, vineyards, and fields of vegetables and wheat.

The luncheon highlighted local specialties: cold cuts and cheeses, meats grilled in the open air, seared tuna, grain and vegetable salads, orange marmalade pie and baskets of exceptionally sweet strawberries, to name just a few of the delectable dishes enjoyed in the extensive gardens. Norman Douglas and Henry Swinburne would have delighted in the afternoon's repast and the Metapontino's gentile milieu reminiscent of the sophisticated lifestyle of the ancients. Good food, good company with no *mal aria* on the horizon.

X.
REFLECTIONS

Old Town, Potenza

31. VALSINNI AND COLOBRARO: *SFORTUNA*

Take, my beloved Siri, great pride
In your rich and fortunate shores,
And the land that your name draws
Upon, which today my heart so gratifies.

Isabella Morra, *Canzoniere*, IV
translated by Irene Musillo Mitchell

STARTING OUT on my Lucanian journey, I didn't know what to expect. A small region not talked about much outside of Matera, how much could there be to see? How many pages could I fill? And then I began exploring and I realized that my book could go on forever. I had to make decisions on what to include and unfortunately, what I must leave out. Some locations made the cut for their successes and others for their challenges. But in the end, the allure at times lay not in the hand that had been dealt but in how the cards were played.

Take the neighboring towns of Valsinni and Colobraro near the Calabrian border in the Province of Matera just outside the Pollino National Park. Due to a couple of noteworthy brushes with *sfortuna* (misfortune), the reputations of the two villages have extended well beyond their confines, and regardless of their other attributes, they are on the tourist map for a bit of historical bad luck. Their stories are very different, and as it usually goes, the most intimate is the most heart-wrenching, in this case, a familial tragedy.

The dramatic, even shocking incident occurred in the period we refer to as the Renaissance, although the world in which the Lucanian poetess Isabella Morra found herself could hardly be characterized as one that had progressed much past a medieval mindset. Morra (c. 1520-1546) carried out her brief existence perched on high in her family's castle in Valsinni, located in the hills of the Sinni Valley on Basilicata's Ionian side. Up until the 19th century, the village was called Favale, which meant land rich in springs.

Closed up in her castle room, Morra took solace in the natural landscape just outside her medieval walls. She rejoiced in its fertility and shared her innermost thoughts with the abundant Siri River. But when overwhelmed with a personal desperation, the river's turbulent waters coldly reflected the harsh realities of her difficult life. In her writing, she references this river, the Siri that is today called the Sinni. (From the 1980s, the river's strength has been greatly reduced due to the building of one of Europe's largest earthen dams, the Monte Cotugno, in neighboring Senise.) The following quotation comes from the opening verse of her eighth sonnet:

Turbid Siri, disdainful of my despair,
Now that I feel my bitter end close,
My pain to my dear father disclose,
If ever his harsh destiny returns him here.

Tragic doesn't begin to describe Isabella's life. Economic or social privilege has no meaning in the face of evil. Without her education, however, we wouldn't have ever known of her story.

Morra was born at a time of political unrest with France and Spain in continual dispute over the territory. Isabella's father supported the French effort to gain control over the Kingdom of Naples and was thus forced to flee to France when Francis I was defeated by Charles V. Isabella was left behind with her ne'er-do-well brothers and ineffectual mother. Tormented by her siblings, Isabella put her misplaced faith in the return of her father, who had become a savior figure for her but who in reality had abandoned the family for the Parisian highlife after the political situation had abated. She became a prisoner in her own home as her brothers did their utmost to squash her spirit. Her poetry is thus very inward and personally expressive, particularly for a woman of the period. In Canzone XIII she rails against the times and her fate.

O sweet and given way,
Truly found in the vile, deceitful century;
And who was the first, showing me from Heaven
Only in a hermitage, the tranquil life!

And as it turned out, it wasn't all the fanciful story of an impressionable young woman, faint from her corset's tight laces. Her brothers were an ignoble brood, who stabbed their sister to death for an alleged affair with a Spanish nobleman living nearby. The accused lover was also killed as was her tutor for his supposed assistance in passing on letters of a poetic nature. Three murders for a romance that was never verified. Shamefully, the three fraternal assassins escaped and lived out their lives in France.

Musing on this violent episode, I am reminded of Gesualdo, Prince of Venosa and wonder how the murderer and the murdered might have gotten along. He with his madrigals and she with her poetry—such anguish and pathos. Alas, he was born twenty years after her tragic demise.

And what if Isabella had lived a freer, more tranquil life, able to travel outside her window and her imagination? Perhaps we would be reading her poetic descriptions of other rivers, woods, rocks and grottos. Nonetheless, her modest output of ten sonnets and three canzoni are greatly admired for their personal depth, and Valsinni actively promotes her memory with castle tours, poetry readings and other minstrel-strolling events that evoke the epoch in which she lived.

In the town next door, the local tourist board fosters a different image, seemingly less sophisticated but no less complex. The village, itself, has a reputation for being bad luck. And its neighbors don't smirk when referring to the place as *quel paese* or "that town" in their various dialects. Seriously, no one wants a chandelier falling on his or her head, and if you can avoid risk with such verbal discretion, who will blame you? Everyone has the right to a little protection.

Today, *quel paese* takes it all in stride. "Magical" events are organized throughout the summer, shops sell Italian horns and amulets to counteract the evil eye, and tourists are encouraged to join in the fun. But how does one find a place that cannot be named? I will cross my fingers and say it: Colobraro.

Remarkably, the stigma has a history of fewer than 100 years. As the story goes, sometime around the Second World War, a Don Virgilio, prominent lawyer from the town, made a grandiose statement when arguing a case in Matera, something to the effect of, "If I'm not telling the truth, may this chandelier fall from the ceiling." At which point, the light fixture crashed to the floor. In some versions, it fell in an empty room; in others, the decorative branches took out several innocent bystanders.

In the 1950s the reputation was reinforced by the Neapolitan anthropologist Ernesto De Martino, author of, amongst other works, *Sud e magia* (1959), translated into English by Dorothy Louise Zinn as *Magic: A Theory from the South* (2015). Already familiar with the nationally renowned *sfortuna* of *quel paese*, De Martino arrived in the town with the prospect of encountering some form of *malocchio* (evil eye) around every corner. He was a scientist, after all, and he and his entourage were traveling through the region to soak up the culture and legends.

As part of their Lucanian ethnographic study, the researchers had an appointment with a local bagpipe player of note, no pun intended, to make field recordings of traditional music. It just so happened that the poor musician met with his own *sfortuna* under the wheels of a cart prior to De Martino's arrival. Staying in *quel paese* through to the funeral, members of the group fell prey to an unusual number of unpleasant incidents: one fell down the stairs and broke his leg, another came down with an unknown fever, and yet another had a serious car accident due to matches that inexplicably caught on fire in his pocket while driving.

And here, it might be appropriate to mention the popular Italian saying, *"Non è vero ma ci credo"*—It isn't true, but I believe it. The proverb comes from the title of a 1942 theatrical comedy written by De Martino's fellow Neapolitan Peppino De Filippo. Thus, the mere mention of inopportune occurrences coupled with the book's documentation of magic potions and incantations, and capped off by spectacular images of funeral mourners sealed the fate of *quel paese*. De Martino's analysis of the conditions that fostered superstitious beliefs faded in the reader's mind: the lack or uncertainty of basic necessities, societal pressures, whims of nature and of the ruling classes, and an unknown future. Those details don't make for compelling tittle-tattle.

In the final analysis, who would you consider more superstitious, those who refer to the town as *quel paese* or those who live there? Dear visitor, you needn't worry about falling chandeliers. Go to the town. The good people of Colobraro will be happy to sell you a lucky charm.

32. MIGLIONICO AND IRSINA: ON AUTHENTICITY

T HE CATCHPHRASE in travel these days is "authentic experience." Facebook is full of Italian travel groups with members seeking out that elusive authenticity by way of the best cooking class in Tuscany or the must-do gondola ride in Venice. Follow-up posts solicit recommendations for the premier outlet mall in the neighborhood.

Basilicata doesn't have such problems. Pretty much everything is authentic. You simply have to show up. On my visit to Miglionico, I had just checked into my B&B after winding up the hill and happily finding a legitimate parking spot off Piazza Castello. I made an appointment to visit the castle for the following day and set off to ramble through the historic center. As I was closing the wrought-iron courtyard gate, I heard a *"Buongiorno"* from the street behind me. A little old woman was sitting on her steps crocheting. We got to talking. She was retired from a lifetime of picking fruit. Her crochet hook seemed to move on its own. Had I seen the mother and child hanging in the Santa Maria Maggiore Mother Church? It was her handiwork. I hadn't yet ventured into the heart of the old town but could see the church at the center of the map supplied by the local tourist office.

The brochure enthusiastically stated that Miglionico was *un paese bello*, a beautiful town, at the same time acknowledging that such an affirmation by the mayor, himself, might seem banal, but his spontaneous sincerity would be revealed to the visitor upon arrival. And I, for one, found Miglionico's first citizen to be wholly honest as the town is quite lovely, indeed. The historic center retains its medieval layout along with several of the old towers. Its perimeter is delineated by the natural hill; the original, fortified city walls have since been replaced with houses and slope reinforcements. Looking out to the north from its height of 461 meters (1,513 feet), there is a wonderful view of the artificially created San Giuliano Lake amidst a patchwork of undulating farmland.

I easily found the Mother Church, which was built during the Renaissance over Byzantine and Norman structures. Its historical highlights include elevation to Pontifical Basilica by Pope Leo IX in 1051 and designation as Episcopal See for over 500 years as a consequence of the protracted dispute between Acerenza and Matera. Its decorative portals beckoned me inside. I was drawn to the wooden crucifix, carved in 1639 by a Franciscan monk known as Umile da Petralia. Apparently, Jesus' face had been used by Mel Gibson in his film *The Passion of the Christ*. I admired the eighteen paintings in the acclaimed polyptych, painted by the Venetian Cima da Conegliano in 1599. Suspended in a balcony, the large Baroque organ was also noteworthy. And sharing sanctuary space with these lofty pieces on a wall to the right of the altar were the haloed heads of the Holy Family meticulously crocheted by the retired fruit picker and lovingly displayed under glass in a gilded frame. It doesn't get any more authentic than that.

The next day I showed up to the castle for my tour together with an Italian couple from Milan. Given its proximity to Matera, just 21 kilometers (13 miles) southwest, I thought more people would have been visiting on a beautiful spring day, but they apparently hadn't taken the mayor's message to heart. Or they weren't history buffs, as the *Castello del Malconsiglio* is rather famous, or it was, back in 1485 when it was the site of Miglionico's 15 minutes of fame. Constructed during the Byzantine period, and enlarged and modified in the 12th and 14th centuries, the castle is an imposing fortress with seven towers, both square and round, in a strategic position that dominates the valley of the Brada-no River. Its nickname, which translates as Castle of the Bad Council, refers to an event that occurred during the Aragon period, a time in which King Ferdinand I (aka Ferrante), ruler of the Kingdom of Naples, was attempting to wrestle power from the aristocracy. The barons re-volted, both militarily and through an alliance with the papal state. The *Castello del Malconsiglio* was where a decisive meeting between the bar-ons and Ferrante took place. At the royal assembly, the king appeared to concede certain points to the barons, who walked away pleased with their position. Subsequently, the king reneged on the agreement, and he arrested and executed the principals of what has come to be called the Conspiracy of the Barons.

The castle's multi-media presentation features a re-enactment of the discussion between the barons and the king held around a long ban-quet table in the grand hall, which for some odd coincidence included a turkey amongst its bounty. Life-size video images projected around the castle tell the story of the famed baronial conspiracy. As for the castle itself, the wealthy landowners walked away with everything that wasn't nailed down and then returned to rip out the rest, but there's an inter-esting niche or two, vaulted ceilings and a beautiful courtyard staircase.

The stone walls of the *Castello del Malconsiglio* have their stories as do those of Miglionico's more modest abodes. The crocheter caught my eye each time I passed her steps. Her adult daughter also joined the conversation, shyly at first, but full of curiosity. She wanted to show me her home. Not wanting to impose, I declined at first, but she insisted when it began to drizzle. Sitting on the rather comfortable sofa, sipping a glass of fruit juice and looking around the good-sized, spotless room, at a certain point I realized that this was it, the whole house. She showed me family photos on top of the cupboard and a special knickknack or two. She lamented that her clients were dying with no one to replace them. She cleaned houses.

Friends had moved to Matera or places farther afield. She wasn't happy, but she couldn't imagine herself away from her town, her home. She didn't know anything else. We were sitting on her parent's sofa-bed in the large one-room, partial basement living quarters. She had her own room off the kitchen area, not much larger than the single bed that filled the chamber. Was this the "authentic experience" searched out by those on Facebook who clamored for the best accommodations under 350 Euros per night?

I can't blame anyone for wanting the Under-The-Tuscan-Sun experience but it's only one of many snapshots of life, and by Italian standards, it doesn't come cheaply. In another town in the Province of Matera, 45 kilometers (28 miles) northwest of the provincial capital, I stumbled on a group of foreigners who had found their own little piece of paradise on Italian soil. In fact, I learned that Irsina actively welcomes new residents to fill the space vacated by their own, who sought opportunity elsewhere. Today, the community has fewer than 5,000 inhabitants. In the 1960s when the big wave of emigration began, Irsina numbered well over 11,000. Many emigrated to the north, specifically the town of Sassuolo in the Province of Modena in the Emilia-Romagna region. This sister city even hosts a festival dedicated to St. Euphemia, the patron saint of Irsina.

Upon entering Irsina's walled town center through the arched medieval gate named after Sant'Eufemia, I was vaguely aware of a small group of foreigners who seemed at home in the large piazza. Later on when I walked into the ladies room of the former 16th-century Franciscan convent that had been turned into a cultural center, I took special note of a sign taped to the wall, not so much for its contents, advising what the toilet could and could not handle, but because it was printed out in three languages: Italian, English and Dutch. Of course, my first thought was, don't the Dutch speak English?

I suppose most Netherlanders could have deciphered the English, but the *irsinesi* clearly wanted to make their Dutch and Belgian guests feel at home. Among the many classes and events hosted by the local cooperative is an international art course that takes place over several months in the summer. I was told that at least one of the participants always ends up buying a place by the end of the session. The Europeans and others moving to Irsina are mostly retirees or people who work from home. They restore historic structures and live a tranquil village life with views of the countryside as they sip their cappuccinos in neighborhood cafes while clusters of old Lucanian men engage in conversation, as always. The newcomers have become part of the scenery.

In addition to the panoramic vistas from the 550-meter (1,804-foot) hilltop position, there's quite a bit to contemplate within Irsina's ancient walls, which follow the line of the landscape's long, narrow butte. Artifacts in the municipality's Janora Museum attest to the fact that people have been living in the area from prehistoric times. This well-appointed archeological museum housed in the former Franciscan complex focuses on objects dating from the 6th through the 2nd centuries BC. Next store, the Church of St. Francis is celebrated for its crypt that was excavated from one of the 12th-century Norman towers. The underground vault is richly decorated with 14th-century frescos in the style of Giotto.

Irsina's jewel in the crown stands behind glass in the cathedral. Actually, she rotates if the priest obliges to flip the switch. The alluring St. Euphemia gazes out with a remarkably human expression, so that I had to remind myself she was carved of stone. One hand is in a lion's jaw, a symbol of her martyrdom, and the other holds a mount crowned by a castle, which represents Irsina, rather Montepeloso, the city's name up until 1895. The painted statue sculpted of Nanto stone was created by Renaissance master Andrea Mantegna around the year 1453. The cathedral, itself, was constructed over earlier churches. After the Saracens destroyed the city in 988, the religious structure was rebuilt right into the new external walls, so that from behind, it takes on the aspect of a fortress.

Irsina's medieval walls, arches and towers frame the old town's interesting mix of simple, religious and noble edifices, all quite historic. With the proprietor of my B&B, I had the opportunity to visit an exceedingly modest home set up as a museum. The two-room, thick-walled house, a handful of steps down from street level, was occupied well into the 20th century. In fact, my landlord, a distinguished, well-spoken man, not a spring chicken but full of energy, told me he grew up in a similar dwelling just around the corner. It's one thing to look at a little fireplace with pots hanging from hooks and a wooden table laid with a simple plate of bread and *peperoni cruschi* and have a guide recite a story of how it was. However, when you enter a partial-basement room with a vaulted brick ceiling and stone walls that have been cleanly whitewashed up to furniture level, in an unassuming space that has been outfitted with wooden furnishings and a large double bed laid with beautiful lace sheets and a lovely jacquard coverlet, and your docent talks about how it was, you get the feeling that those linens, lovingly ornamented by hand, may have been part of his own mother's dowry. And then he wistfully indicates the slightly raised curtain that reveals a tall, lidded chamber pot decorously placed in the corner of the room. He remembered it well.

Times changed long ago for those who left Irsina and those who remained. Now, we enter such museums and think fondly of our grandparents or even our great-grandparents, but as time marches on, these bastions of cultural heritage will be regarded as remote history, a topic studied at school. Just outside of town, another piece of history runs below ground, an ancient system of water canalization, referred to as the *Bottini*. I walked through a portion of the subterranean culverts with a guide, mindful of the tiny bats intermittently clinging to the ceiling. The water, drawn from the water table, is purified in decanting tanks and then channeled to above-ground fountains. Near the *Bottini*'s entrance, pure drinking water still runs continually from the thirteen spouts of the communal 18th-century fountain. Animals had their own trough and an area for washing clothes was used into the 1930s. Historical practicalities can make an old fountain come alive, but the system is not just an antiquated pastoral image. As with Matera, such ancient techniques of water collection and usage are being studied for their application today.

Back in the old town, I walked up and down the medieval lanes, taking in the architecture and breathing in the atmosphere of days gone by. At one point, a large container full of some sort of herb caught my eye through a sparklingly clean window. I stopped for a closer look, at first thinking it was a shop, and then raised my glance upwards into an old woman's eyes that crinkled with her little smile. I waved and she waved. She got up from behind the large plastic container full of orega-no, came over to her front door and beckoned me in. She had been rubbing the dried herb between her hands to obtain the seeds that were gathered in a big square cookie tin. Those seeds could have seasoned the food for an army. She cooked mostly for herself and her husband, with one child living far away and the other, always busy. That oregano was destined for the tables of others.

Times have changed. People come and people go. In many ways, Irsina has stayed the same, true to its origins, but in others, it has moved on. In order to survive, it must create new beginnings. Is a medieval church any less authentic than a Byzantine chapel? Times have always changed and authenticity can only be judged with the passing of years. Someday, this new authenticity will be just as bona fide as the old.

33. ARRIVEDERCI

M Y TRAVELS THROUGH Basilicata tell of the past and recent pres-ent. What will I find when I return in the future? And what will be waiting for you, the reader, when you wander off the beaten path? In 2018 the *New York Times* honored Basilicata with the number three position on its annual international list of "52 Places to Go," and I couldn't help but notice the repeated use of the word "secret" within the brief presentation. Visit "before the world catches on." It was Ita-ly's 'who knew?' of the year. Since then, the word has been getting out fast, with Matera's prominence as Europe's Cultural Capital in 2019 and James Bond screeching tires through the Sassi's ancient streets in 2020.

With Matera as the linchpin, the *lucani* are working hard to pub-licize their region. First Jesus, then 007, who will be next? It's raining in Italy as I write this and much of the *bel paese* is under water. Social media is inundated with pleas to help Venice, which is treading water under a particularly devastating *acqua alta* or situation of high tides that cause flooding. At the same time, a friend from Basilicata sends me a video that shows category-6 rapids coursing down the Sassi's staircases.

A special Italian bank account number is set up for easy donations to Venice's relief fund. Organizations in America scramble to request money for La Serenissima. And Matera? Pino Aprile, writer and advocate for South Italy, blogs, "It rained only in Venice. In Matera, the streets were washed for free."

Articles about Venice's MOSE, acronym for a costly, troubled project intended to protect the city from flooding, expound on the system's inherent problems as well as the deep corruption associated with the enterprise, including the misappropriation of 400 million Euros earmarked for Italy's south. An old story quickly forgotten with the mayor's shout of climate change; and as the water flows, so does the money. Should Venice's spectacular beauty be safeguarded? Absolutely. It's just curious how natural disasters, human error and corruption are treated differently from one end of the boot to the other.

Another breaking news story recently hit the Italian airwaves. RAI, Italy's national public broadcasting company, presented an extensive report analyzing the amount of money allocated to communities based on citizens' basic needs. Were federal resources being distributed equally as mandated by a law enacted ten years earlier to correct historically inequitable spending patterns that favored the north? Naturally, Pino Aprile had something to say on the subject and summed up the report by giving a bizarre twist to the Robin Hood story: "The state robs from the south to give to the north." And in fact, the financial discrepancies are chilling. RAI's coverage was even entitled *Miseria e nobilità dei comuni italiani* or Misery and Nobility of Italian Communities. Rather than making basic necessities a priority as prescribed by law, the public entity doling out federal money considered a town's historic spending. And in the case of the south, it was determined that since southerners were used to less, they could get by on less.

Many more words have been and will be written on the subject. Such reflections can't help but enter a discussion on the current state of affairs and why so many Southern Italians are forced to emigrate not only to foreign countries but to the north of their own country to find work that just isn't available at home. To encourage a resettlement of the south, the government recently enacted a law giving tax breaks to foreign retirees who move to Southern Italian towns with fewer than 20,000 inhabitants. Although without the same level of incentives, Italy hopes to follow in the footsteps of Portugal, which has been able to augment its gross national product in the process. There have also been proposals to include Italian pensioners who reside in or have already retired to other countries, which might ironically bring back a few of those highly trained young people who left Italy as part of the nation's much-discussed *fuga di cervelli* or brain drain, in the great return of the gray hairs.

As I ponder on these discrepancies and the difficulties of the south, a common Italian quotation, attributed to various politicians and which I'm told even appears in elementary schoolbooks, comes to mind: *"L'Italia sarà ciò che il Mezzogiorno sarà."* Italy will be that which the South will be. Food for thought that has been chewed on for a long time.

As I travel, I try to understand why a place looks like it does, the people act like they do and what makes it all tick. Why are brigands revered? How can people firmly believe in the sanctity of marriage as well as the wedding of two trees? Where did all the harp players go? And what motivates a community to celebrate the history of a ship sailing on an unnavigable river?

Perhaps due to Carlo Levi's bravura in telling an unforgettable story or to the nature of the region's remote mountain villages and the associated colorful folklore, Basilicata has, for some, remained suspended in time, a clichéd image, a Disneyesque land of a destitute peasantry at the mercy of witches and the local priest. Some *lucani* rail against this anachronistic depiction, a few market it. Regardless of perspective, however, it can't be denied that this compact, rocky region packs an incredible richness and diversity into a package that appears small until opened. In an interview for the online journal *Talenti Lucani*, native son Giuseppe Lupo, contemporary writer and journalist, describes his homeland as being "full of contradictions, curiosities, ambiguities, extraordinary virtues and symbolic values that can no longer be attributed to myths of the earth and the ancestral world."

Many ancient traditions may still be followed, but Basilicata and its people have moved on. Lupo, himself, went to Milan to study and follow his dream of becoming a writer, but as with so many who departed before and after him, Lucania came along for the ride. Curious about such an experience, I consulted his memoir *Breve storia del mio silenzio* (Brief Story of My Silence), as I worked to finish this book. His personal journey gave me another window on the more rural southern context of his childhood and his emotional displacement in the move to a large northern city in order to realize his literary goals. Incidentally, his parents were schoolteachers who leaned towards the intellectual, so his experience had nothing to do with the hackneyed, stereotypical culture shock of the savant goatherd.

Lupo's narrative radiates a deep connection with his homeland. Reflecting on the long train rides north, he doesn't wax poetic about a suitcase full of his grandfather's sausage or his mother's tomato sauce (valid and important Southern Italian images, mind you). Rather, at the end of the interminable transfers, he recalls the sensation of not wanting to leave the train car at all, so as to *"conservare l'aria di casa nei vestiti"* or hold on to the feeling of home in his clothes. To step outside the train was to leave his home behind him.

Further along in his life's journey, Lupo shares an anecdote regarding his attempt to visualize the foreign world of the skyscraper as he worked on a novel about a Lucanian immigrant in New York. And I had to ask myself, would just any Italian writer, conceptualizing a story set in New York City and not sure about the shadow left by the Empire State Building, construct an elaborate nativity scene of the Big Apple? This Neapolitan-style tradition of the homemade creche that makes the Christmas story a part of everyday life is quintessentially southern and never fails to bring a smile to the beholder's face. It's the *aria di casa* that can make a grand project feel intimate and is what a southerner luxuriates in at home and clings to when on foreign soil, whether a brief sojourn or a permanent move.

L'aria di casa is what the *lucano* looks for when away from home or when encountering a *forestiero*, who could be a foreigner from another land, a stranger or a tourist. That outsider may come from the same country or even the same region, but he or she is still unfamiliar. I've noticed that when Americans travel abroad, they're often concerned with blending, not wanting to fall victim to the white sneaker syndrome. And on this count, I won't lie. Italians are fashion conscious and they do notice what everyone is wearing; however, it's not all about the footwear. It's the connection. *Nonna* doesn't wear six-inch Ferragamos.

A connection to tradition and ancestors, community and landscape, an appreciation for the small things, contact with people — these fundamental values and links are what the Lucanian clings to, and this *aria di casa* is what the traveler searches for when after that authentic experience, that special moment in which one feels a part of something. I found this in Basilicata, and I have many a warm feeling as I reflect back on the B&B hosts who took special care of me, the women who invited me, a complete stranger, into their homes, my numerous guides, the people I met in the street, on public transportation, in restaurants, museums and shops, in large towns and on a lonely mountaintop. And this *aria di casa* is what inspires me to return, to reconnect and to seek out new experiences. Amazingly, there is always something new to see.

I couldn't possibly fit it all into one book, the diversity and detail contained in this small region that I've often described as Italy's instep, although perhaps the mostly mountainous landscape would be better characterized as its anklebone, that important connective component keeping everything above and below in balance. On my quest, I have traversed Alpine forests and Mediterranean beaches, visited medieval castles and modest homes, attended folkloric festivals and sampled earthy local cuisine, uncovering Basilicata past and present, from pre-Greek to the story of emigration that continues today. And for now, I must bid the region farewell with an *"Arrivederci,"* not goodbye, but until we meet again.

When will that be and what will it hold? Thus far, I have traveled to six of Basilicata's seven *Borghi piu belli d'Italia*: Acerenza with its majestic cathedral, Castelmezzano and Pietrapertosa, between which I flew like an angel, Venosa of ancient Roman fame, Irsina with its walled, medieval center and Viggianello in the Pollino Mountains. Perhaps the exclusive club of most beautiful villages will have grown by the time I visit Guardia Perticara, an attractive medieval town, the old stone construction of which lent atmosphere as one of the cinematographic sets for Rosi's *Christ Stopped at Eboli*. Luckily, the community has always managed to bounce back from the battering of the earth's many quakes.

As I crisscrossed Basilicata, I learned a great deal on my visits to seven of the region's eight fine national archeological museums, those of Potenza, Melfi, Venosa, Grumentum, Matera, Metaponto and Policoro. Muro Lucano would round out the list. Like so many communities, Muro Lucano is built on a castle-crowned hill and is often characterized as resembling a nativity scene, particularly at night as its lights twinkle along its slopes. I have explored numerous castles and admired many from afar. Of a large part, only ruins or towers remain; however, when I reflect back on the towns and villages, these stalwart structures anchor the memories as they have the communities for so much of their histories.

On my travels, I have also found that so much of importance lay hidden, whether in natural or manmade caves or in oil fields deep underground. Who knows what still awaits contemporary explorers, like La Scaletta, the group of young people resolved not to be victims of their fate but to actively influence their own futures as well as that of Matera? I would like to study such work even more, learn of discoveries and follow restorations. As I scan photos of the region's rupestrian culture, I realize I've yet to make it to Pietragalla, an atmospheric complex of rural caves near Potenza. Called *palmenti*, the grottos were excavated from tuff stone and used for winemaking with vats for stomping and fermentation. What an image that brings to mind!

The numerous festivals I enjoyed were so colorful, but there are so many more. Saints, wine, olive oil, cheese, truffles… and not to forget the *"U Strittul ru Zafaran"* (*Giornate del peperone* in Italian or Pepper Days) in Senise, home of the region's *peperone crusco*, that crispy sweet pepper, so unusual and crunchy, that I have munched noisily in dishes throughout Basilicata. So much to eat, so much to experience, I just need the time.

In an adventurous moment, would I set off across the 300-meter single-span Tibetan bridge suspended 120 meters between two hills in Sasso di Castaldo? The 328-yard heart stopping experience was closed on my visit to the town — a good excuse not to venture over the 132-yard plunge down to the Mediterranean gray-green below. Interestingly, there was a group of students from Bari studying the geology of the area, which must have been wondrous judging by the undergraduates' riveted attention. I thought that would have been more my speed.

With the *Volo dell'Angelo* (Angel's Flight) behind me, who knows what my next daredevil stunt will be? The Tibetan *Ponte alla Luna* (Bridge to the Moon) or the *Volo dell'Aquila* (Eagle's Flight) in San Costantino Albanese or another thrill ride with a view at the *Parco delle Stelle* (Stars Park) in Trecchina. Of course, you need to stay calm to appreciate the panoramas.

And then there's the summer theatrical extravaganza *La storia bandita*, the backdrop of which is the village of Brindisi di Montagna. With its scores of characters, music, dance, horses, donkeys, oxen and ducks, not to mention the natural wooded setting, this production tells the Brigand Story of Carmine Crocco and highlights the social and cultural realities of one of Basilicata's most controversial and significant periods. The more I learn, the more history comes alive.

I began this Southern Italian journey further south, in Calabria, the toe of the boot, where I taught English for four years. The experience turned into a book *Calabria: The Other Italy*, then a blog where I continued my explorations, and now I lead tours to the region. Perhaps Basilicata will follow the same course. Once you commence, the *briganti* get under your skin. You listen to their stories and they listen to yours. You have elbowroom. You need to make a reservation not to beat someone else out, but because you're the only guest who planned on taking the tour that day.

Dear reader, will you stray off the beaten path? Basilicata, the Great Lucania, awaits.

Palatine Tables, Metaponto

SELECTED BIBLIOGRAPHY
Quoted and Consulted Material

Acerenza, un fiore sulla roccia. Acerenza, Basilicata: Pro Loco di Acerenza, 2007.

Cascino, Mariateresa. *Action...and Go! Film locations in Basilicata*. Potenza: Agenzia di Promozione Territoriale Basilicata, 2016.

Cornelisen, Ann. *Torregreca: Life, Death, and Miracles in a Southern Italian Village*. South Royalton, Vermont: Steerforth Press, 2002.

De Martino, Ernesto. *Magic: A Theory from the South*, translated and annotated by Dorothy Louise Zinn. Chicago: Hau Books, 2015.

Douglas, Norman. *Old Calabria*. New York: Harcourt, Brace & Company, 1956.

Gissing, George. *By the Ionian Sea: Notes of a Ramble in Southern Italy*. London: Richards Press, 1963.

Horace. *The Complete Works of Horace*, translated by John Marshall and Christopher Smart. London: J. M. Dent & Sons, 1945.

Horace. *The Odes and Carmen Saeculare of Horace*, translated by John Conington. London: Bell and Daldy, 1872.

Kingston, W.H.G. "Ninco Nanco, The Neapolitan Brigand." *Foxholme Hall and Other Tales*, Project Gutenberg Ebook #40692, 2012.

Lear, Edward. *Edward Lear in Southern Italy: Journals of a Landscape Painter in Southern Calabria and the Kingdom of Naples.* London: Kimber & Co, 1964.

Levi, Carlo. *Christ Stopped at Eboli,* translated by Frances Frenaye. New York: Farrar, Strauss and Company, 1947.

Levi, Carlo. *Cristo si è fermato a Eboli.* Torino: Einaudi, 1967.

Lupo, Giuseppe. *Breve storia del mio silenzio.* E-book, Marsilio, 2019.

Manfreda, Salvatore et al. "La gestione delle risorse idriche nella città dei Sassi (Matera)." *ResearchGate,* June 2016, www.researchgate.net/publica tion/305921047.

Morra, Isabella. *Canzoniere, a bilingual edition,* edited and translated by Irene Musillo Mitchell. West Lafayette, Indiana: Bordighera, 1998.

Morton, H. V. *A Traveller in Southern Italy.* New York: Dodd, Mead & Company, 1969.

Museo Archeologico Nazionale della Basilicata "Dinu Adamesteanu." Potenza: Soprintendenza per i Beni Archeologici della Basilicata, 2005.

Nitti, Francesco Saverio. *Eroi e briganti.* E-book, Antica Biblioteca Rossanese, 2017.

Petraglia, Vincenzo. *Basilicata: Viaggio d'autore.* Potenza: Agenzia di Promozione Territoriale Basilicata, 2010.

Pino, Angela. *èPotenza.* Potenza: Agenzia di Promozione Territoriale Basilicata, 2014.

Pino, Angela. *Miti e riti di Basilicata.* Potenza: Agenzia di Promozione Territoriale Basilicata, 2011.

Principi ed eroi della Basilicata antica. Potenza: Soprintendenza per i Beni Archeologici della Basilicata, 2009.

Randall-MacIver, David. *Greek Cities in Italy and Sicily.* Westport, Connecticut: Greenwood Press, 1970.

Ribolla, Romolo and Salvatore Ottolenghi. *Voci dall'Ergastolo.* Roma: Loesher, 1903, E-book, HathiTrust Digital Library.

Scotellaro, Rocco. *The Dawn Is Always New: Selected Poetry of Rocco Scotellaro,* translated by Ruth Feldman and Brian Swann. Princeton: Princeton University Press, 1980.

Scutari, Pasquale, editor. *Gli Arbëreshe e la "Rilindja."* Rende, Cosenza: Università della Calabria, 2010.

Siepe, Maria Antonella and Antonello Di Gennaro. *Matera: Guida alla città dei Sassi.* Matera: Edizioni Giannatelli, 2018.

Sinisgalli, Leonardo. *Un disegno di Scipione e altri racconti.* Milano: Mondadori, 1975.

Slaughter, Gertrude. *Calabria: The First Italy.* Madison: University of Wisconsin Press, 1939.

Swinburne, Henry. *Travels in the Two Sicilies, Vol. I.* London: P. Elmsly, 1783, E-book, HathiTrust Digital Library.

Tacconi, Franca and Centro Studi Federiciani. *L'eredità di Federico II in Basilicata.* Potenza: Agenzia di Promozione Territoriale Basilicata, 2010.

Theroux, Paul. *The Pillars of Hercules, A Grand Tour of the Mediterranean.* New York: G.P. Putnam's Sons, 1995.

Yeadon, David. *Seasons in Basilicata: A Year in a Southern Italian Hill Village.* New York: Harper Perennial, 2005.

Agenzia di Promozione Territoriale Basilicata, tourist board, www.basilicataturistica.it.

Carlo Levi Fondazione, carlolevifondazione.it.

Città di Venosa, city website, www.comune.venosa.pz.it.

Città di Viggiano, city website, www.comune.viggiano.pz.it.

Craco Museum, park-museum website, www.cracomuseum.eu.

Fame di Sud, cultural magazine, www.famedisud.it.

Il Maggio di Accettura, festival website, www.ilmaggiodiaccettura.it.

Maratea Info, city guide, www.maratea.info.

Parco della Murgia Materano, park guide, www.parcomurgia.it.

Pino Aprile, blog, pinoaprile.me.

La Scaletta, cultural society, www.lascaletta.net.

Talenti lucani, blogger newspaper, www.talentilucani.it.

Terra Ribelle 1860-1865, university project, ribellidelpollino.wordpress.com.

WikiMatera, open encyclopedia of the City of the Sassi, www.wikimatera.it.

About the Author

Knowing the meaning of *al dente* before it was in vogue, **Karen Haid** inherited her love of Italy and its traditions from her parents. She went on to study the Italian language and culture at schools in Rome, Florence, Lucca, Sorrento, Taormina and Reggio Calabria, and earned Dante Alighieri Society's Advanced Certification of mother tongue equivalency, as well as credentials to teach the Italian language and culture from Reggio Calabria's University for Foreigners. Her first book *Calabria: The Other Italy* grew out of a four-year immersion, observing, interacting and absorbing the wonders of the society and its traditions. She continues her exploration of the bel paese with *Basilicata: Authentic Italy*, in which she presents a region of incredible depth and diversity packed into the unassuming instep of the Italian boot. *Publisher's Weekly* has praised her work as "an intoxicating blend of humor, joy, and reverence" for the people, their land and culture that she vividly brings to life in her writing. Join the virtual conversation on her blog or travel with her on a tour to Italy! Visit her website at www.calabriatheotheritaly.com.

The Author in Matera

Also by Karen Haid

"A phenomenal book that captures the heart and soul of one of Italy's most obscure and attractive regions"   *PRIMO Italian American Magazine*

"Part history, part travel guide, part memoir – and as informed and informative as it is engaging and entertaining"   *Midwest Book Review*

"Upbeat and inspiring tour into a lesser-known part of Italy" *Publisher's Weekly*

"Charming and refreshingly honest"
        Ambassador, Magazine of the National Italian American Foundation

"When I started reading this book, all I knew about Calabria was pizza calabrese. Now it's on my list of places to visit!"   *Women on the Road Travel Website*

Once the hub of the Mediterranean, Calabria now dangles, largely ignored, at the bottom of the Italian boot, struggling for survival, acceptance and a place in modern Italy and the world. Little-known even to Italians outside the nefarious activities of its 'Ndrangheta mafia organization, Calabria allures with its simplicity and rewards with an underlying complexity, as in the savoring of an artisanal cheese, appreciating an ancient Greek masterwork or interpreting a particularly expressive phrase in the local dialect.

Based on the author's experiences, living, working and traveling throughout the region, *Calabria: The Other Italy* paints a compelling picture of contemporary Calabria. At times humorous, at others poignant, this fascinating work shares the joys and challenges of the "other Italy."

Widely available in paperback and electronic versions

More information: www.calabriatheotheritaly.com

CPSIA information can be obtained
at www.ICGtesting.com
Printed in the USA
BVHW032306120122
625986BV00016B/107